No Lack of Madmen
- you can never be too paranoid

David Porter

First published in 2023 by

Walk in My Shoes Publications
36 Silverwood Close
Lowestoft
NR33 7LX

All rights reserved
Copyright © David Porter 2023

The right of David Porter to be identified as author of this work has been asserted in accordance with Section 77 of the Copyright, Designs and Patents Act 1988

This book is sold subject to the condition that it shall not, by way of trade or otherwise, be lent, resold, hired out or otherwise circulated without the publisher's prior consent in any form of binding or cover other than that in which it is published and without a similar condition including this condition being imposed on the subsequent purchaser.

ISBN: 9780993489877

Walk in My Shoes
PUBLICATIONS

Also by David Porter:

Old Men's Dreams, a novel (2015)
Walk in My Shoes Publications
ISBN 9780993489808

A Rebel's Journey, my life and times (2017)
Walk in My Shoes Publications
ISBN 9780993489822

Wild Beasts and Plague, short stories (2018)
Walk in My Shoes Publications
ISBN 9780993489839

Scoffers Will Come, short stories (2019)
Walk in My Shoes Publications
ISBN 9780993489846

Detestable Things, a novel (2020)
Walk in My Shoes Publications
ISBN 9780244866228

The Scapegoat Keeper and other short stories (2021)
Walk in My Shoes Publications
ISBN 9780993489860

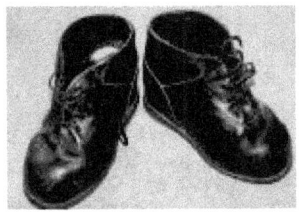

**Walk in My Shoes
PUBLICATIONS**

DEDICATED
to Sarah
who after 45 years of marriage
still inspires, encourages
and challenges me

Based on an untrue story, with thanks to all the people and places, events real and imaginary and those that are a little bit of each who often unknowingly helped make this tale.

Prologue

On an early evening in late summer, the sky gathering dark but everywhere still warm, a man, well into his 70s, embraces a younger woman on her doorstep. They are saying goodbye.

A teenage girl emerges to push past her mother and gives the old timer a quick hug.

'Bye, Grandpa, see you soon.'

Her big brother shakes the gnarled hand, 'Laters, Grandpa.'

'You make sure you practice your chess. Play with your Dad, Joseph. Anyone play at school?'

'I'm signing up for *Total Checkmate*, Grandpa, online against a computer.'

'Remember, while you're guarding your defences, think how to kill the enemy. You can never be too relentless in chess.'

'Teach *me* next time, Grandpa.' Emily is interested, too.

'I will. Start to learn the moves. Bye Emily. Bye Joseph. And Rebecca, you take care, my love. Thank Simon for putting up with me for a week!' The kids head back indoors. The woman hugs him. 'And you, Dad. Drive slowly and carefully.'

'Oh, but the music from that great 1967-70 era...'

'You must be so familiar with all that stuff, it'll send you to sleep. Will you stop on the way home?'

'No, I'm OK for petrol. I'll keep going.'

'Did you pick up that bottle of drink I made you from the kitchen?'

'Yep, if I get thirsty, I'll be fine. Don't worry, Rebecca.'

'I can't help it, Dad. I hate you being in that house on your own. Even though you're by the sea and surrounded by all your familiar things.'

'I told you I'm not ready to leave it yet. Too much of your mother in every room. I happily sit in my lounge, shouting at the telly and drooling into my frozen dinners. I'll move to that funny farm when the time is right. They've even got artificial staff in there so you're never alone!' They laugh; she shakes her head at him and gives him another hug for good measure.

Carrying around a little more weight and nursing blood pressure higher than his doctor likes and struggling with the progressive deformities and pains in his feet, he climbs into his old Fiesta, slams the door and opens the window. 'Don't hang around outside, Rebecca, an army of killer moths will get indoors attracted by the light!'

'Nobody else is scared of moths, Dad...'

They wave as he puts the car into first and takes off, no more than crawling, imagining speeding boy racers pursued by kamikaze cops crashing into his front, back and sides, though the road is a cul-de-sac.

She watches his red taillights into the distance till he turns onto the link to the A12 and out of sight.

She locks the front door, goes though to the kitchen and sighs deeply spotting the soft drink she'd mixed him for his drive sitting on the draining board.

He's grateful that Rebecca, her two girls and husband Simon live exactly 100 miles from him and no more, on the outskirts of London. Essex really, but he always thought of Essex as rural London. He drives carefully, comfortable in the slow lane.

He loves his music choices. The Beach Boys to Jefferson Airplane; the Four Tops to Dave Dee, Dozy, Beaky, Mick and Titch. He's got either the early Van Morrison or the John Denver hits album to play next. He rubs his eyes – headlights are so wearisome, attacking him from the other side of the road.

They could be the thought police softening him up for interrogation in a cellar of some abandoned warehouse where nobody can hear him scream as they proceed to dismember him limb from limb, awake and alive till his head finally parts company with his body.

Should he keep the window down for fresh air, hot and turgid as it is? But not long ago some insect got into his ear and became entangled in the tough hair sprouting from it, so he won't risk any repetition of that horror.

Homeward side of Colchester, feeling thirsty, he reaches in the side pocket of the door for the flask of squash. Damn it. He pictures it on the draining board, being swallowed by a moth the size of a small child burglar inside Rebecca's house.

Thinking through what garages lie ahead he spots a refreshment van pulled into a lay-by. He's not clocked it before, must be new. It looks open and will do for a drink to keep him going.

The lay-by leads to a gravelled area behind, a former rest stop, partly concealed by scrubby, litter-strewn bushes, offsetting two piles of fly-tipped junk. The A12 in Essex at its best. Roll on being back in Suffolk and nearer home in East Point.

He turns into the area, off the lay-by. A battered refreshment trailer is parked, lights blazing while legions of those killer moths flutter around, ignored by the handful of men in dark clothes, some with hoods, faces concealed even on a warm night, others with hands in pockets nursing weapons.

He notes a couple of parked cars in the gloom and a tow truck; no other vehicles. He pulls up adjacent to a car, gets out, sees he's not square to the neighbour, climbs back, and shunts back and forward to make it neat and at a precise right angle to the trailer.

Satisfied, he takes his walking stick from the back seat and limps across the gravel, glad to stretch his legs, flinching as man-eating moths circle his head. He's watched; eyes never leave him and his stick.

'Can I get a can of drink, some sort of cola, please?'

After a pause, the man behind the counter, with just a glance at one of the others, answers, 'Yeah, OK, mate.'

He's handed a can, not as cold as he would like. 'That's a quid, mate.'

Everyone watches him. They're criminals up to no good, pretending to be a roadside stopover. There is one staring at the back of his head. He waits for the tell-tale click of a gun hammer or the swish of a machete in mid air.

Having found a coin among his pocket change to drop into a sweaty palm, he turns towards his car, catching a flash of what one of the men is wearing under an outercoat. Looks like a police uniform.

They're police pretending to be a roadside stopover to catch criminals. That's a relief. They continue to watch him get in, slam the door and belt up.

As he reaches the lay-by, he brakes, all clear and edges forward ready to rejoin the A12, needing a reasonable space in the fast moving cars, vans and heavy lorries.

Stationary, his lights not yet on as he reaches for the switch, he's inches from being crushed by a white Ford Transit coming off the A12 at speed before screeching to a halt at a lopsided angle by the refreshments, dirt flying all ways.

In his mirror he watches the passenger opening his door to exit but falling back, shot. A man flings back the drivers' door and fires into the cab five times, the noise lost against the A12 traffic.

What the hell? Shaking hand paused on the light switch, he clocks the pickup truck roaring into life and immediately swinging round, reversing to the van.

In less than a minute the hook is attached so the van's front wheels are hoisted up leaving the rear wheels on the road. One of the men attaches a set of trade plates to the rear of the van.

The truck will veer round towards him in a second, so he pushes forward, praying out loud for a gap in the relentless traffic flow. Finding one, he puts his lights on and foot down, being rewarded with a loud, angry, extended horn blast for his trouble.

He turns off The Four Tops mid-flow though *I'm in a Different World*, gasps warm air from the open window and drives automatically as he makes sense of what just happened.

Police or criminals, he's just witnessed two men being murdered and their vehicle is on the road in his direction.

Maintaining 50 miles an hour and staying in the nearside lane, it isn't till north of Ipswich on the last bit of dual carriageway before the miles of single lane to home, that the truck overtakes him, the Transit still hooked behind.

As it passes, the passenger stares at him, hard, and then it's gone, ahead. He eases to a steady 40 as he presses on northwards.

The man had looked at him; he will be remembered and now they're going towards his home town. They'll surely track him down, they have his registration number. Ring the police? Report the number of the truck? He's gabbling aloud so E403 CDP sticks in his mind.

Replaying the execution over and over he tries to fix the faces in his mind and what the voices said, but they're already a soup of nightmare dimensions, figures, threats and horrors. He changes the CD and allows Steve Reich to calm his nerves.

Ten minutes from home lies the village of Clottingham. On the sea side sits a holiday camp complex for happy tourists; directly opposite that is a permanently closed refuse tip.

In fact, it was always known as the toxic tip before it was sealed and abandoned through environmental pressure. Seepage into the sea, under the holiday camp, was feared. The chemicals dumped in there before it was fully regulated made it a poison playground.

How much time had he wasted on the competing pressures of that place, back in his day? Anti-campaigners versus supporters of sensible waste disposal. And he, caught squarely between them.

James Ellington, Member of Parliament for this very constituency from 1987 to 97, slowly cruises past, grabbing a glimpse of the place he hasn't entered since just before closure and the official sealing off.

The gates stand open; E403 CDP is towing the Ford Transit in. Flashing torches point the way deep into the site.

Dear God! Two dead men and their van are being dumped into the toxic pit, never to be seen again.

And the killers saw him at the crime scene.

Some relief fills him as he arrives home, safe enough. He hurriedly grabs his case and locks the car on this little drive. With careful glances up and down the road, behind him, he unlocks his house, steps over the post, nulls the alarm and turns on lights, lots of them.

With no noises in the house and no household items moved, he closes curtains, straightens the settee cushions and makes for the kitchen for a much-needed drink. He decides against coffee, but goes for diet cola from the fridge, the warm can still on his driving seat.

Home, he feels less tense. Better get the lights down and make for his bed. Oh but they have his car number, they can trace him.

Failing to quell fresh rising panic, he pictures the scene in every dark corner of his street, men dressed in black falling over each other to shoot him and drag his bloody body to the tip.

He's seen enough films and read sufficient crime literature to fully imagine five miles away Ralph Dines, not unlike him, a fraction taller and putting on weight too, ear hair growing abundantly, a stick-clutching limper, Member of Parliament from 1987 to 2019, one-time minor whip and very junior minister in the business department, answering his phone.

'Job done; all good,' he is informed. 'Fee received.'

'Thank you.' He listens to a question from the other end before stating, 'Oh, the secret of successful lying is to include as much truth as possible, don't you know.'

The caller is satisfied. Dines wishes him or her, 'Good night.'

Act One, Scene 1

The woman with the green front door was spitting-teeth furious; livid. Her face unhealthily red, unkempt hair standing up from her head, she looked every inch her fifty odd years. She was beside herself in a way not witnessed locally before.

If she'd known her father would die only two weeks after her mother, she'd have held off her funeral till they could be buried together. The undertaker had just offered discounts for multiple disposals on any midweek day.

With no idea what had upset his neighbour, he enjoyed watching her stomp around her garden, kicking the little wooden table, rattling the clay plant pots and scattering the early autumn leaves she'd earlier tidied.

They'd shared a garden wall for a couple of decades, yet he knew little about her. He'd occasionally wondered if she was as daft as she looked and finally concluded that she was, but more so.

James Ellington prided himself on knowing and remembering things about people. Throughout his years as an MP he'd successfully recalled faces and places – people expect their representative to do that. And to remember their partners, kids, domestic arrangements and burning problems, too.

Over a quarter of a century since those days, he reckoned he'd not been bad at it. He was readily recognised, of course, even with the advancing evidence of wear and tear in his body, his walking and his hearing.

If all else failed, a trick he still used occasionally was to say to the person who stood waiting for recognition, 'I'm sorry, I've just lost your name....'

'Bob,' the man might say, which triggered the response, 'no, no, I remember you Bob, obviously, I just can't reach your surname in my head...' It worked, too, if they gave him the surname first.

Standing in his kitchen that an estate agent would describe as 'open to modernisation', he loaded the coffee filter machine, staring at the woman with the green front door through the little window as she continued to spit venom, furiously telling herself off. While he waited for the bubbling to start, he straightened the knife holder and gave her some thought. A couple of hearses had been driven past recently; he heard she'd lost both parents. Perhaps that was making her angry.

Whatever caused her tantrum was as nothing compared to the weight on his mind. Over the past two days he'd replayed that shooting over and over; imagined the bodies and the van turning to something putrid in the toxic tip and expecting the killers to crash through his front door at any moment.

It felt better to picture fighting back, being more than ready for them, capturing the lot with just a cricket bat or killing them in an orgy of thrilling switchblade combat, their heads and arms flying all over the place. The reality was neither agreeable nor satisfying.

Even when younger and fitter he'd have been no match for their brute strength. Now, he wouldn't even expect to win by confusing their minds with his superior verbal tactics.

It was the butterfly effect. A butterfly flaps its wings in Brazil which causes a tornado in Texas. His forgetting the drink at Emily's in Essex led to the lay-by and then to the unintended consequences that would follow when they found him cowering in his home.

A piece of litter thoughtlessly dropped. Somebody bends to pick it up. Stumbles forwards, pulls over a rack of tools, a passer by steps aside to avoid the falling tools and is run over by a truck which causes her loved one to change personality and become a rabid vampire wolf.

Small events have large, widespread consequences. He must really get hold of his irrational fears – a dead fireman is not going to drop on him from a great height; he's unlikely to crush a cyclist by driving too fast; a deer is not going to appear in his garden at night causing him to shriek in terror and trigger a heart attack.

But one or more of those murdering thugs on the A12 could suddenly knock on his door; bomb his car or spring from his wardrobe brandishing a needle of Russian Novichock poison. Small things lead to big outcomes.

Who was it said, 'for want of a nail the shoe was lost; for want of a shoe a horse was lost; for want of a horse a rider was lost; for want of a rider a battle was lost and for want of a battle a kingdom was lost?'

Shakespeare, surely? Or was it Benjamin Franklin? He should get a grip. Had he said all that out loud? Could that mad old woman next door have heard him? What if the gangsters identified her as his weak spot and forced her to lead him into a trap?

James took his coffee to the lounge and checked for the millionth time the locks on the French windows to the garden. If they decided to enter that way they'd probably just remove the entire panel of doors and surrounds.

His landline phone rang. He had a mobile somewhere,

perhaps in his jacket pocket. He just didn't get on with digital devices.

It was Rebecca. 'You got back alright then, Dad. I thought you'd ring.'

'Sorry, love. Been very busy. I saw...' He suddenly decided not to share with his older daughter his A12 and toxic tip experience. Nothing had happened since then, so although he couldn't relax, perhaps he was over exaggerating.

She waited to hear. 'I saw a man with three heads in Clottingham as I drove through it.'

She chuckled. It was an old story he'd made up for the girls when they were little. He'd carried on with the grandchildren but Maisie had suffered nightmares so he let it rest.

'Dad, I said I was worried about you. We all are. After you'd left, Emily and Maisie separately asked why can't you come and live with us. And before you say it, Simon is totally happy with it. We may have his mother coming to us next year...'

'And before you start matching me up with your mother-in-law, I'd rather chew a bag of wasps.' This, despite being terrified of wasps, bees, gnats and dragonflies.

'I know, nobody can replace Mum. We get that. But you're a worry.' There was silence while he watched a massive spider cheekily appear from under his hall table and moved to crush it with his foot. 'By the way, Dad?'

'Yes, Rebecca?' he gasped as he solved the problem of the spider in his house. 'What is it?'

'Did you enjoy your drink I made for your journey home?'

'It was lovely, my darling.' She waited. 'Oh, I remember, I forgot it.'

'And that's only half why we're worried about you.'

His attention was caught by the front door mat which had ridden across to the left – it always did. It irritated – it always did. She sensed he was done so signed off the call.

Straightway he pushed the doormat square and after fetching the dustpan and brush from under the sink, straightening the cutlery tub and realigning the washing up liquid, he knelt to remove the remains of the spider and pulled himself up on the hall cupboard, releasing a little cry from the stab of knee pain.

In the lounge, his coffee was too cold to enjoy; he preferred it piping hot. As he returned to the kitchen, his neighbour kicked garden furniture and mouthed incoherent curses afresh.

The phone rang again. He knew she wouldn't wait long. It was Samantha, his younger daughter. She lived with her family a five-minute drive away. He knew, just knew, that Rebecca had called her to say that the old man was seeing things and shouldn't be left alone.

'Hello Dad, how's it going today?'

'I'm fine, Samantha. And what about you? How did Henry do in that school assessment?'

'William had the test, Dad, and he did well. Is everything OK there?'

'Been talking to your sister, have you?'

'Haven't talked to Rebecca for ages.'

'Two minutes. And you're a lousy liar, Samantha, that's why you couldn't have followed me into politics.'

'Speaking of which,' Samantha took the opportunity to broach the care home issue yet again. That one full of old politicos, where he'd be right at home.

Ellington was saved by his doorbell. He signed off with a solemn promise to think deeply about it, give it serious consideration, mull it over, take advice, not kick it into the long grass, not park it and reach a consensus round the table very soon.

After a quick squint through the pin hole, he unlocked and stood facing his neighbour, the one with the green door who'd recently been in a froth of rage. He wished he could remember her name.

'Sorry to disturb you, James,' she started off, cheerfully enough.

'That's fine, Judy,' her name rushing back at the right moment. 'How can I help?'

'I need advice.' It was his political days all over. Someone needing help would come to him as he was the right man with a few contacts he could still call, a few favours he was still owed. Also, in her case, he lived right next door.

Faced with no choice but to invite her in, he stepped back and indicated that Judy Blowers should step inside. Her foot dislodged the mat. James smiled to cover his irritation.

In the kitchen his cold coffee sitting on the worktop prompted him to offer her a cup. She accepted and while he went to brew two cups, she had a good nose round. At almost five feet, one inch, she was not tall but made up for that with her girth.

Certainly in her late 50s, she could have been ten years older or younger, now he'd seen her close. Her blouse, cardigan and grey trousers were widely deployed by the elderly in the 1970s. He thought about putting rat poison in her cup so he could get some peace, but then feared mixing the cups up.

While the coffees filtered and he imagined killing his neighbour and burying her in her own garden to escape her, she examined his framed photos of Rebecca and Simon's wedding, Samantha and Paul's wedding and various stages of his five grandchildren's lives so far.

Head on the slant, she stepped back to admire his Don Rout original circular painting from 1974 of Arctic microcosms that Elspeth had tolerated but never loved. Stepping closer to peer at the detail, it still made no sense. Don had been a one-off, a local character with a sense of humour that strangers took for rudeness, uncouthness and bigotry.

'Worth a lot, is it?'

'Sentimental value,' he replied, carrying coffee.

Still standing and looking at the painting, she began asking everyday fool questions about his health, the weather, his family, his garden and the price of bread. It gave her time to slurp the hot coffee. He'd never asked if she wanted sugar or milk. She lapped it up as it was.

'Good coffee. Costs a lot, does it?'

'You can never pay too much for good coffee,' he replied.

Then she switched tack. 'You know I recently lost my parents, James.' It was statement, not question. Brushing aside his mumbled regrets, she dropped down heavily into his favourite armchair while he perched on the settee.

'There's a bunch of kids, teenagers I suppose you'd call them. One or two from Hall Lane and St Jerome's Road, that area, but most come from the estate.' He nodded. This was a huge pile of tall flats and empty shops built to take London overspill and poor locals in the 1960s.

As she warmed to her saga, he was right back in his surgeries of yore, when he'd listen, write notes, promise action and did his best to get them out the door before they repeated the same tale of woe. But that was then; he'd moved on.

'There's one. His name is Dizzy or something. Not that I've listened. But they play in my garden, they smoke and daub stuff on my walls. They urinate on my dahlias. And when they see me, they make rude remarks.'

James was all ears now. If they were next door, were they also in his? 'What do you think I can do, Judy?'

'You were the MP, weren't you? I want you to take action to protect me.'

'You need to talk to one of our councillors, or the police responsible for this area or even our present MP. I have no powers now.'

'Useless. And half mad, some of them. They don't understand.'

'I'm too old and unsteady of my feet to confront them, Judy.'

'Listen, James.' She put the mug on his little table, missing the coaster he'd carefully placed. 'My old dad, God rest him, always used to say that bullies must be stood up to. Opposed, with full on war. And if you cut off the head of the ringleader, the others will disappear, scared shitless.'

'Blimey, Judy,' he said with a laugh as he stood and placed her mug on the coaster. 'You want me to execute the ringleader!'

'Exactly. Dizzy. He said the way to deal with bully boys was to decapitate the leader. You have old friends and contacts. You can arrange it. I have some money, don't worry, though it's not much.'

With a vague promise to 'look into it' and 'don't fret, I'll see what I can do' James ushered her out of the room and to the front door.

She turned outside his house, 'Remember James, I'm alone now and I keep watch through my windows, as always. You can never be too careful.'

What looked horribly like a dead mouse lay on the side of the front garden path leading to the gate. Dear God. At least it was dead.

With a more resounding shove than intended, he closed his door, stood against it a moment trying to forget the dead mouse. What replaced the image was the face of a constituent asking him in all seriousness thirty years ago to arrange the liquidation of a business rival.

Ellingham needed a change of scene. But did it have to be a care facility, as his family were urging?

And not Sir Thomas More House. It was by design stuffed full of former MPs, Lords, civil servants and the like. Not there, he'd never be free.

It was as he walked back to the lounge to retrieve the coffee cups that his right ankle twisted outwards, and he crashed to the floor with nothing close by to grab.

He lay, biting down a howl of pain and rage. He hadn't fallen for weeks. Months even. If he could just get himself up, he could recover and the family wouldn't know.

The pain subsided – he'd wrenched his shoulder a bit and grazed a knee on the carpet through his trousers. The ankle might be a problem. Hands and knees to the hall chair and hauling himself up so it tilted precariously, he was upright and gingerly hobbled to the lounge to rest.

Wincing on the ankle, he made it to the settee. Shutting his eyes for a little, he realised he was tired. But those cups were annoying, still in the lounge. Oh damn, hobble through with them to the kitchen? Or leave them there irritating him?

Before he decided, he lost 40 minutes of his life asleep, dreaming of a circus of bats that were debating invading his loft with a Spanish flamenco dance, but hadn't yet. He woke aware of noise nearby, outside. Was it another white van? Or the tow truck come for him?

Or had the teenagers moved from Judy's garden to his? Had those A12 killers found him? Had they done both – found him and recruited the teenagers to harm him?

James Ellington rarely thought there was an innocent explanation for any threat. He always lived the fearful possibilities on endless loops in his mind, so every fear was magnified.

And if you fear something enough, it will become true. While some entertained angels, James gave mental hospitality to legions of anxieties. You can never be too careful with entertaining fears.

Act One, Scene 2

This fall proved to be one of his less serious. Recovering enough to stagger about, cautiously furniture-walking, he was grateful to have escaped an ambulance call out or his family renewing their campaign for him to move to a place of safety.

After Elspeth had died, they worked in collusion with brochures, hints and outright asking him to look into some possibilities. It was for 'their sakes as well as his; his falls would not disappear; they would only increase.'

He'd had the loft emptied in order to get them off his back for awhile. Boxes of photos, election posters and handouts, press cuttings, diaries and constituency records that he hadn't been obliged to pass on to his successor through gritted teeth, covered the double bed, floor and overflowed from his wife's wardrobe in their marital bedroom.

James now slept in the spare room, preferring it to lying in a big bed with that empty space beside him. Whenever he felt strong, he gave an hour to sorting his MP papers with the intention of scrapping and shredding most.

Whenever he sat in that room crammed with memories – it was where both Rebecca and Samantha had been conceived – the records of the only job that had really mattered took him right back.

Squeezing into the one sitting space left, at the foot of the bed, his eye was caught by his box of diaries. He picked one at random. One page every day. He'd kept it up almost daily without fail ever since he was fifteen.

He and Elspeth did this; Elspeth said that. The little outings, the family raising issues all parents have to deal with. The balance between work and family, not always right. Parliamentary work was unique, an MP (or putative candidate) is never off duty.

After a row there was the making up. James read it, recalled it and felt a tear in his eye. Elspeth would never row and make up ever again.

Time to focus on the job in hand; back to searching for his files on the toxic tip. As MP he'd been pressurised by an effective 'Close the Toxic Tip' war waged by genuine environmentalists, regulars from the ranks of anti-everything protestors and a few recurring, serial mentalists. All MPs had to deal with them, the protest bandwagoners, the single-issue obsessives and the handful of genuine worriers.

On the tip, they'd actually had a point. Nobody could guarantee that there wouldn't be leakage under the holiday camp, through the sand cliffs to the beach. The news that over one week four dogs from different families were taken severely ill before passing away in agony was credited to the tip and clinched it for public opinion.

However scientific the team from EnviroSafe Waste were, after dogs died, were on a hiding to nothing. The council adopted a voluntary closure stance ahead of a compulsory one and the company meekly complied, only hanging on for a few hundred local lorry loads of ordinary domestic waste to fill it fully to minimise their costs.

Several times he'd visited in the run up to the end and on the first day of actual closure was filmed by the local

TV news among partying protestors outside the locked gates, his well-washed hair flying wildly in the wind.

He'd chatted amiably, his hand enthusiastically shaken by a man who turned out to be the vet who'd carried out the autopsies on the dogs.

Of course, EnviroSafe Waste was obligated to send in maintenance crews periodically to inspect the place and report to the council. But who'd let in the disposal crew from his A12 murders? Was there corruption in high places?

While an issue to get his teeth into would have excited him years ago, now it simply added to his fears. If the killers could arrange the perfect disposal of victims and their van, then they could give him and any other witnesses the same treatment. And James had rather set his heart on a pitch in the local cemetery where several generations of his paternal family rested under a fine off-centre stone cross and angel, tastefully dressed in moss and bird shit.

Still nursing the pains of that last fall, he hobbled through to the hall to check his front door was secure. In the lounge that extended from the front to the garden, he looked up and down the road from behind his window and at his garden through the french windows and the kitchen.

Not for the first time, he was glad they lived in an expanded bungalow and not a big house with stairs. The ankle throb would die down. He had all he needed here; why would he move?

Returning to the lounge, he flopped down, cursing that he hadn't made coffee before sitting. The brochures the family had left sat on the coffee table. They were everywhere, like love notes that young couples leave for each other.

Picking up the Sir Thomas More glossy booklet ready to rip it to shreds, he opened it. Top of the list of directors and chairman of the company behind the home was his old Parliamentary Honourable friend, Ralph Dines.

Rare were genuine friends in the Commons, or Lords for that matter, but Ellington and Dines had known each other a long time. Their love-hate relationship had filled hours in and about the Palace of Westminster while Dines climbed the greasy pole, less high than he'd have liked.

Of course, Dines compensated for that shortcoming by having a finger in many pies, a hand in every nefarious business/political scheme going, his snout in several troughs and two fists clamped round the neck of anyone in his way.

Well, if he was Chairman of Sir Thomas More House, there was no way on earth James Ellingham was going to move there. And that was that.

He looked up as a vehicle slowed outside. The road was a quiet, minor one in a nice part of town, a mix of bungalows and medium to large homes with a mainly elderly population who kept themselves to themselves. Apart from Judy Blowers, next door, of course.

It was a white van, not unlike the one he'd seen going into the tip. The driver was peering at his house. A sudden chill running down James' spine, he slid to the floor, crawled to the window, hauled himself up on the radiator and watched, half hidden as the van stopped and the driver climbed out.

Already he was confusing tow truck fear with white van obsession. From the angle he couldn't read the number plate of the van. And was the tow truck number, E404 CPD? They'd probably changed it. Would they come for him in broad daylight? But those people would do anything. Carry out an activity that looked normal and nobody would even notice it.

Villains dressed as workmen or engineers could close roads, enter houses and sever utilities. Even if they bore signs on their fronts and backs saying, 'criminals at work', no resident would notice. James hoped that Judy had got the details down – she rarely missed a trick.

The driver, a young, short-cropped hair, ugly-mug, wanted-poster male hooligan approaching six feet and dressed in a filthy white jump suit, opened the back doors. Ellington froze, waiting the machine gun.

But it was a small parcel, the size of a medium domestic tool like a kettle in a box, which he carried to the Carvers, his neighbours on the other side from Judy, and left on their doorstep. As he wheel-spun drove off, the thug gave James the finger, taking exception to being stared at.

It all looked innocent, but the parcel could be a bomb powerful enough to demolish the Carvers' house and his own. Or it could unleash clouds of mustard gas. Ellington stood still by the curtain, till he had to go to the toilet. There was no bomb; no mustard gas.

Fear is a killer. James had read it several times. But he was unable to stop entering that dark world. People can be destroyed by fear of attack, loss, escaping animals or gasses, fear of plague and disease, famine and drowning, war or even just making a dick of oneself. Fear. He'd been fearful of Dines in his time.

And now Dines was slap bang in the middle of his mind, the link with a criminal underworld was astonishingly logical to James Ellington who now needed to remind himself from his diaries, notes and comments on all that he'd recorded about Dines amidst that material in his bedroom.

There was a relegated wife in his back story, he recalled. Nice Sloan-ranger type from a wealthy county family with high expectations of her marriage to an aspiring politician. James and Elspeth had met her early on in their Westminster days.

Unfortunately, as Dines failed to even make Parliamentary bag-carrier for a junior minister within a year of first election, she'd taken herself off to richer pastures with their single child. Or he'd had her taken off.

That was more likely.

Or had there been a scandal? Infidelity of some sort? Such things were not only frequent in the Westminster hothouse, they seemed to be the price many players were happy to pay to take part in the great political Game.

Grateful for having missed out on that side of his political life, James recalled more detail of the first post-election meeting the four of them shared on the second day at the Palace of Westminster, before things got under way with the election of a Speaker. Dines had taken James and Elspeth for a drink on the terrace to a) impress and b) eye James' wife up properly.

The Dines already lived in London in an apartment funded by her parents with a little middle class terraced house in the constituency they'd bought when he was first selected as prospective Parliamentary candidate.

The drinks had been awkward, metropolitan versus living yokels. Trendy London school compared with the local comprehensive because that is what Elspeth and James had wanted for their girls.

Despite a gushing 'yes, you must come' invitation to dinner they never met up again in or out of Westminster. Even when Dines visited James' constituency to grandstand at an after-dinner speech for a constituency function, his wife didn't accompany him.

Dines was filed in a unique category of his own, with some impressive cross-referencing, which James admired, though he said so himself, out loud. Files were vital to sustain his memories as he found he couldn't always grasp past details.

However, somehow Dines loomed larger in the mind than most others. Why was that, James wondered?

And he certainly had no intention of being parted from his files – too many memories, too much information that could prove useful one day.

Act One, Scene 3

In the House, one early evening, James worked as usual at his desk in the Cloisters, below the chamber and lobby level, a long corridor with desks paired back-to-back. The East corridor was for his party; its parallel, the West Cloisters, was for the opposition, but their leader in waiting had gradually cleared out his fellow MPs to claim the whole stretch.

Ralph often walked through that enemy side, just to wind up the ambitious MP and his endless staff. Then he breezed into the East Cloisters, his own party side, with his constant air of entitlement, looking at what MPs had on their desks and at what was decorating their pinboards that divided one MP's tiny space from another.

Constituents who imagined their MPs luxuriating in personal, spacious, state-of-the-art offices would be horrified if they saw the pre-war conditions many Members laboured under in those days.

'Evening, James, my good man!' This was always in the tone of addressing a butler. 'Time for a spot of supper in the cheap caff, as my appointment worthy of a proper Strangers' Dining experience has baled on me.'

James was regularly second choice when Ralph didn't get a more important person who'd help him and was to be guested in the Stranger's room (all non-MPs or staff were Strangers) or he didn't have an offer to dine off site at the expense of some lobby group, trade organisation or special interest campaigners.

Ralph Dines was an expert – he rarely paid for his own dinner and when he did, it was in the subsidised Members' cafeteria. James Ellington was ideal company on these slummed down occasions.

'I can, Rafe, yes, give me a minute,' he nodded, returning the waste bin to its normal spot after Dines had kicked it aside, and imagining slapping the man senseless till he stopped annoying everybody.

Ralph Dines was commonly called Rafe or Raif; it was a snobby affectation that helped reinforce his sense of self-importance. Dines was an apt surname for this man who relished his breakfasts, luncheons and dinners. Or just a drinks bash, he was always good company, good value.

Such people were known as 'trenchermen' in Westminster – those who dined well at the tables of others and Ralph, Rafe, Raif certainly gorged for his constituents. For his country, in fact.

He sat on the only empty chair beside James', the seat usually occupied by secretaries when taking dictation. He flicked through the pile of letters at the side of the desk.

On the pinboard he disorganised the family photos and a scribbled note from the PM congratulating him on a speech last year and bent to fiddle with the waste bin and hummed a tune that could have been anything at all.

Slamming his pen down, James snapped, 'Alright Ralph, I'll come now, shall I? Would that make you happy?' Where were the assassins when he needed them?

'Delirious, old boy. I'm getting peckish for a plate of caff haddock and chips followed by a bowl of spotted dick with custard.'

And off they set, greeting people all the way. This was another thing Dines did that drove others mad. If he was walking with a colleague or visitor, he'd always stop to flatter someone more useful en route. When he talked to anyone face to face, say standing in the Members' Lobby or the Library, his eyes darted ceaselessly over that person's shoulder hoping for a more interesting colleague to appear.

His front door opening brought James back from the bedroom-study-archive of the past into the lounge of the present. Those memories were on paper, newsprint, video and in his head. Those wouldn't shift, though they were less clear than years ago. He was glad of the break; he didn't take to Ralph Dines any better in retirement than he had at the time.

'Hi, Grandpa!' It was Henry, bright middle child of his daughter, Samantha, who'd stayed local. Nearby. That seemed more natural than how Rebecca had moved away, as far as Essex.

'Hi Henry! Hi William! Hi Maisie! Hi Samantha! Hi Paul!' James sang out, as his hi-five local family trooped in.

'Just me and the kids, Dad,' Samantha informed him, plonking her capacious bag on his settee. 'Paul's at work. Some new contract they're excited about.'

'That's great, my love. The last thing we need is that joinery company going bust.' She kissed his cheek and looked at him closely. 'What's the matter?'

'Nothing, I'm pleased to see you all. Do you want to hear about my trip to your sister in Essex?' He looked round. His three grandkids were deep into their mobile phones. 'Yes please, Grandpa.'

'Rebecca gave me an update, Dad.' A pause followed which was the natural moment for him to share the A12 event and his recent fall. He said nothing. With a smile she got up to go the kitchen to grab coffee and observed the spare room door open.

'Been doing more sorting, Dad? That's a good thing to get on with. When we all helped you get everything down from the loft, it was a halfway house to the bins and shredders, not the bedroom.'

'I know, Samantha, I know.'

While she made coffee and seized cans of cola from his fridge for the kids, she pushed a little harder about him needing more care than they could give.

'Which reminds me, would you have a look at the washing machine, please? I seem to have got the programs in a muddle' he said to change the subject.

As soon as she'd gone into the utility room, he approached Maisie, tapping a message, but before he could press her about how far the campaign for him to move had developed, she said, without looking up, 'my sixth driving lesson tomorrow, Grandpa, remember you promised?'

Nodding, he accepted that he'd agreed to take her out for a few practice drives once she'd had the basic six lessons from the driving school. 'Yes, of course, my love, later this week?'

'Cool. Thanks, Grandpa. Thursday morning is good.'

'Have you overheard your parents talking to each other or your aunt Rebecca about persuading me to leave here?'

As she opened her mouth to reply, her phone actually rang, so with a shrug and sorry face, she replied into it, 'Hi babes, how's it going?'

Turning to Henry he repeated his question. He was answered with, 'hang on a sec, Grandpa, I'm just three points off the next level.'

With a smile and a nod, he put the question for the third time to young William, still of an age when he might tell the truth to his ancient granddaddy.

'I've heard Mum and Dad talking and Mum on the phone to Aunt Rebecca, yeah, I have.' Ellington nodded, his suspicions confirmed.

'Mum put some brochures in her bag, Grandpa. I think there's Fitzgerald Home and Thomas More hostel or asylum. She's got two.'

Thanking the boy, he fished in his daughter's bag. Fitzgerald Hall was a residential village of miniature villas in gorgeous grounds around an old house that was the actual care home for those too far gone to self-cater in a villa. He'd seen their sales material before and thought it was just too commercial for him.

Sir Thomas More House – well, here would be his seventh copy of that brochure. This was the home stuffed with people who had known or administered high office and he knew many of them, including that bloody Ralph Dines.

'Have I got anyone on my side in not wanting this?' he asked the kids. Henry nodded. Maisie finished her call and told him, 'we're all your side, Grandpa. We just think you'll be better looked after than managing alone.'

Samantha reappeared, holding the instruction booklet of the washing machine. 'I've reset it, Dad. You just have to put in the program number on this list on page 7, depending on what sort of things you want to wash.'

'Sounds simple. I'll get the hang of it, Samantha, thanks love, just need more practice. I thought I might flood the utility room and be unable to stop water, find the stopcock rusted open and me drowning in a trapped room when the door self-locked on me.'

As he reached to take the booklet from her hand he missed the back of the settee that supported his normal furniture-walking and stumbled, arms flailing like windmills to stay upright.

The boys clapped. Samantha shook her head as she stepped sharply to help him up. Maisie said, 'see what we mean, Grandpa?' as another call came in to her phone.

Samantha said, 'this can't go on, Dad. You're not safe alone.'

He muttered, 'it was just a missed grab at the furniture. Could have happened to anybody.'

'We're not worried about anybody. We care about you.'

Act One, Scene 4

In his plush office on the ground floor of Sir Thomas More House, Ralph Dines, former MP, former government whip and former junior minister in the business department, stood staring through the window, across the grand sweeping drive skirted by well-kept flower beds.

He felt comfortable in the old place, the next best thing to being in that great gentleman's club, the Commons. By an unforgivable administrative oversight, he'd not been elevated to the House of Lords, but here he was de facto the boss of a growing business empire so he could lord it over staff, inmates and their grateful families alike.

Leaning on his stick and shifting his weight from the left leg to the right, he bent it at the knee a few times midair to stretch it. Damned knees, damned feet. He'd been alright when he was younger. Now the years brought physical challenges to complicate his schemes and dreams.

To end up as the chairman of a trust running a glorified old folks' home seemed perfectly natural. Just as drawing comfortable retainers from two investment companies, a lending firm, several retail outlets, pubs and hotels was no more than what he should expect.

After all, what he'd worked assiduously at since just before leaving the Commons, was to be the puppet master with many strings to pull in business, public relations and affairs and the lives of an increasingly large number of citizens.

'Politics is never black and white; it's always at best grey,' was a favourite adage of his. And the greyer the better, he could have added.

Imelda, his willowy, unsmiling secretary slid in, treading quietly on the rich pile ochre carpet and approached his desk like a child to the teacher. He'd seen her in the window reflection.

'Mr Dines,' she said quietly, 'Dr Zoe asks for half an hour on the patients in the dementia ward, if you can? The Brittle Bone Society called to ask if you could make a speech at their annual dinner and Maintenance suggest replacing a window unit upstairs in Room 45B where that damp came in.'

'Yes, to all three, Imelda,' he barked, clutching his walking stick – a fine wolf-headed silver-topped art deco specimen appropriate for his position. He limped over to his records cupboard as a signal that she could go now, passing and correcting the hanging angle of a framed photo of him shaking hands with the Prime Minister before last.

His internal phone rang, causing him to curse quietly. He hated being stopped when he was on the way to doing something he wanted to do. He fancied a delve through his cuttings' books. He'd been thinking about his finest hour, when he was a junior whip. 'One should always have something sensational to read about other people and oneself' was another of his oft-stated adages, unaware it was remarkably close to an Oscar Wilde quote.

Lord, what a lot he'd discovered about his colleagues. Peccadilloes, downright vile habits and secrets galore. Oh the power of the Whips' office keeping their little black book, vehemently denied, as a means of enforcing discipline, doling out rewards like Parliamentary trips and punishments like 'no pairing' or a 'gossip hare' set running in their constituency.

'Yes, Imelda, what now?' he snapped.

'Our new guest, Mr Douglas Gardener has been a little over familiar with one of the cleaning staff.'

'Female, of course? Alright, I'll give him some thought. Move the shifts around so Douglas Gardener sees only male cleaners.'

Dines had never been imprisoned and forced to run his operation from inside and he'd never been in the military, but he was a man used to getting his own way. People always arrived at his way of thinking. He'd reduced Members of Parliament to tears; done deals with ministers to increase his wealth and perfected his air of entitlement that reached privilege proportions.

Gardener would be a pain in most organisations, a man to be avoided. But to Dines, Gardener was putty in his hands, living in the constant stomach-churning fear that his flaws would reach the ears of his family, especially his son who had a high moral attitude that wouldn't have been amiss in a Victorian clergyman.

Returning to his cupboard where he was headed, he had a new mission. The press cuttings could keep; the files on Douglas Gardener had become urgent.

Long ago, Dines had concluded that it was never safe to keep anything of value in digital form. Somebody would always work out how to steal it. The head was the best, but minds turned doolally and forgetful. So, good old-fashioned paper was his preferred way of storing the information he needed to maintain his hold over people.

It could always burn, be flooded on, tear, fade and, of course, be stolen. But thieves would have to know what they were looking at. So, his cupboard store behind his drinks cabinet with the imposing portrait of himself on

Westminster Bridge with Parliament as a backdrop housed his personal archives.

The Gardener file was found quickly, under his junior Whips section. Gardener had reported his wallet stolen to the Commons police one night two hours after the sitting had ended when he drove to the Kings Cross area to buy a first edition of a national newspaper.

That's what he claimed, anyway. He'd left his jacket on the back seat of his car, parked on double yellow lines, nipped round the corner to the newsstand outside the Post Office. The wallet had been snatched because in his rush he'd neglected to lock his car.

It was kept quiet, of course, discretely handled by Commons' police. A new Commons pass was issued and he ordered new credit cards and his Tescos' loyalty and roadside rescue cards. The matter was closed.

Except of course it was recorded in the Whips' archives. Dines refreshed his memory, locked his cupboard, then his office and set off on one of his casual strolls around the house and grounds. Thank heavens for the Whips.

His apparently random meandering, nodding here and there, sharing a few words with one or two staff and residents and glad-handing was a masterclass in working the room in a style much beloved of politicians. It was mechanical, allowing him to reflect on the Whips.

Whips, short form of 'whippers-in' from fox hunting with dogs days, described their public role in Parliament – to ensure all their MPs respond to Government or Opposition directives, to support or oppose.

Who was it had described the Whips system as essential to the smooth running of Parliamentary business as the sewers were? Whips were the 'usual channels' stitching up deals between Government and Opposition to suit and managing day to day Parliamentary business.

In the corridors of the old house he passed the nursing wing where the sickest were cared for and then the Dementia bays, heading for the residential wing for former MPs and in a few cases, their partners/spouses.

The entrance contained a magnificent window looking across the courtyard and beyond to the old kitchens where they had just secured planning permission for a crematorium.

Noting one old buffer hiding an e-cigarette as he walked past, Dines mentally noted to make a big announcement about the safety and health risks of smoking in his care home. And what the hell was the name of that fool?

He found Douglas Gardener hiding a magazine under a desk in the lounge. Dines didn't have to see it to know it was pornographic. 'Ah Douglas, my dear chap, settling in, are you?'

'Oh, yes, thanks, Ralph, never been happier, really.

'Well, I'm over the moon to hear it. You could have a very long and fruitful residence here, Douglas, if you keep your nose clean.' He paused to see if Gardener knew what he was talking about, while he slowly tapped his stick on the floor between them.

'Throw myself into all the activities', you said.

'And that's the ticket, old chap. However, if I may speak man to man,' and he pulled a chair adjacent to Gardener which brought his face almost touching the man who was beginning to sweat.

Dines removed the magazine from Gardener's clutch and tossed it into the waste bin. 'Douglas, not a smart move to start fiddling with the staff, the young lady staff, when they're trying to clean your grubby room.'

Light dawned in Douglas' brain. 'Oh, yes, I'm sorry.'

'Good. Consider this a friendly chat with a tiny warning. Not a good move. Just as driving to Kings Cross to buy a paper and not locking your car wasn't a smart move.'

Flustered, going red and wiping what used to be a fringe from his forehead, Gardener swallowed. 'That's below the belt, old news from long ago, only a few knew about it.'

'An unfortunate term, in your case old cock, below the belt. And few know to this day. But I'm one of them. And I also know about the night of your drive around Kings Cross after buying your paper. You picked up a man with a young woman who was almost certainly a prostitute...'

Gardener began to push himself up from the chair. 'Now, wait a minute. That wasn't me!' Dines just watched him, eyes almost closed, a lizard on a rock.

'No, you must be mixing me up with someone else. I saw other Members in that area. There was Andrew Findlay one time. And I saw old Lord Bilcham a couple of times.'

Dines knew of Findlay, but not Bilcham. Useful information. Still, he said nothing to Gardener, knowing it was best to let suspects condemn themselves in the panic of interrogator silence.

'No, that wasn't me; I think I'd know if I'd been there, Ralph. Be reasonable.' Now Dines had been accused of many things in his life, but never of being reasonable, so he waited, silent, watching Gardener squirm, weighing it up.

'Look, listen. OK, so it was me. I never reported it, nothing was taken and nothing happened. I just offered a lift to a young couple who thumbed me and who looked lost. He sat in the front, she in the back. We drove around but he wouldn't say where they wanted to go. She said nothing. He got out at a traffic light saying something about I could do what I wanted with her. I couldn't wait to get rid of her, back near the station.'

He stood fully, so Dines could look him directly in the eye. 'Your word against hers. Twenty quid on the back seat, was her word. The incident was recorded in the Book.'

'What, even then you were following all of us around all the time, interviewing anyone and everyone we talked to!'

'Not everyone, Douglas, that would've been silly. No, only the iffy ones, like you. Now relax...'

'But to think you know anything about what was a short, unimportant moment in one evening.'

'You can never be too paranoid, Douglas. And in this place, think of it as an extension to the Parliamentary estate.'

Dines turned, leaving Gardener too shaken to retrieve his magazine, which Dines pushed deeper into the bin with his stick.

He smiled at Gardener, like a cat to a trapped mouse. 'Oh, I might have a little job for you, later, Douglas. We'll have a drink and discuss how you can help me make Sir Thomas More House run smoothly. Do you still drive?'

'No, I don't Ralph.'

'A pity. I need a driver or somebody with one for the job I have in mind.'

Dines set off, stick thumping the carpet, smiling broadly.

You can never have too many people shit scared of what others know about them.

Act One, Scene 5

James couldn't have got out of bed the wrong side because it was against the wall. But he was certainly in a disgruntled mood.

He'd wrenched his leg while hobbling through to the bathroom in the night, wall-holding all the way. The coffee machine needed de-scaling and he had no chemicals to push through it. And to crown it all, he caught sight of Judy Blowers rolling up the path.

His promise to investigate her problem with that bunch of young yobs had completely slipped his mind. In fact, it had vanished the moment she left his house after her last visit. He had to come up with something.

Flinging wide the door before she could bang on it, he pulled his dressing gown tighter around him in the stiff autumn breeze and croaked, 'Hello Judy, I'm so sorry, I think I'm going down with a serious cold or even, God forbid, man-flu. I have made some enquiries about those kids but my contact hasn't got back to me yet.'

He pretended to be holding back a sneeze through pinching his nose.' 'I'll chase him up, Judy, trust me, and I'll get back to you.'

It was at that moment he wished he'd had the sense to clutch one of the old Covid facemasks from a few years back when the pandemic swept the world and face coverings became mandatory.

'OK, James, wouldn't want to put you out if you're going down with man-flu.'

Not the only actor in the doorway with a sense of timing, she added, 'my mother died of flu last month and my father a few days later of grief. So, you get to bed and get better, James, don't worry about me. There is no grief counselling on the NHS, so you just get better.'

She turned to leave. Of course, he felt bad. But the really important issue was that he needed a break from everybody. He closed the door gently, straightened the mat and gave her a moment in case she decided to return at once. She'd not let it go now. He'd promised, after all.

Determined to get her off his back for good, he clumped straight to his study, rummaged around the dusty Council drawer to find the number he needed.

'Hello, could I speak to Hilary Sinclair, please?'

'Do you want Mr Hilary Sinclair or Mrs Hilary Sinclair?'

'What?'

'Both Mr and Mrs Sinclair work here at the council now and they're in the same department.'

'Mr, please. It's James Ellington.'

He sat, calmly waiting. After clicks, a snatch of recorded voice lying, 'your call is important to us' and a fragment of some ghastly 1950s' lounge music, Hilary came through, 'Hello, James, how in the world are you doing?'

'Rarely better, Hilary. I hear your wife is there with you now!'

'We have a pact that we never talk about work when we're at home. Now, how can I help?'

As James outlined what he remembered of Judy Blowers' fears and problems with the kids, he felt, fleetingly, as he did in his glory days. Then, a phone call from the MP to council officials had them jumping to it, standing to attention by their desks before solving the issue at once and reporting to him so he could inform the constituent and bask in their brief gratitude.

'I'll pass it on, James. One of my juniors will deal with it. I'm more into bigger pictures these days. I'll ask Hilary to do some digging.'

'That's what Judy Blowers wants, I think, somewhere to bury the bodies.'

'Very droll, James, you haven't lost your edge. Talk to you soon.'

No sooner had the call ended than the phone rang again.

It was Samantha. 'Hello Dad. Just to give you a heads up, that Rebecca is coming; on her way now. The kids are at school and Simon will be there when they get home so she has the whole day.'

'That's nice. Is something the matter?' He sensed trouble coming if both daughters were on their way.

'We're going to solve what's the matter, Dad.' His heart sank. He was the matter. 'Get ready; we're going for a little drive.'

He waited a moment. 'And where are we going, my love?'

His front door opened and in she walked, still talking on her mobile to him. Rebecca followed.

'We've arranged a little tour of Fitzgerald Hall and we're coming with you.'

He'd been ambushed. Neither daughter would take no for an answer. He wondered about feigning the cold that had worked with Judy earlier, but it was already too late to swing that one.

His old indoor surgical boots were being taken off and replaced with his newer outdoor surgical boots. They were handling them, so he couldn't claim to be bootless. Of course, they'd borrow a wheelchair.

Asked if he wanted the toilet as if he was five, he was led out the door with Samantha locking it carefully behind them. Rebecca took his arm, which was just as well as he stumbled on the path. He glared at the spot as if it had done it deliberately.

Trying to make entirely natural his glimpse to both left and right for the A12 killers that he hadn't forgotten about, he stood at Rebecca's turquoise ten-year-old Ford C-Max. He was pushed into the front seat and buckled up as if he was still that same child of five.

He kept his silence while they drove, the sisters sharing an endless stream of information, anecdotes and jokes about his grandchildren. The radio played music from the 60s – she'd chosen an oldies station – but he couldn't concentrate on it through their chatting.

He recalled Fitzgerald Hall well enough. In its heyday it had been a fine stately home for the Fitzgeralds who were big in the 18th century. After the line died out the house had, over the years, been variously a country club, a hotel with a golf club and then a hotel and high-end function facility.

It had decayed a little every time it changed hands.

Maintenance costs rocketed while more modern alternative facilities grew up in the locality. The golf course was sold to the neighbouring farmer; the old house lost half its roof in a winter gale and a bunch of travellers wreaked pointless vandalistic damage when they removed all the copper water pipes, fireplaces and half the floor planking before being evicted.

During his time as the Member, the house and grounds, including the entire farm with what had been the golf course had been bought by a consortium with deep pockets that restored the house into a modern, specialist care home. It had been given planning consent and most locals were happy the shabby eyesore was transformed.

'Sharp left turn here, be careful Rebecca.' He had helped his daughters learn to drive, but they certainly pushed at speed boundaries these days. He pictured coming across a tractor from the opposite direction that shunted them into the ditch where they were set upon by a gang of rowdies pouring from a Transit van wielding clubs, maces and sawn-off shotguns.

In the grounds they'd built a hundred villas or small bungalows, each designed for the elderly and infirm. Nobody under 65 was allowed to buy any and cleaning, feeding, shopping, medical help was provided to all residents until they were too ill or frail to cope alone at which point, they moved into the Hall.

To be fair, they'd landscaped the grounds beautifully, James conceded silently, as they swept through the restored gates and up the drive. Tall trees not only swayed in the easterly off the sea, but shed their leaves in an almost constant shower.

Each villa was slightly different from the next, well-proportioned and attractively laid out among the swaying sycamores, oaks, ash and lime trees along with shrubs circling a duck pond he didn't recall being there before. And he didn't really know the names of any of the trees,

A Fitzgerald Hall staffer, shivering a little, his slick black hair all over the place in the breeze, was standing at the doors to greet them after parking in a disabled bay, placing James' blue badge on the windscreen.

'Greetings,' the man in the smart suit and eyes that were sharp and cold in a face well shaved apart from a cut on the neck that was still fresh. 'I'm Elvis Bicker,' and he held out his hand to James.

'Elvis Bicker, I'm James Ellington and these are my daughters, Samantha and Rebecca. I'm guessing your parents were fans of Elvis Presley.'

'They were indeed. They liked retro-rock 'n roll. I was nearly called Little Richard and if I'd been a girl I would've been called Janice after Janice Joplin.' It was an explanation he'd had to give most of his life. Everybody smiled.

'Well, I imagine we don't want to look round the main house, James?' The use of the personal address was unavoidable these days. 'You're keen to see inside one of our individual, independent-supported living hubs. We have two vacant and for sale at present.'

He set off at a snail's pace as if leading a bunch of ancient oldies clutching walking frames and each other for support. James pulled ahead to make them move faster, while Elvis kept up his estate agent patter to the women.

When vacant, the hubs could be sold on the open market since residents and families owned them. They could be altered within reason. Outside each home were little wooden sheds with charging points to hold disability scooters. Refuse was collected weekly. Staff would shop, prepare meals and clean. Residents often ate in the restaurant in the main house.

Medical help was on tap 24/7 and they had a direct line to the local surgery, when needed. One of the units for sale had been stripped, cleaned and repainted. The other was full of the possessions of the old dear who'd either passed away there or been moved to the house. Her head shape was indented in the pillow; her slippers still on the floor at the bedside.

James acknowledged the exquisite design and planning with every state-of-the-art aid to support living for the disabled and/or elderly. The grounds were superb; pleasant walks were certainly to be had. Several faces peered from windows, most looked hostile, one or two curious. One woman who appeared to know him grinned and waved inanely.

'That's Elsie. She's doing remarkably well. Has dementia, but her family support her here every day, working in shifts,' Elvis told them, waving back at Elsie.

Samantha and Rebecca kept up a stream of questions about costs, what independence actually meant, what activities were laid on and were they optional and what was the food like if James chose to eat in the restaurant?

'Let's have coffee and some of Mrs Agal's cheesecake, what do you say?' said Elvis, longing to be indoors if not to sample the cakes.

The coffee shop was adjacent to the restaurant and shared the same kitchens. The food offer looked appetising and everywhere was spotlessly clean. James made the effort for his daughters, as they had hopes he'd love the place. If he played along, they'd be happy.

He asked questions that had already been answered, chatted about the highlights of his life and his daughters' relationships and children. Elvis and his brothers Roy (after Roy Orbison) and Gene (after Gene Pitney) were setting up a little retro band and had rehearsed in front of some residents, which James might like. Nodding enthusiastically, he asked for a coffee top up.

Passing an old man giving himself a thorough telling off, his toast neatly cut into tiny cubes on the table before him, James limped to the gent's toilet, to allow them time to talk about him and because he was busting for a pee. Coming out was an old boy he knew he'd seen before. 'Hey, Mr Ellington, hello!'

He shook the proffered hand, hoping the man had washed it. 'Peter Houseman! Your favourite student!'

'Peter Houseman? Student?' James was confused. He'd heard the man say 'I'm your favourite constituent.' But he'd said student.

'Yes, you remember, when you were at Lord Henstead High School. I was your favourite student!'

'Of course, sorry, I don't recall names as well as I did. And you must have been what, 15, 16 when I taught at Lord Henstead?'

'I know that was before you went into politics, but I thought you'd have remembered me and the first class you ever taught there.' The man was disappointed. James could do nothing.

'Well, Peter, I'm sure we'll have a chance to catch up very soon.' Peter Houseman nodded with joy, shook his hand again as James tried to recall his teaching years before the political ones. He barely could, the politics having been so all embracing.

On a note of jollity, optimism and basking in high expectations they made their way from the coffee shop to the car where Elvis slipped away. As the girls were keen to ask what he really thought, James was allowed to get in the car and buckle himself up.

His door was still open when he was hailed by name by a couple of women wrapped to the chins in old fashioned greatcoats perched on a wooden bench in front of a nearby unit. 'Hello, it's James Ellington! Hey, James Ellington!'

One stood and shook the other. She was thrilled to have seen her former MP. Unbuckling, he limped to them knowing it was a bad idea. They'd want something from him.

'Well, if it isn't James Ellington. I'm Margaret Lindley, you remember.'

'Of course, Margaret, how are you?'

'This is Margaret Francis, you remember?'

He recalled neither, and it was clear that Margaret Francis had no clue who he was.

'You'll love it here, James Ellington. Everyone is so friendly and lovely. They really care. Don't they Margaret?'

'Yes, Margaret. Is it time for our snack?'

Helped by his daughters with small talk for the next two minutes, James started to move off with a look at his watch and exuding the air of rush, hurry and purpose MPs put on when meeting everyday constituents.

Margaret Lindley was having none of it. 'James

Ellington, now you're here, I wonder if you can help. I used to live in Clottingham, you remember. My dog died on that beach from the toxic tip, you remember?'

He went cold, there it was again, the bloody toxic tip. 'How can I help?' he heard himself asking, out of habit. Samantha tried to nudge him towards the car, recalling so many times as a child she'd had to wait when he'd been waylaid by constituents with problems and now this one was going to sour their successful visit to Fitzgerald Hall.

'Well, my family pestered me about coming here, and they very carefully arranged everything and made a plan for paying for it. It's not cheap, you know! And now I think they've sold my house so I can't go back home if I wanted to.'

Catching a glance from Samantha, James mumbled, 'I'll look into it, Margaret Lindley. I have your address here. It was lovely to see you again. And you too, Margaret Francis. But if you'll excuse us now, my daughter has a child to pick up from school.'

And with that they managed to slip away, back to the car, belted up and Rebecca hit the road. Once through the gates, Samantha said, 'Don't let that old constituent with a problem thing bother you, Dad. People always do that when they recognise you.'

'What did you think of the set-up there, Dad?' asked Rebecca, changing gears angrily. 'Worth at least thinking about?'

'I saw it. I asked a lot of questions. It was all very nice indeed. I actually think it's a great concept. For other people. Not me.'

Nothing further was said in the car as they drove back to his home.

On the bench in Fitzgerald Hall, Margaret Francis spoke to her companion. 'Who was that? Didn't he used to be James Ellington, our MP?'

Margaret Lindley gave it some thought. 'I really have no idea who he was.'

Act One, Scene 6

Nobody spoke as Rebecca pulled into his drive, deliberately driving on his grass. The women hurried out, but Ellington dawdled. That is, until he saw Judy Blowers leaving her front door having obviously waited for him, when he put on the best spurt he could manage.

Indoors, he stepped sharply, thumping his stick on the carpet. He fell in the lounge doorway with no warning as usual as his ankle just gave way and he went over sideways.

He clutched, like he always did, for anything or anyone to grasp as he fell. Nothing wrong with his reflexes, despite them being absent from his knees. As it happened Samantha was nearest to him and he yanked her arm as he tumbled, pulling her almost on top of him.

Rebecca thought it hilarious. 'You remember, Dad, when you pulled that stunt falling out of the coach on our excursion on holiday in California? Mum pulled you up and we got your bleeding knee looked at there and then!'

'Not funny,' Samantha muttered. Remember that afternoon you walked me home from primary school, which you did about once a term and fell pulling me down so you actually landed on top of me? Get up, Daddy. I remember saying that to cover my embarrassment.'

Crawling on his knees to the lounge, he pulled himself up on the settee, which was misshapen enough to indicate it had been called into that service more than once.

'No, I don't find any fall funny, Rebecca, thanks a load. And you really are a menace, Dad, you can fall over in a puff of wind, how the hell do you think you can manage on your own here!' Samantha's voice rose to a shriek of irritation and frustration.

'Occasionally I stumble a bit. Hardly surprising at my age and with my feet condition,' Ellington shouted back at his daughter.

Not to be outdone Rebecca decided it wasn't funny after all. 'Dad, what is it going to take to make you see sense and think of us for once and not yourself?! Break a few bones in your leg? Fracture your skull?'

'You'll both damage your vocal cords shouting like that and I can see your blood pressures rising, I couldn't bear...' he yelled.

And the daughters were off, riled even more. In the minute that they kept up the row, Judy Blowers reached the front door, listened a moment and turned back to go home, deciding this wasn't the right moment.

'Right, enough of this. Go and have a pee, Dad, we're going for another drive. Right now.' Rebecca had made her mind up.

'I'm not going back to Fitzgerald Hall.'

No, Dad, 'we're going to look at Sir Thomas More House whether you want to or not. I haven't given up a whole day to this and you carry on like a spoilt child refusing to eat his cabbage.'

The atmosphere was knife-cuttingly deep, but he went to the toilet wondering if a snake emerging from the bowl would stop them, put his coat back on and slowly shuffled out to the car, summoning as much dignity as he could, doing his best to hide the knee pain from that recent fall.

It took twenty minutes to drive there at what James would have described as breakneck, reckless speed. Rebecca and Samantha chatted about the forthcoming autumn half term break, about their men's jobs and Samantha's idea to train as a teacher next year.

Neither addressed their father; he contributed nothing except private thoughts about country lane pile ups and bloody rioting in the villages.

As he wondered how they knew the precise way to go without consulting a map and whether they'd just drive straight in, he saw a white van coming towards them, leaving.

Not unlike the one he'd seen towed into the toxic tip, this was clearly a different vehicle but it had been there ahead of him. Rebecca pulled up on the verge by the entrance to the House.

The van driver thought she had stopped for him to exit, but she was only going to park outside and look. The van crawled past them, both driver and passenger staring hard at James as they passed.

A chill went down his neck and he turned away. But they'd clocked him. They knew where he was going. 'That van, did you see those rough men inside?' he muttered.

'Contractors, I guess, Dad. Were they rougher than any others?'

'They saw me, they know.'

'What are you on about?'

'It was the same men who saw me on the A12 when I

was driving back from yours, Rebecca. They're the ones who overtook me, saw my face and know where I live.'

His mouth closed, stubbornly silent. The women looked at each other, both in the dark. 'Well, if you move here, you'll be safer, won't you, not to mention having people around to pick you up when you fall and see to your every need,' Rebecca said, turning in her seat to look at him closely.

'Oh yes, with old Ralph Dines in charge and a bunch of other clapped-out, mad as hatters, swivel-eyed dinosaurs from Parliament and the Civil Service, their batty spouses and half the staff either former constituents or the children of constituents. I can't face it.'

They thought a minute. Samantha gripped his wrist, 'don't you see former constituents remembering you as a touching thing? It shows you had an impact, you made a difference to their lives.'

Rebecca sensed they might have found a more fruitful line of persuasion, so she turned, too. 'Dad, when people ask you for help now, as if you were still their MP, it's because they don't know where to turn, who to ask. You are the answer to their hopes and fears and you did it well. You cared.'

'As we care. We're not asking you to go somewhere for our sakes, but because we need help in helping you. Can you see that?'

'You still have value. Your self esteem should be high, as your head held high.'

He looked from one to the other. This lengthy battle was one he'd have to lose in the end. With a sigh he said, 'Not Fitzgerald Hall and not here. Especially not here.'

That was something; the best they were going to get. They smiled and nodded, Rebecca looked at her watch, started the engine and they returned to his house.

Act One, Scene 7

With the increasingly sinking feeling he was going to have to tour Sir Thomas More House, at least, James perched himself in the study.

Starting with his diaries for 1987, 1988 he skipped to 1993, dipping and skimming over the personal comments about life with his Elspeth. He turned to a couple of dog-eared *Hansards*, the verbatim record of Parliamentary debates.

Except, of course, the record was never fully word for word. The editors removed all the ums and arrhs that people found vital to speaking; they corrected grammar without altering the essence of the point. James always admired how they were able to translate every possible regional accent with uncanny accuracy.

Sometimes they sent messages to MPs inviting them to read the draft of their speeches before publication and fill in the odd word the shorthand writers had missed.

Keener backbench MPs climbed to the Hansard offices upstairs and waited for at least half an hour before a draft was available. He regularly tried that, after obeying the convention that you should stay in the Chamber to hear a chunk of the MP who followed in case he or she referred to you.

Five times he'd been granted an Adjournment debate – the final half hour of debate at the end of each day's business when an individual MP could raise any issue of pressing concern, almost always local, and have a relevant minister reply.

This debate could start at 10pm when business ended, or at any point in the middle of the night. James had waited for his drafts at 3am and 4.30am, falling asleep in the waiting chair both occasions.

There were other occasions for Adjournment debates – sometimes a whole day on a Motion to Adjourn the House for Easter, for example, which saw perhaps a dozen MPs get their slots to speak out on behalf of their voters, usually to an empty Chamber.

James unfailingly followed the advice he received from an old hand – Lady Winifred Carswood – on his first day, 'always have an Adjournment speech ready in your pocket.' Sometimes an MP or Minister was ill; occasionally they put on a couple of debates to fill in time. You never knew when your moment might come.

Almost every time he browsed his archives, he encountered Ralph Dines. Sitting for an inland urban constituency, Dines had no interest in the issues that preoccupied James – fishing, dredging, coast protection, the gas/oil industry, farming, coastal economies, rural schools and unemployment.

Nonetheless, Dines was everywhere. James assumed he was popular, but looking back it was more that Dines was building alliances, making deals and harvesting information of potential use. Dines had a flair for publicity and often managed to shoehorn himself into others' photos or publish a comment on a press release before it was issued.

There was the time James returned to his desk in the Cloisters to find Dines on his hands and knees methodically going through the wastepaper basket.

'What the hell are you doing?'

Dines tossed the paper back into the bin, stood up and brushed his knees. 'Oh, there you are, James, I thought you might have fallen into your rubbish bin!'

'I asked what the hell you were doing?'

'Fact is, James, old man, I was bored and finding myself in need of a press release on something, anything, thought I'd see if you had some scribbles that might inspire me.'

He was completely unapologetic and didn't think it was at all odd. 'So, you thought I might have an idea you could steal?'

'Borrow, James. I'd have given you back my press release and you could have adapted it for your own grubby local rags.'

James had never shared that with anyone else. But it said all he needed to recall about Ralph Dines. No, he couldn't face Sir Thomas More. He could see no reason to put himself in the hands of Ralph Dines ever again.

And he'd tell his Samantha and Rebecca so, firmly.

He was fine at home. Yes, an occasional fall. He'd pick himself up. He loved this house that he and Elspeth had lived in, expanded and made their own over four decades. He'd accept some daily care coming in for half an hour to clean the toilet and make him breakfast, even twice, if that was the price of reassuring his girls and grandchildren.

Coffee time. Switching the machine on reminded him it still needed de-scaling so would take ages. He went through to the lounge to look out the front. A mistake.

As Judy Blowers appeared in his drive and waved, he leapt to the side and fell over his walking stick. He lay still, grimacing at the pain. Perhaps she hadn't actually spotted him. If he lay still, she'd go away.

She knocked. He waited. The door opened and in she came. He was outraged, but she swept into the lounge, 'Oh James, I saw you fall, and I had to come in to call an ambulance.'

'No, don't you dare, I don't need a bloody ambulance. They'll take me to hospital to check me over. I'm fine. Just caught my leg on the stick as I moved to let you in,' he lied.

With a nod, she bent to try and help him up. Fearing that her effort would result in her collapsing on top of him and them both lying there till their skeletons were discovered next year, he crawled to the settee and raised himself.

She made sure he was sitting, smelt the coffee and went through to his kitchen to pour two mugs.

'I see your daughters were here. Worried about you?'

'Yes, they are. Won't leave me alone. I'd be obliged if you said nothing about this minor incident. Judy.'

'My lips are sealed. No charge.' After a beat, 'and how are you getting on with my little problem?'

'My contact at the council hasn't got back to me yet. I'll chase it up later today; he should have rung me by now.'

After a sip of his coffee, she put the mug on his table without a coaster, stood and fetched over his landline phone on a long cable. 'Now's a good time. Half term coming up and those blighters will be out and about all day.'

Caught without further excuse, he pointed at his phone book, which she passed him. He found the number and dialled. While he waited, he wondered if staying next door to Judy Blowers and encountering the occasional constituent was the lesser or greater danger than being incarcerated among dozens of former MPs.

'Hello, could I speak to Hilary Sinclair, please?'

'Do you want Mr Hilary Sinclair or Mrs Hilary Sinclair?'

Act One, Scene 8

After double checking every lock and looking meaningfully at the dummy security cameras on his house front, James limped out to his car, crossing his fingers Judy Blowers wasn't watching from her window.

She wasn't, the coast was clear and he clambered into his old Ford Fiesta, belted up, cleared the leaves and raindrops off his screen and drove off, ignoring the fist raised from an old boy walking a terrier. Probably another former constituent – they weren't all admirers.

Pressing his radio, he realised he didn't want the news or some very worthy people criticising the government and arguing for more money to be spent. He clicked the CD on and smiled to hear The Byrds' greatest hits. But when did he insert that album?

Quite soon it was going to need a service and government road test that it would probably fail, but he was fond of his old Ford. Nothing flashy. Just a workhorse.

The drive to Samantha's was about ten minutes on roads not over busy for a late autumn Thursday morning. He pulled up outside her 1970s private estate detached house with multi-coloured tile cladding on the upper floor and weathered rusty red brick on the lower.

Outside the attached garage, Leroy was bent over Henry's upsided bicycle replacing its front wheel. Henry shouted out, 'Hi Grandpa.' James didn't bother to lock the car. Maisie and he would be off for the promised drive soon. In fact, if they could get off swiftly, Maisie's mother wouldn't start up again about his welfare.

'Leroy, how's it... going on the bike?' When Leroy first came on the scene, James had made the mistake of addressing him as if he was a template black ghetto drug dealer who needed to be spoken to in a particular patronising rap style.

In fact, Leroy, with two children of his own by a woman he was separated from, was extremely likable and really seemed to love Samantha and had taken on fathering her kids with energy, consideration and perception.

James asked for no more. He'd never fully trusted Paul, her first husband, and events proved him right when the man was unable to stay on the straight and narrow. However, he'd fathered three great kids which were the delight of James' old age.

Maisie emerged through the back garden gate clutching a pair of flimsy plastic L-plates to show the world she was a learner driver. She tied one on the front bumper and taped the second inside the back window.

'Six lessons already, then, Maisie?'

'Yes, Grandpa, six and I've done the basics.'

'Right, so now it's reverse parallel parking, hill starts, emergency stops and three-point turns.'

'Bring it on!'

'Good luck, James, with that!' Leroy grinned, tightening the wheel nuts. Henry shook his head, 'Hope your life insurance is up to date, Grandpa.'

The boy was right; you can never have too much life

insurance.

With a wave to Samantha in her front room window he buckled in the passenger seat while she climbed in behind the wheel and went though the ritual. Clunck, click, check gear in neutral, clutch in, start engine, check rear mirror and side mirrors, indicate, engage gear and gently off.

Despite her confidence, they kangarooed down the road and stalled before she reached second gear. 'Sorry, Grandpa.'

'No worry, my love, I was thinking of updating the clutch soon, anyway.'

'Why not update the whole car? Soon all cars will be electric and then autonomous, driven by an algorithm.'

'You should learn to drive properly, in a manual. You never know when you might need the skill.'

'Yes, if I suddenly find I've time travelled back to the 1950s.'

Once she got used to the vehicle he relaxed his hold on the side handle and replaced it with a grip on the outside of his seat so she couldn't see. 'Perhaps a left here, Maisie, and then stop fully at that junction where you don't have right of way?'

'It's OK, Grandpa, I have a destination in mind. A surprise.'

'I don't trust surprises.'

'Just wait and see.'

They continued the journey she'd planned in her mind. He kept the chatter to a minimum so she could concentrate on driving, and confined his remarks to simply pointing out a wobbling demented cyclist and the hare-brained pedestrian with a dog determined to commit suicide under her wheels and the pensioner who seemed to have forgotten he was crossing a road.

He pictured her suddenly braking, veering, getting in a skid and ending up facing the wrong way while a twenty-tonne truck ploughed into them and carried them over the quayside where they drowned inside the battered car.

You can never entertain too many unintended consequences and bad outcome butterfly effects.

She was doing well, changing gears, indicating and actually going in a circle, so she'd probably end up near the seafront where they'd park and she'd allow him to buy her a hot chocolate in the little café.

'Speaking of surprises, did I ever tell you about when I was first in the Commons?' She shook her head, though she'd heard many tales before.

'There was a Family Room for MPs and their spouses and children to wait in. It was quite comfortable, lots of big settees, a large TV and cupboard with a selection of board games and a few novels. The kids and Elspeth often sat in there when we were all in London, waiting for some Division of the House or a long enough gap for us to get out for a burger.'

'I sometimes slept in there before we got a flat of our own in London, rather than a hotel. I settled down as the House finished. *Who goes home?* The cry of the policeman shouted throughout the building to show end of the day.'

'Once I was woken in the middle of night by the security staff on duty. All quiet so they'd go in there to enjoy a break before morning. We startled each other, screaming in terror. I thought I was at home in bed and they thought I was an intruder!'

He looked across at his granddaughter, finishing the dutiful laugh and still driving brilliantly, carefully and with growing confidence. She reminded him of Elspeth.

'She never thought she'd be an MP's wife, you know, your grandmother. When we met, Elspeth knew I was interested in politics. But me getting elected, and all that she had to do to carry the family through that. She was remarkable. I miss her so much.'

After a moment, she said, her hand on his arm, 'I miss her, too Grandpa. We all miss her.'

He lifted her hand back to the steering wheel and drifted into a reverie. Family life was often a casualty of MPs' work; divorces were frequent. He suddenly recalled the messy one that Ralph Dines went through, with nobody mentioning it in public. What had put him back into his mind?

But once Dines had returned to his mind the incident of the constituents' tour came back. The Commons allowed licensed guides to conduct tours for MPs when the House was not sitting and mornings when it was. Tax-free cash only; a nice little earner. Sometimes, for special constituents, MPs would do them and cut out the guides.

On this occasion Dines had asked, begged, cajoled and threatened James to do one for his constituents. 'Say I'm in committee and you have stepped in heroically to help me out at the last minute.'

'Why, Ralph?'

'One is the wife of an Association officer. I don't want to see her.'

'Why not, Ralph?'

'If you really want to know, it's because she gave me a blowjob in her car at a function last month and I haven't called her since.'

It was a rare sharing of personal information from Dines.

James did the tour but failed to identify the woman in question. Dines really owed him a favour after that, but it was never repaid.

Now they were approaching the terrain around Sir Thomas More House and as she indicated to turn into the grounds, he realised she'd tricked him.

He looked sharply at her. 'I know Grandpa, I'm sorry, but you wouldn't have come if I told you I'd arranged an appointment to see round the place. Would you, be honest?'

'Of course, I wouldn't.'

'It's just that I was reading some of the history of this place. It's fascinating. It's on the site of what was a leper hospital. It then became the Second County Imbecile and Feeble-Minded Asylum, later amended to The Second County Home for Mental Defectives, a far less offensive name.'

'How very appropriate, given the inmates there nowadays.'

'It was remodelled and renamed, St Christine's Hospital, after Christine the Astounding, the patron saint of insanity and lunatics.'

'I refer my honourable granddaughter to my comments a moment ago.'

'During the First World War it was a treatment centre for war wounded, particularly those gassed. After 1918 it became the regional TB hospital.'

'Yes, one of our ancestors died there with TB, so she got no benefit of fresh air, rooms without walls and bedrooms without glass in the windows.' Maisie hadn't known that.

'In the Second World War it was a naval barracks, *HMS Christine*, for sailors being shipped off and returning home. From 1950 to I think 1986 it was the Grand Empire Hotel, serving seaside holidays and with ambitious plans to develop a superior tourist trade.'

'It was 1985, I remember. It was condemned to be demolished. It was almost derelict. In 1990, a consortium bought it and a mass of agricultural land around it for a song and made it the care home and related businesses it is today.'

'That's in your time. And do you know why it was called Sir Thomas More House?' He shook his head, trying to recall. 'Sir Thomas More, patron saint of politicians, a man of moral integrity, beheaded by Henry VIII for treason.'

'Yes, a good history well told. You could work as a guide during next summer before you go to university. I'll put in a word for you.'

'That's an idea, Grandpa!'

'I was joking, Maisie. I wouldn't want you in this place anymore than I'd want myself in it among the other historical relics.'

In the parking area he looked around for Samantha's car ahead of them, with the family waving. He expected Rebecca to have come up from Essex as part of their plan to stitch him up.

But all he saw was a worker's van, not unlike the one he'd seen at Fitzgerald. In, fact it was so alike it was the very same vehicle. She braked, switched off the engine.

They'd parked by a faded sign, 'Keep your social distance. Save the NHS.' It was from that corona virus pandemic. For a second James considered fabricating Covid symptoms and saying he needed to self-isolate.

Maisie had an attractive smile to top off her warm, helpful, caring ways. She treated him to one as she unfastened his seat belt. 'Let's go and have a look, Grandpa. Just to please me.'

He couldn't recall the Covid symptoms and didn't really notice how the car was parked across two spaces.

Act One, Scene 9

The imposing front view of Sir Thomas More House warmed many hearts as a fine old English pile that soaked up maintenance money like a sponge but was worth preserving as a shining addition to the fabric of the countryside. The weak sun emerged to bathe the scene in pastel warmth.

Nonetheless James' heart sank as Maisie stepped out of the badly parked car and led him to the front door, giving the quaint old dangling bell a fulsome tug. Neither knew that their approach had been videoed and recorded the moment they turned into the oak and dead ash tree lined drive.

'There's nobody here, Maisie, let's come back later,' James began as the old wooden door rescued from a fire-damaged Victorian folly in Yorkshire creaked open. A gormless young woman stared at them through misaligned bulbous eyes, under a dead black head of nylon substitute hair as if she'd just arrived from the Planet Vacant.

'Hello, I'm Maisie and this is my grandfather, James Ellington. I made an appointment for a visit?' She said it with that annoying sing-song question at the end of a statement much favoured by her generation.

The servant shuffled aside, presumably to indicate they should enter. The immediate reception area was a cage, a structure designed to hold them imprisoned for a moment while they sanitised their hands and had their faces filmed and their eyes scanned for security passes, which plopped from a machine after a matter of seconds.

If they hadn't passed whatever the test was, they'd have been penned in the cage till armed forces arrived. As a buzzer sounded, the gate swung open allowing them access to the main hallway. To James it sounded and looked like the entrance to one of those high security American prisons he'd seen in films.

He imagined the outer gate to their exit was now sealed, so they couldn't escape if they'd changed their minds. The underling indicated they should leave the cage.

The enormous foyer, the height of faded glory, was dominated by a central staircase curving round, boasting silver balustrades and plush carpets. They didn't know it was rescued from an old house in Devon that was in the way of an essential road. A calm quietness pervaded, yet in the distance, from upstairs and on the ground floor what seemed like a dozen corridors there was a sense of activity.

People talking, occasional laughter and some gentle but jolly music from upstairs floated around. The functionary stood behind the reception desk – a fine Edwardian example bought at a bankruptcy sale in London. She fumbled with a set of switches on the walls behind her.

The first one she stabbed instantly stopped the ambient warmth, the music, the laughter, the serenity. It was replaced by the real atmosphere. Screaming in the distance, doors slamming, high-pitched arguments, shouting, swearing and madly running feet. 'Oh, sorry, wrong switch, I need light.'

She stabbed back the pleasant, smooth, soothing background recording and the madhouse disappeared. The foyer was flooded with light, like a stage set and Gothic windows were projected on the walls. 'Oh, sorry, that's the night-time lighting.'

The voice was rough, as if she smoked a hundred nicotine tubes a day, yet she couldn't have been more than twenty. She peered at the passes that had just been issued and wrote them into a big, old-fashioned folder in big childish writing.

A metallic voice from a silo behind startled them. 'Thank you, Imelda 4, I'll take over now.' It came from a tall, gangly woman dressed in nurse costume, devoid of normal human features. Her face was smoothed out, with tiny eye sockets, small protruding nose and a mouth that barely twitched.

'I'm Matron Mercury. Welcome to Sir Thomas More House. We hope you will be very happy here.' She turned to the skivvy. 'I said I'll take over now.'

With a scared little 'yes, Matron,' Imelda 4 curtsied clumsily and made her escape. 'That is one of five Persons of All Trades that we use to carry out the menial functions of this great home.'

Nurse Ratched from *One Flew Over the Cuckoo's Nest* came to James' mind, the archetypal battleaxe nurse, yet this one was more robot than human dragon.

Jerking one leg down heavily after the other, Matron moved off, leaving them to follow and James to glance at his granddaughter who seemed to be regarding everything so far as perfectly normal and reasonable.

All that entry palaver was the curtain raiser for three hours of madness. He was trapped in a cross between a circus of lunatics and an old-fashioned asylum where people visited on Sunday afternoons to be entertained.

He didn't come across them all at once; encounters

were spaced to string his ordeal out to the maximum. He even spied one that he probably wasn't meant to see. An old man with livid red rope marks round his neck was being guided towards the central lobby.

Someone suffering advance stages of Parkinson's disease was being helped down the staircase, hands and arms frantically shaking in the tell-tale tremours of the condition. It was a woman, James noted. He'd never seen her before; he hoped he never saw her again.

A pervasive smell of urine gave James a moment of nausea before catching a dash or two of some sort of perfume squirted from little jets at strategic intervals along the walls, designed to mask the piss. It didn't work.

Their first designated port of call, ushered in by the Artificial Intelligence Matron, was to the former MPs' wing, where a long, wide corridor with about ten doors each side stretched ahead.

'Former Honourable Members and Members of the House of Lords who were once MPs live along this wing. Here are two day rooms with relaxing facilities where families can visit, there is a unique medical facility here and a small dining room and a mini cafeteria.'

They looked around, Maisie starting to make appreciative noises as if she was going to move in. James kept his noises to himself. Dotted about were faces he recognised despite the ravages of the years they'd endured. Some were so aged that they must have predated his years in Parliament.

One face he recalled but not his name approached him with a broad grin, grabbed his shoulder and pleaded, 'Hello, Dad, can we play football now?'

Recoiling, wiping the spittle off his face, James looked

to the Matron for some help. 'This is Bill Forbes, one-time Leader of the House.' James remembered him, now mad as a hatter, but back then, he was just a little barking.

Avoiding being clutched, Maisie shifted smartly away and asked about the view of the grounds through the tall windows. 'This is lovely, Matron.'

They passed a tall, painfully thin, stooped gentleman who was staring intently at a bowl on a little table. It was full of assorted false teeth. He raised a twisted hand above the bowl, poised.

Suddenly the man dropped his hand and grabbed a handful of dentures. He dropped them in trying to select just one. The arthritis was not going to beat him, but it was putting up a good fight.

After several attempts, he was left holding a single lower dental plate, which received a cursory wipe from his worn jacket sleeve before being popped into his mouth. Moving his jaw about, he nodded. Just right.

An overweight man in an armchair put down *The Times* as they walked by. 'Hello, James Ellington, isn't it? Ronnie Wyford!' He struggled upright, dandruff showering off his shoulders, wincing from knee pain, to offer James his gnarled hand. 'You'll fit in just fine here, place is made for you, James.'

James looked doubtful so Wyford wagged a fat finger in his face and said, 'many of our residents have been here for years, this is their home, they now know no other and they receive the best care that money can buy.'

Wyford watched James closely. A shrewd old bird in his day, he now had something of a child's drawing of an owl about him. His total baldness was neatly compensated for by copious tufting from his nostrils and ears.

The Matron mechanically recited Wyford's CV. 'Lord Wyford was an MP for twenty-five years, followed by fifteen years service in the Upper Chamber. Nowadays he helps the management run the place. Lord Wyford is the deputy chairman.'

That meant he was close to Dines. James shook the big hand that couldn't open fully and smiled politely, trying not to inhale the pungent smell of nicotine falling off his Lordship.

'Lovely to see you again, Ronnie. Haven't seen you since that reception you organised in the Other Place for big-league builders and I came because of a constituency interest.'

'Remember it fondly, of course! Matron, have you shown James the room we set aside for him? One of the best in the wing.'

Matron took the hint and led them away from the lounge and that almost palpable circle of nicotine hanging around Wyford, further down the corridor, passing a crone having drool wiped from her mouth and an ancient hairless man banging his head on the wall.

They passed a mini bar built into a corner space between two adjacent rooms. 'There are 19 bars in the House, open all hours just like in Westminster,' the matron informed them, with just a slight hint of disapproval.

'Open all hours only when the House is sitting,' James replied, but was rewarded with a blank expression. He was off script.

'This is the room previously occupied by Mrs Clemmy Denton, one time Member for Shrewsbury. Now she's vacated, it's been redecorated and will be yours.'

'Where has she gone?' Maisie asked, rather naively.

'She was buried last week and no longer needs the room. We'll soon have our own licensed crematorium in the grounds. Departures will be simpler and less expensive.'

It was an unremarkable, standard big house bedroom, with a king size double bed, two not quite matching wardrobes, a tall cupboard, a bookcase, modern ensuite with a shower and bath and carpet so thick he found it difficult to walk on without his ankle twisting.

Both windows afforded an excellent view of the well-laid out garden and a hint of the woods beyond. Yes, it was agreeable. But not where he wanted to spend the rest of his days till he too moved to the licensed crematorium.

'Well, many thanks for your time, Matron, but it's getting on time for lunch and with my stomach ulcer I need to eat small amounts regularly, so we'll be ...'

'Lunch is arranged for you both.'

'Don't worry about that, Grandpa. We might as well see lots more while we're here.' Always so sensible, that girl, just like her mother and late grandmother. 'And, since when did you have a stomach ulcer?' she whispered to him.

Matron led them back down the corridor towards the central area beside the magnificent staircase. As they passed one room a door was hastily slammed shut by someone wearing a Halloween mask. In that split second

James saw a head being held aloft while its former body dripped blood onto the carpet.

In the main foyer a double door sported a huge plate marked: Rt Hon Ralph Dines, MP for West Norton 1987-2019, Junior Whip, Under-Secretary for Industry, Chairman of Sir Thomas More House.'

Matron stomped straight in; they followed into a medium-sized reception area. Imelda 4 sat behind a modern desk with a bank of screens. 'This is Imelda 1, Mr Dines' secretary.' They mumbled greetings and James suspected all the Imeldas were identical. This was an old-fashioned place staffed by robots who'd run amok sooner or later.

Magnificent double oak doors were flung wide revealing a large room, splendid, speaking of power. A single screen adorned an oversize Queen Anne desk bought from an industrialist's mansion when it was turned into multi-occupied flats.

Desk and a chair, something like the throne an Archbishop might sit upon, were mounted on a platform giving the whole the appearance of an altar.

'Mr Dines sends his apologies for being out at a business meeting this morning. He hopes to catch up with you later.'

Showing the office at this point was meant to reinforce who was the boss around the place, and James felt that inside the drawers and secret cupboards in the oak panelling, originally from the House itself, would be all sort of gizmos and gadgets for watching the unfortunates.

He'd spotted cameras in every room so far; but not here.

He stood clutching his stick for support looking up at the huge portrait of the great man, hanging above the fireplace that had come over from an 18th Century chateau in the Loire. In the ghastly, mock classical painting, Dines held a silver ornament of the Commons portcullis logo, his face a smirk of pompous self-satisfaction.

As they returned into Imelda1's domain, Maisie spotted behind Perspex a massive pictorial map of house and grounds, while James straightened the desk calendar that was awry. Matron stopped too, and pointed out with jerky arm gestures, that on the ground floor opposite the MPs and Lords was a smaller corridor for rooms and lounges of Lords who'd never been MPs.

A third corridor, almost behind the stairs, led to a nursing wing for the sickest residents. 'It's almost full at the moment.' She told them of the state-of-the-art medical facilities the management had provided, 'more advanced in many cases than the local NHS hospital.'

James waited for her to inform them that the ill were better being treated in the facility. He watched her artificial mouth for the words, 'once here, there is neither reason nor hope for leaving, except in a box.' She didn't say it, so his thought remained unspoken.

'When you talk to some of our guests you'll find they don't finish sentences, can't always find the right word to use. This is normal. Old age often brings short term memory loss and forgetfulness.'

Now matron had the air of a lecturer addressing novice nurses. 'I can think of the right words for them,' James offered. 'Dotage, doddery, drooling, dribbling, incontinence, senile, decrepitude, feebleness, second childhood.'

He waited for her response to his insult, but then realised he'd said it in his head. Maisie took his arm, 'come on Grandpa, there's more to see. Isn't it fascinating?'

Above the MPs' corridor was a further set of rooms and lounges for civil servants, bureaucrats and officials who'd served the nation well. There were offices, an extensive kitchen area and three dining rooms with a large cafeteria that was 'extremely popular, as prices are subsidised, just like in Parliament. At least they appear to be so. In reality, guests subsidise themselves, of course.'

Three small bars were tucked away near more offices. At the rear in a newish block were rooms for widowed spouses and partners of residents who could no longer afford the fees in their own right.

'They're part of our charitable work. We don't tip them out. We look after them when they fall on hard times. Until they need no more care.' Her monotonous voice made it sound more sinister than he could have thought possible.

She pointed down another corridor. 'That's the wing converted into a replica Commons chamber. It's the most popular leisure space. Lighting can make it green for Commons or red for Lords. They're rehearsing for our annual Speeches of the Year contest. Mr Dines said to look there before lunch.'

Maisie pointed at the buildings in the grounds she noticed through the windows. 'The licensed Crematorium. will be built next year. We'll rent it out to the community; will help the income stream.' And a warehouse labelled Archives and Records.

'That's where every member is allowed to store their material, notes, anecdotes and records of their

Parliamentary time. One large lock-up each; it's an add-on fee, but everyone pays it.'

'Fascinating,' James smiled, looking at his watch, pausing while he did so to avoid falling. Suddenly with cries of 'stop it!' there darted past a cat. Gone before anyone had really taken it in a short, well-fed woman with staring eyes and a wig askance, hobbled to them, 'that's a Turkish Angora, recognisable for its silky white coat.'

Matron looked the old dear up and down and said, 'all pets are banned, as you know Mrs Smythe-Smith, and it will be reported. The animal is a health hazard.' The old woman nodded as if she was being praised.

As if from nowhere two white-coated assistants appeared and set off after the cat. 'Some residents miss their animals,' Matron explained, pointing them forwards, but she was livid.

'The rules are quite clear. Mrs Smythe-Smith thinks she has to look after every stray, including a rabid bat. The last thing she befriended turned out to be a fox.'

'Really?' Maisie was intrigued.

'Yes, the rules about no smoking indoors and no pets are the hardest for some residents. One who is no longer with us broke the two rules simultaneously, forcing a dog to smoke!'

James looked at his granddaughter. 'It's the stuff of comedy, a laugh a minute!' James said.

'Lunch, very soon, now, Mr Ellington. After the Chamber.' She made it sound like the Chamber of Horrors.

'Haven't you got a meeting, Maisie? Somewhere

urgent?' Sixth form lesson you're late for?' It was a futile attempt to appeal to her good nature and let them escape.

The overriding impression the last lounge made on James was of a madhouse, where the deaf tried to communicate, nobody listened to anything, all overlapping in a hellish cacophony.

Leading to the toilets on the way to the Chamber, they passed an old dear being helped to swallow medicine and making more than a meal of it. James' gorge rose; he was not good at swallowing medicine either.

They passed the same old man banging his head on a wall as two white-coated assistants rushed to help him. Help him do it properly, James thought.

Act One, Scene 10

In its specially built wing, the replica Chamber was busy. A dozen or more residents were rehearsing for their annual Speech of the Year contest, sitting around and going through the debating motions they'd enjoyed years ago.

The stage lights were off – the place was flooded with natural light from the autumn sky outside through the high windows. More stage set than reality-copy, James saw that it was smoke, mirrors and lights that created the full fantasy. Plus what was inside their heads.

Typical. But if it was what these old buffers still clinging to their glorious past when they lived under the illusion they were important needed, so be it. Not for him to criticise. And certainly not for him to count himself among them.

They stood watching at the bar of the house, the little space that was not technically in the Chamber itself but was in reality an extension of the chamber floor.

He was recognised by several who waved or called out, to the irritation of Dame Winifred Carswood, standing with the aid of a walking frame on the back row of the backbenches, who was gathering her vocal cords for the climax, for her peroration on the shocking treatment of the mentally unwell.

'Is this what it was like, Grandpa?' Maisie asked, quietly.

'Yes, in some ways it was. More like a freak show now,

though. I remember the thrill I got every time I sat on the green leather benches. They wore your suit trousers threadbare in a few months, you know."

Someone began to gibber from the gallery on the mezzanine above the Chamber, which faintly replicated the press gallery. James saw it was Timmy Greenwood. Even in Parliament representing the London seat of North Westway East, Timmy had been regarded as mad as a box of frogs.

Now he was completely gaga and hanging on the rail of the press area, swinging himself backwards and forwards, shrieking 'Me thinks the honourable Lady doth protest too much!'

James had never been close to Greenwood, regarding him as more liability than lovable oddity. Someone loved him. As James recalled, he sat on a comfortable majority of over 20,000, even in a bad election.

But he was in danger of either falling backwards onto the bench behind or forwards over the edge onto the Dispatch Box sitting on the Table. James imagined the horrible mess and noise. Surely, they had already seen enough, despite Maisie staring almost open-mouthed at the display.

'He thinks he's an actor, does old Timmy Greenwood,' Sir Gerry Manders muttered in James' left ear; he'd not noticed the old buffer sidling up. He could have been an assassin; must keep wits about me, James sent himself a mental memo.

'Don't we all, Gerry?' He turned and shook the hand of the large, well-fed octogenarian in fine fettle, a few silver strands on his shiny head, cold blue eyes that would watch emotionless as you were hanged as an aperitif and several chins that wobbled when he spoke.

The noise from Timmy Greenwood stopped as two nursing assistants arrived to calm him down and lead him away – for a lobotomy, James imagined.

'How are you, James?' When he wasn't whispering plots and rumours in someone's ear, Manders had a booming voice and belly laugh that drew attention from a room and embarrassment from the person closest at the time. James guessed he was another of Dines' right-hand men.

'Lord Wyford and I look after things on a daily basis. Helping out old Dines, you know. We're God's representatives on earth, in a manner of speaking.'

James nodded, his suspicion confirmed. 'Very nice. Good to keep busy, hey?'

'Indeed. And this delightful young lady is?'

'This is Maisie, my granddaughter.'

He gave her the same manly, fist crushing shake, looked her in the eye, smiled coldly and nodded. 'Don't tell me, she's making you come here with the support, one might even say, connivance, of your family because they want you to be safe.'

'Spot on. Maisie, this is Sir Gerry Manders, one time MP, PPS to the Prime Minister for a time and a fixer. Then and now I suspect.' He decided not to tell her the man's inevitable nickname had been 'gerrymandering' for all the fixing and interfering he'd done over decades.

Timmy had reached the door leading out of the upper part of the Chamber to which he clung and yelled one final outburst. 'To be or to be? Now that is the question to debate, Mr Speaker. To be alive or to be dead?' And with that he was stuffed rather than led through the exit door.

The practice speech contest had been interrupted and as Dame Winifred Carswood was unable to continue, she carefully made her way down to the doorway to join James and Maisie.

Peering at him, she pronounced, 'I recognise you. James Eddington!'

A fine, upright woman with an air of natural authority that came from a lifetime of living in hunting, fishing and shooting circles, Winifred Carswood had earned her title through hard work and longevity in Parliament, chairing the Education Select Committee with distinction till she was removed in an opposition coup several years before she retired from the House.

'Ellington, James Ellington, Winnie.'

'And which was your seat then, James?'

'This one, this very one where we're standing.'

'You should be on the Board, James. If we're in your old stomping ground...'

She trailed off. The speech practice, the interruption and the effort to talk politely to visitors were already too much.

She glanced at Maisie, hoping the girl could bring her a coffee and three of those lovely caramel biscuits, so James introduced her. 'Oh, is she making you come here with the connivance of your family because they want you to be safe?'

Sensing a pattern beginning, James looked at his watch, at Matron Mercury with an eyebrow raised questioningly and smiled at Dame Winifred, taking her arm.

'It was lovely to see you again, Winnie. I remember our late-night chats round the table in the Member's Tea Room waiting for votes with great affection.'

James was actually moved; he'd been close to old Winnie, she was like everyone's grandmother in those days and he was upset that she was so far gone now.

'Ah yes, the Tea Room,' Manders said, taking hold of James' elbow to lead him out. 'Be good if you work up a little speech on the state of mental health. It's our theme this year. Ralph thought it amusing. As the newcomer you will be called first after the opening speech. Be good to make your maiden as soon as possible. Just like the good old days, you know, no interruptions of your first speech.'

'Gerry, I can't stay. Maisie is taking me back home. Things to sort, fish to fry, walls to wash, people to see, opponents to skin alive. You know how it is.'

'Oh yes, I do. You've got a few months before the contest. Word to the wise, don't deliver your maiden without rehearsing it. Doesn't go down well. People find that sort of behaviour rather rude.'

'Well, wouldn't want to be appear rude, Gerry, not to inmates in a madhouse, hey! You can never be too mad, yes?'

Matron suddenly announced in a curt bark, 'time for lunch, Mr Ellington, Honourable Ladies and Gentlemen.'

'And you can never be too rude, James.'

Act One, Scene 11

Uncertain whether he felt hungrier or more anxious to get the hell out, James followed Matron and Maisie from the Chamber. With a final look behind, he stood a second in the double doorway and noted that the speech rehearsal had dissolved into anarchy.

Members were talking to themselves. One, clearly blind, missed her step and fell headlong. As a nurse rushed to her aid, Manders began berating some hapless, bent double centenarian for failing to anticipate the problem and have done something about it.

James turned to follow the others and with a jolt came face to face and close with Ralph Dines who grinned without mirth, looked him up and down without warmth or concern, offering a hand from habit rather than welcome.

'Am I so short of madmen that you have to bring this fellow here to carry on like this?'

'What? Hello Ralph.' He deliberately avoided calling him Rafe, but shook the offered hand. During the Coronavirus pandemic of 2020 and onwards, handshaking had been discouraged; now it was creeping back.

'From the Bible. *1 Samuel 21*, if I'm not mistaken, and I rarely am. You just have to feign madness - make marks on the doors and gates and let saliva run down your beard and you will be the Old Testament David before King Achish.'

'I never had you down for a Bible quoter, Ralph.'

'You can never have a pocket too full of appropriate quotes, you know that. How are you doing, you old renegade?' Dines had aged as well as James. In fact, in a dim light they could have been brothers or cousins.

'I'm doing quite well, thanks, but I know I will feel greatly improved when my granddaughter Maisie drives me home and I put this visit down to a bad dream.'

Dines laughed loudly. He gripped James' shoulder. 'Very droll. Now listen, you haven't had your lunch yet. I believe old Gerrymandering has told you about our annual speech contest. Timing couldn't be better. You weren't a bad speaker in your heyday, whenever that was.'

James waited, hoping this would all end soon. 'Fuck all good at anything else, but you could speak! That is, when you weren't fishing round in my wastepaper bin for ideas.' The infernal cheek! If this was making him feel welcome and impressed by a friendly management, then it wasn't working.

But perhaps that was the purpose. In here, as in Parliament, you had to make your own way, your own luck and your own allies. Your enemies came of their own accord.

As an anonymous MP once said of Prime Minister Blair who came after James' terms in Parliament, 'you have to take the smooth with the smooth.' So with Dines. You had to take the megalomania with the megalomania disguised as insincerity.

They were silently joined by a tall, slightly stooped man in a suit and faded military tie with grey thinning hair, a tan and an air of calm confidence born of being in authority for decades. 'James, you remember Sir Ronald Hasbery, former Clerk of the House?'

James certainly recalled the official, the most powerful in Parliament after the Speaker. He controlled the interpretation of Parliamentary laws, rules and precedents. When he whispered in the Speaker's ear, his word was the Ten Commandments being delivered through the Speaker.

James remembered the man's superior, but not arrogant, way of peering over tiny frameless glasses at the end of his nose and sense of entitlement he wore like a robe as he floated around the grounds back then and understood why he'd replaced Westminster for Sir Thomas More.

'Ronald is resident in the wing for former senior civil service mandarins and does a magnificent job overseeing that area. Runs the lounges like a gentlemen's club, despite there being more women than men!'

'You must come up and visit us as soon as you've settled in. We don't bite, unless you want us to!'

James nodded his thanks with a smile; he'd always respected Hasbery, and still did.

Wondering how much longer this was going to be dragged out, enthused, 'well, time flies...' At that precise moment his ankle chose to give way and he reached out wildly with his left hand, his right releasing the stick that flew sideways.

In that split second his left hand connected with one of Hasbery's lapels and in an awkward fall, managed to both push the man over and topple onto him. Shutting his eyes while the pain eased a little, the Clerk of the House waited patiently under him.

'Never mind, never mind. It's not altogether perculsive, a Latin word meaning something that gives you a shock.' Everyone nodded politely.

James was back that day when he'd been teaching and as the class gathered by the classroom door to await the bell, his ankle gave way and he fell, taking three teenagers down with him.

They took it in good spirits and James apologised profusely. From then on, they asked at the end of every lesson if Sir wouldn't be better sitting at the teacher's table than standing by the door.

James was hoisted off the hapless Clerk and stood upright by a male nurse, the Matron and Ralph Dines, who then helped Sir Ronald Hasbery to his feet.

'Well, James, my old friend, didn't realise you were so fond of Ronnie Hasbery. But we'll mark you down for extra monitoring as you're clearly a serial faller.'

'Sir Ronald, I am so sorry...' Hasbery brushed apology aside, straightened his tie and smiled as if at a child who'd lost control of a dog.

'Don't you ever fall, Ralph? Surely with your feet...?'

'Lunch, everybody!' Dines ordered, cutting the conversation short and cueing the party to obediently troop towards the dining room.

When Dines whispered at him, 'have to watch those ridiculous clown feet of yours, James!' James realised that he'd asked Ralph if he ever fell only in his head, not out loud.

Overcoming irritation at his fall, James found a rhythm

with his walking stick while Dines found his own rhythm with his heavier, longer and more impressive walking stick.

He muttered, 'says the man with his own ridiculous clown feet.'

Act One, Scene 12

Universally referred to as 'The Members' Dining Room' it was only superficially like the real thing in Westminster, but its impression reinforced memories for those in need of them.

Formally attired waiting staff hovered while serving up the standard three course luncheon – soup, terrine or seafood cocktail with lettuce and tomato, followed by roast beef or gammon with a range of seasonal vegetables.

The cheese platter was popular as were the public school puddings of spotted dick, jam roly-poly or semolina with jam. However, there was also a dessert trolley, refreshed for the evening dinner, and ice cream or sorbet, too. Coffee was always served at the table.

One convention from Westminster was scrupulously followed. Most tables were 4s or 6s with a couple of 8s. If a Member arrived alone, he or she was expected to join the nearest table, regardless of the political affiliation of the diners, provided they hadn't got their mains in front of them.

Dines was greeted at the door and shown to a table, ignoring the vacant spaces on a couple of tables. Maisie followed, with James next, looking round at faces, nodding to a familiar couple.

One poor old sod sat in her wheelchair, head down on the table while soup was spooned sideways into her mouth by a waiter. James had to look away in embarrassment and revulsion. 'It doesn't come to us all,

James, don't worry, I'm sure you'll be fine,' Dines hissed, taking him by the arm to direct him to their table.

Matron remained at the door and was replaced by Lord Wyford who hurried in showering both nicotine stench and dandruff and made a play of holding Maisie's chair out for her and stroking her back as she sat. At a nod from Dines, the men sat and at once a waiter appeared, dealing menus like cards at the gambling table and waited, pen poised over his pad.

'Share a bottle, James? Or are you still teetotal?'

James smiled, 'Fancy you remembering that, Ralph.' It was Dines' turn to smile. 'Like the Inquisition, we forget nothing, James.'

Wyford piped up, patting his pockets for his reading glasses, 'I'll split a bottle with you, Ralph.'

'Better not. Work to do this afternoon. We need to go over the small print on the crematorium project. Sparkling waters all round, not French.'

Maisie, reading the menu with something approaching embarrassment, muttered, 'I'm sorry, but I'm vegetarian.'

A bomb didn't explode. Nobody raised an eyebrow. 'Oh sorry, Maisie, I expect...' her grandfather said, looking at the waiter.

Dines dealt with it. 'Vegetarian lasagne good, Maisie? I'll have soup, no bread, roast beef with only potatoes and peas followed by two coffee éclairs from the sweet trolley.' Wyford nodded his agreement to have the same and James felt obliged to nod likewise.

The waiter wrote notes on his pad and went off backwards, like departing the presence of royalty. He never reappeared, yet drinks, starters and main meal followed seamlessly. All was calm.

But it was a front. Every time the door opened, noise of circus animals flooded in. Elsewhere in the house, residents were feeding in the cafeteria, swallowing medication, exercised or enduring therapy. Others were being encouraged to unburden themselves of their innermost private secrets and fantasies.

Why all this should be so loud in the Dining Room escaped James and Maisie. But suddenly the sound system they'd seen earlier was switched to fill the room with *Silent Night, Holy Night* from Westminster Choir which thrilled some diners who thought it was Christmas.

'For God's sake,' Dines slammed his fork down. 'Recycle whichever Imelda is responsible. I do apologise Maisie, James. Don't let it spoil your lunch.' Wyford wiped his jowls with a napkin, echoed the apology, rose and scuttled off to sort out the Imelda and the background music.

The old MPs' and Lords' trick of dining in company came back to James. Eat at speed, keep others talking before trying to answer your guest's endless questions. Once, out at a dinner for interested MPs hosted by Multiple Store Retailers he'd answered a question about Parliamentary business during the starters and found the plate whipped away before he'd had two mouthfuls.

Nobody waited. It was repeated again during the mains. Organisations who paid for meals to lobby MPs on something in their interests never knew when the Division Bell would ring and all their guests would be ferried back to Parliament within the eight minutes before the voting lobby doors were slammed shut.

So, the art of wolfing quickly and copiously without being

rude, joking without being distracted and all before serious discussion set in was mastered early on by most MPs. Maisie couldn't keep up eating her passable veggie lasagne because Dines had asked her about her A-Levels, her dreams for university and beyond while tucking into his lunch.

When he'd eaten enough, he pushed the plate aside, cocked an ear to the new ambient sound-tape and leaned on his elbows towards James as if he was about to share a confidence.

He told James and Maisie about the plans for the crematorium – 'I wish we'd had it during the Covid pandemic, we lost one every four days' – the ins and outs of the annual Speeches contest, how they cared for old MPs and Lords and civil servants and had even started taking in senior council officials and elected members to help grow the business.

He stated, proudly, we've even got a slogan for the crematorium. *'Never fear being buried alive at the Sir Thomas More Crematorium!* What do you think?' Maisie laughed politely, hiding her shock; James nodded sagely.

'And how much did that corporate marketing mumbo-jumbo cost?'

'The director of the promotions company is a resident, so we got a good rate. He's even offered to be the first customer. He's not well and we're not quite ready yet. But it's a nice offer.'

Dines drained his water. 'Our minds are constantly trying to run a tight ship but bring in little luxuries and needed supports for our residents. Old age is not cheap. Neither is medicine. Put the two together, and we have a cost situation.'

Maisie agreed and added, 'Everything looks in very good condition. It has the air of being well looked after, and obviously that applies to the residents.' James wondered if Maisie hadn't been drugged with some hallucinogen.

'Thank you, my dear,' Ralph purred. 'Many grateful residents leave us a little something in their wills, James. You might consider a modest bequest, too?'

The background noise rose so James didn't have to respond – it now sounded like some creature from a horror film being strangled under water and when Wyford slid back to his seat just as his unfinished main course was taken away, Dines snapped, 'What the fuck is that noise, Ronnie?'

'It's dolphin and whale music; they say it soothes women in labour and people about to undergo deep brain surgery.' He waited; his hand poised to heave himself up on the table to stop it.

With a curl of his lip expressing distaste that James had forgotten, Dines launched off telling them about his plans for a state of the art mental treatment facility to cater for world leaders suffering stress and burnout.

It was like a signal. An alarm bell rang nearby. 'Not the fire alarm, my friends,' Wyford assured them, before starting but not finishing a tale about a fire alarm he once experienced in the House of Lords. There was shouting. This was not recorded. It was real and present.

Just as his dessert arrived, catching Dines' eye, Wyford stood again, apologised and left. Dines ran over their moving in protocols, their essential regulations, the contract James would sign, the expectation that he would participate and cause no trouble. The full assumption was that he was a definite.

Maisie surreptitiously texted her mother on her lap. 'Good so far. They think he's in.' Dines invited questions. Maisie asked about visiting, about freedom to go off site, about what would happen if her Grandpa had a big fall. All sensible stuff that James should have asked.

Wyford rushed back in time to see his untouched dessert being cleared away. 'My apologies. Someone has done a runner from the Dementia Ward. It happens from time to time. In a lucid moment, she thought she had to catch the train to her house. It took just two minutes for her absence to be realised, so take comfort in that.' He beamed at the guests.

Coffee arrived with a fizzy cola for Maisie. At that moment the door burst open to admit two residents. First came Timmy Greenwood who stood, arms akimbo, as he spouted 'Out damned spot, will these hangman hands never be clean?' before being removed by two assistants in white coats.

Immediately behind him and pushing to get past was Lennie Sanders, former Member for another East Anglian seat, now in his late sixties, thin, lean even, a well-worn shiny suit hanging on his frame. He'd lost weight.

'I'm sorry Ralph. Ronnie. And hello, James. I hear you're moving in. Hello, miss.' James opened his mouth to put right the false impression, but Ralph raised his hand, palm facing James, a gesture that shut anybody up. James recalled it. He'd often received it; now here it was again.

'This had better be important, Lennie.' Sanders bowed to whisper in Dines' ear. He continued for a full minute, while both men watched James' reaction. Obviously this was part of the spectacle laid on for his benefit.

When Lennie was clearly starting his points all over

again, he was brushed off by Dines' hand and waved away. Wyford opened his mouth to address a passing waiter, but Dines spoke.

'You remember Lennie Sanders? In your league as an MP, I'd say. Good at some things. Generally solid, reliable, good lobby fodder when the government was hard pressed. Never amounted to more than a couple of elections and some local coverage.'

James recalled him vividly. He was always a bit of fast-boy, keen to kowtow to people who mattered. His reward was to keep on doing what he did and being made a Parliamentary Private Secretary, a bag-carrier for a minister, the lowest rung on the payroll.

In fact, it was an unpaid role, James smiled. Eyes and ears for his/her minister, in the House and out, good training for a fully-fledged sycophant. 'Sorry to wipe that smile from your face, James, old man, but Lennie has just reminded me – it had slipped my mind – that if you are moving in here…'

'I'm not, but what if?' Nothing ever slipped Dines' mind, so what was coming?

Dines indicated to Lennie he could say it. 'For the help you gave that prisoner, all the help you gave him after what he did, you'll have to pay. And you will pay big time, James Ellington, be certain of that.'

And he stormed out of the Dining Room causing several to tut gently and shake their heads sadly. Old Lennie Sanders off on one. Again.

Act One, Scene 13

Matron saw them through the security cage, out the door and into the carpark, maintaining an uninterruptable flow of upbeat chat about his freedom to have his room decorated to his taste, securing his archives in his personal locker and his participation in the speech contest.

Maisie pointed out she'd report all to her mother and aunt, they had arrangements about his house to make and Grandpa hadn't actually committed to it yet. James said nothing.

That is until he saw a white van slowly making its way through the carpark headed down the little side drive. 'That van...'

Maisie looked at him. 'I mean, I've seen that van before.'

'It's a white van, Grandpa. They're everywhere.'

'Well, this one is everywhere. Everywhere I am.' Clearly shaken he put a spurt on to get back to his car.

'They're going down to the new crematorium. Probably just bringing supplies to start the alterations.'

'Of course, they are. But what else will they be doing?'

He waited impatiently for Maisie to unlock the car. He'd

have preferred to drive this time. Across the car roof he looked back at the house.

Matron had gone back in. Ralph Dines watched him from his office window. Of course, and he'd be checking the recordings made during the visit.

'Who watches the watchers?' James asked.

'What?'

'Look, there's Ralph Dines watching us like he's God. But who watches him? It's an old conundrum, along with nature versus nurture. And if Labour is the answer, what on earth is the question?"

'He's just interested in you, Grandpa.'

'Let's go back a different way, Maisie. I just don't feel comfortable having seen that van again.'

'What happened with a white van?' she asked before she stalled on take off. He shook his head while she concentrated on getting a smooth away in first gear.

James pulled down the sun visor above him and attempted to see the house in the little vanity mirror. He couldn't. He missed Dines answering a phone from his left inside jacket pocket.

'Hilary?' he opened with.

'Afternoon, Ralph. You asked me to keep you in the loop on any council connection at all with any former MP, Lord or senior civil servant.' Ralph waited. 'Well, Sir Michael Michaelson got a parking ticket on the seafront yesterday. I didn't know he was still driving. Or was still alive for that matter.'

Dines chuckled. 'And James Ellington, MP for our very own area.' Dines still listened. 'He rang to ask a favour for a neighbour having a spot of bother with some youths. I believe she is Judy Blowers, next door.'

'And what did you tell James Ellington?'

'I said I'll look into it.'

'I'll do the same.' Without thanks he cut the call.

From his cupboard store already open, he produced another phone from a charger, scrolled the contacts and pressed one.

'Boss?'

'Look into a bit of bother with some youths that a neighbour of James Ellington is having. They need taking down a peg or two. Perhaps time in intensive care, but not the mortuary.'

'OK. Well, the A12 team have been watching him, as you know. They're not over busy now. I'll look into it.'

'You can never have too many people looking into a problem.'

He put the phone back on charge, locked his cupboard and walked through to Imelda, still behind her desk.

'Imelda, send a message to James Ellington who was just here. *Dear Mr Ellington, we hope you enjoyed your visit today and are looking forward to fixing a date for your permanent arrival. If you put your house up for sale, rest assured that your neighbour's little problem has been looked into and solved. Yours ever, etc. PS.You owe me one, my friend.*'

'How do you want that sent, Mr Dines?

'Get someone to hand deliver it to him. In a white van.'

Act One, Scene 14

Less than a month later, a For Sale board was planted by the gate in his front garden. James stared at it from his lounge window. The place had been featured in the weekly local rag and according to his grandkids was 'almost trending' all over the internet.

Cars brought an endless stream of the curious to drive past slowly or stop and walk nearby a few times, necks craning, fingers pointing. Several white vans joined the onlookers. It was greater traffic than a house opposite had enjoyed one Christmas when they lit their home with lights, plastic grottoes and flashing reindeer sufficient to make the local news.

Every passer by added to his feeling that he'd go to a home if he had to; but not there. He'd be fine, even with the odd fall or two.

'What about this file, Grandpa?' It was Emily, up from Essex. They all were. With his two daughters, his sons-in-law Simon and Leroy and his five grandkids ruthlessly packing up, James had thrown in the towel and let them get on with it.

He yawned. He'd agreed to put the house up to test the market as a means of gaining some space to himself. He really needed to preserve his strength to resist being pushed into Sir Thomas More House. That visit had strengthened his resistance.

'Over my dead body,' he told himself. Several times. William had even heard him saying it aloud and informed the family with delight, 'Grandpa's talking to himself.'

They'd have a crematorium there soon, so over his dead body was distinctly possible.

He hoped he'd priced the house high enough to prevent a quick sale.

Judy Blowers had reported a kerfuffle a week or so back when young men in hoods and balaclavas had encountered her youthful annoyers. There'd been a bit of a fight and the strangers left in a white van, apparently.

Those local kids took a beating; five were still in hospital. Judy was over the moon, couldn't thank James enough and several times a day offered to help. With his entire family assisting, she busied herself in support, making tea and coffee to accompany her home-made rock-hard buns.

One thing that had bothered James at Sir Thomas More was the Lennie Sanders incident. What had he meant about a prisoner and he'd pay for what he'd done? He could recall dealings with only one prisoner during his Parliamentary career.

Throughout his time, he held Saturday morning surgeries for constituents to come and sit in front of him for twenty minutes or so, each pouring out their woes, their problems caused by the Government, local councils, big companies, neighbours, their families or to express their views, usually about how lousy the Government was.

It was occasionally rewarding; frequently impossible. Often all he could do was secure responses from ministers or the council – hence his work with Hilary Sinclair over the years.

Most responses he made or forwarded prompted constituents to write back to ring or contact somebody close to him. He shuddered to think how the widespread use of emails and social media nowadays made MPs dance to their tunes.

He alternated surgeries in East Point with ones in Broadland and Bristledown, and Amberbridge and Coldpulse out in the country. Amberbridge ones were in the chamber of the Town Council, up a steep narrow staircase. With no waiting room, after one supplicant or supplicants had struggled downstairs, he'd call up the next.

For disabled people or the elderly, he stomped down to talk to them in the street. One day, nearing the end, he realised a man was loitering in the tiny foyer. He wouldn't come up, but insisted on waiting till the end. James obliged him. He called the man up in the end, but he indicated James should come down.

So, ever willing, he did. And in the street outside Amberbridge Town Hall he met Tommy Cross, a constituent coming to the end of a 'life sentence' for murdering his wife. He was out on day release to give him a chance to see if he felt safe about moving back to his home area.

As they talked in his car, while sudden rain pelted down, James got the story. Cross and his wife had kept *The Golden Fleece* public house. He'd suspected and then discovered his wife was having it away with a regular. In a moment of savage rage he beat her to death with a crystal soda fountain before calling the police.

He reported he'd just killed his wife and sat on the floor beside her amidst the blood from her head and waited for the police to arrive. James vaguely remembered the case, long before he was an MP.

What Tommy Cross wanted was some help with the bureaucracy surrounding his release to the area. His in-laws objected to him returning near them. He'd been a model prisoner and as he kept pointing out to James, 'I've nearly done my time. I just want to come home to die here in old age.'

What he also wanted from James was a visit to the prison. He thought James could put in a good word for him. It was early enough in his MP time for James to agree to visit the jail – MPs could apply for a permit and travel at public expense to talk to 'their' inmates.

Having put his personal diaries into five well-taped boxes to secure his private and personal thoughts, he invited the family to help search the files. 'Look out for one marked Tommy Cross, or prisoner.'

The kids were wearying of loading dusty old files into packing boxes. But Henry piped up, 'I saw that one a minute ago, Grandpa,' and set about delving in a box they'd already loaded and then another.

As they worked, James recounted his experience of going early one morning on the train from Kings Cross to Yorkshire, a taxi to Her Majesty's Prison Grange Howe, showing his Commons Pass and the visiting permit, being admitted to an interview room and watching Cross brought in.

They had half an hour together for the man, tall but bowed, a pasty face, big calloused hands and a certain wariness which showed in his eyes constantly flitting about to talk and talk. He heard afresh the story of the murder – James had checked the case out since the surgery – and what long term prison life was like.

'I've nearly done my time. I just want to go home to die there in old age.'

James had promised to do what he could, agreeing

that the man had almost done his time. As a guard showed James out he said, 'so you're Cross' probation officer?'

'No, I'm his MP.'

'Oh sorry, you look like his probation officer.'

And he'd written to the prisons minister; in due course Tommy Cross was quietly released and lived with no fuss in a rented house in East Point, earning pocket money helping behind a bar. James thought no more of him.

Flipping through the file that Henry held aloft with triumph, he saw nothing that connected Lennie Sanders to the case. Perhaps old Lennie had finally lost it, like most of them in that place.

His landline rang so he left the family at it, Maisie and Joseph now distracted by their phones and William playing with some old toys Samantha had enjoyed as a child.

'Hello, Mr Ellington? It's the secretary at Fitzgerald Hall. I'm asked to ring you to ask if you're still interested in the villa you were shown as there is a keen buyer and we were hoping...'

'Let me stop you there. Thank you but no thank you. I'm not going to be moving into Fitzgerald. Let it go. Thank you anyway.'

The air of palpable disapproval could be cut with a knife as he returned to the study. Samantha looked at him crossly; Rebecca wouldn't look at him. 'Bacon rolls, anyone?' he asked cheerily.

'And veggie burger for me, Grandpa,' Maisie reminded him.

'Of course. Anyone else?' Amidst a chorus of yeses, he went into the kitchen. After a few minutes the crashing, swearing and stumbling about told them James would be unable to produce lunch for everyone. His daughters stepped into the breach.

To make themselves feel better about the whole day, Samantha and Rebecca reminisced about the time the old man stockpiled baked beans and other food products against the fears floating around that the dawn of the year 2000 would make computers fail so supermarket doors wouldn't open.

'They called it Y2K, or some such, and it was real enough' Samantha laughed.

'Yes, it was, though turned out to be nothing, but Dad ensured we weren't going to be hungry.'

'Mum kept asking what about when starving neighbours realise we have a secret food horde here?'

'Yeah, I remember. And Dad's answer was we'd fight them off. On the beach, I presume. We must be fed first.'

The landline ringing again kept James from returning to the kitchen to 'help' and he hurried to answer in case one of the girls did and it was Fitzgerald again. This time it was Imelda from Sir Thomas More House asking if he was ready to sign up now that his house was for sale? 'Mr Dines has suggested soon after Christmas. New year, new James Ellington?'

He swallowed in order to stay polite. 'No, thank you, no.' How did they know it was for sale? Then he firmly declined all the blandishments of Sir Thomas More House. 'No, no, no. Thank you.'

Bacon smells filled the house and hungry people gathered in the kitchen. Maisie took her veggie burger into the back garden to escape the stench of grilled pig.

'So, where are you going, James, man, when this house is sold? Leroy asked gently.

'I'm going on a little holiday while I make my mind up.'

He left them so he didn't have to explain any more. The afternoon wore on. Somebody washed up the lunch stuff. Boxes were labelled and stacked in the hallway. With James' warm thanks ringing in their ears, Rebecca and her family said goodbyes and set off for Essex.

Joseph said as he got into the car, 'You might really have to go on a long holiday, Grandpa.'

Half an hour later, Samantha rounded up hers and with rather stilted goodbyes, they left. Maisie said, 'Tuesday OK for another driving lesson, Grandpa?'

'Of course, Maisie.'

Once alone, he closed the front door with relief, looking sadly at his boxes. There were still his clothes, cutlery, crockery, bedding, furniture, garden tools, CDs and books to deal with.

He walked into the kitchen and fell so badly he ripped the tall cupboard door right off, smashed his head on the table and brought down the pile of freshly washed crockery from lunch.

Which was worse? Sudden falls or incarceration in Sir Thomas More Asylum?

Act One, Scene 15

James was fully conscious all the way to the general hospital in the ambulance called by his neighbour, Judy, in another expression of gratitude by a fresh daily act of kindness.

One day it was a couple of fairy cakes; the next a chicken casserole. She happened to be on his doorstep, hunched against the rain, about to deliver half a sponge cake she'd made for her visiting family, when she heard the noise of James falling. She'd called 999 from her home.

A white van, just driving around the area which drove off sharpish when the blue flashing ambulance lights came into view, had not escaped her notice. But she said nothing. It was all he could do to stop her getting into the ambulance with him; but she promised to ring Samantha and Rebecca to inform them.

He was in a bed at the end of a row of men in various stages of assessment. A few were wheeled off to theatre; some to other specialist wards while one seemed at the point of death so would soon be going to the morgue.

James dozed. When he came round his arm was being wound in tight fabric for blood pressure. A thermometer was pointed at his forehead. Something was plugged into the canula they'd inserted into the back of his left hand.

He felt hot, very hot. A man down the row voiced the

same thought to the nurse working on James. 'I'm hot, nurse, can't we open the windows?'

'Best not.'

'But I'm hot! Too hot to live!'

'You've got a temperature.'

"No, I haven't, all the men in here say it's too hot.'

'That's because they've all got temperatures.'

A man almost opposite started waving frantically when James looked around. Another bloody constituent. James pretended to doze.

When the tea trolley arrived mid afternoon, James had to open his eyes. The action was met by an immediate cry from opposite, 'James Ellington! It's Sebby Catchpole!!'

Heavens above! Sebastian Catchpole was the MP for a constituency in the same county. They'd often shared car drives to and fro Westminster and snacks late at night waiting around for votes.

'Hello, Sebby, good to see you,' James lied.

James hated shouting across the ward; it was just embarrassing. 'Perhaps we can talk later on when one of us can get out of bed.' He hoped Catchpole would take the hint. But he didn't.

He pushed aside his sheets, 'I can come over, crossing no-man's land between us and talk to you!'

Catchpole forced his swollen ankles into faded carpet slippers from home, grabbed an old brown woollen dressing gown to cover up the ridiculous backless hospital garb he'd been provided with, and ambled over.

James pictured a nurse arriving and pushing the man back to bed, injecting him with something which sent him to sleep. Permanent sleep. And James walking over and pressing his pillow down over his face to make certain.

Not that he disliked Sebastian Catchpole. Like James, he'd been native in his own constituency – a rare situation – he enjoyed their talks, though Sebby did most of the verbals. Whenever James' mind wandered off during a lengthy and detailed account of a conversation or action, Sebby would suddenly ask James a question like a teacher to catch him out.

Indeed, in their pre-political days, they'd both briefly been secondary teachers. Sebby was notoriously unfit. Rumour had it on one famous occasion when asked to cover a sports lesson, he wrapped up warm and spent the hour on the field trying to stop freezing to death while the boys kicked balls about doing their own thing.

When he was asked to explain his failure to teach them a single thing about football, he said, 'Is that what it was, football?' He was never given sports cover again. So, he was not as daft as the impression he sometimes let people entertain.

Sebby plonked himself in the visitor chair at James' bedside. 'What happened?'

'I had a fall, not too bad, I'm going home tomorrow, I hope. What about you?' Now they weren't shouting across the ward but merely talking loudly, James felt better about a modest conversation.

'Something wrong with my hands, they think. They thought I'd had a stroke as my face was a bit odd. But nothing unusual; I'm right as rain. Some more tests – have you seen that attractive Indian doctor? I'll be home later in the week.'

Sebby was always drawn to exotic women of every skin tone and had frequently been photographed by the gutter press cavorting with them. One at a time, but some turned out to be married.

What the women saw in the then late-50s, short back and sides, tubby, dogmatic, unmarried Sebastian Catchpole always eluded James.

'You still in East Point? Sorry to hear about your lovely wife, by the way.'

'Yes, but the house is up for sale, my family – '

'I heard that you're set for Sir Thomas More after Christmas.'

'No, I'm not. It wouldn't suit me at all. Where are you living?'

'Ahead of you. I have a room at Sir Thomas More. About two years now. I like all the care and attention you get.'

'That's what I'd hate. You're never alone in the Sir Thomas More asylum.'

'They don't leave you alone in case you harm yourself.'

'Or somebody else.'

'Are you that bad, James?'

'I would be if I moved in there with relics from my past.'

'You'll have to watch that Ralph Dines, slippery bastard. Always was. And Lord Wyford, another one. And old Gerrymandering. Some things don't change.'

'You can never have too much of the same old, same old, it seems.'

'That's wisdom. Like a sitting chicken don't get no feathers on its belly.'

The bell for afternoon visiting rang. A man appeared in front of them. 'Two for the price of one,' boomed Douglas Gardener.

'A reunion of honourable gentlemen!' sprayed Catchpole, prone to spitting when animated.

'A reunion of clowns from the ship of fools,' James muttered, happily mixing metaphors.

'Blimey, James, you're in a bad way.'

'You'll be fine in Sir Thomas More House. Always room for one more depressed, antisocial cynical borderline lunatic.'

'I hear you're speaking in the contest, James,' Gardener said, sitting on the bed, despite the frowning and pointing from a passing nurse. Normal rules don't apply. Don't you know who we are? Or who we were?

'You could always speak well.'

'Yes, but, listen carefully. Watch my lips as I speak. I'm not moving into Sir Thomas More House. I'd rather take my eyeballs out with a fishhook.'

Douglas Gardener thought wisely for a second. 'They cater for all tastes.'

'Yes, it'll be good to have another friend there.'

'But I'm not that friend, Sebby. Believe me.'

'Of course, you are. You're a politician. We're all the best of friends, all the time!'

Act One, Scene 16

The very next day, while awaiting the doctor's round, the medication and someone to sign his discharge permit, James received two visitors. Samantha turned up with Maisie, carrying his raincoat, a scarf and gloves.

'Come to take you home, Dad.'

'You can enjoy me driving Mum's car all the way back, Grandpa.'

'Lovely,' he enthused in a downbeat manner.

'I just have to wait for a permit to leave and medicines. You've come just in time to stop me digging a tunnel. Sebastian Catchpole was in that bed opposite, so either he's escaped or has been wheeled to the morgue.'

'Dad! That's enough.'

'And we had a visit from Douglas Gardener, can you believe it?'

'You seem to be bumping into a lot of former colleagues lately. Just as well, as we've booked you a fortnight's convalescence among them. Got a good discount from Mr Dines and he says -'

'What! No. Kill me now. You might as well have booked me a one-way ticket to Switzerland. I told you …'

'And we made it clear that we couldn't go on coping with your falls. This last one put you in hospital, for goodness' sake!'

'Over-reaction. I'd have been fine after a short rest on the settee.'

Maisie added, 'Leroy mended the cupboard door you ripped off when you fell!'

A nurse asked them to wait outside while James dressed himself and a doctor so young he was barely shaving rocked up to check James' name, date of birth, full address, who the Prime Minister was and the dates of the First World War.

'I'm not demented, Doctor.'

'No, but Doctor Zoe Frayn, a former colleague of mine now at Sir Thomas More House has asked for a full cognitive report before you arrive. We haven't time for that.'

'I'm only booked to convalesce!'

'Mr Ellington, has anyone ever diagnosed you with paranoia before?'

'Is that what you're saying I have?'

'Well, I shouldn't feed the paranoia by telling you have paranoia, of course. But signs have been noted. Excessive fears, OCD a little off-beam sometimes.'

The man dropped his backside onto the bed and lifted the weight off his right leg. 'Paranoia is thinking and feeling you're threatened in some way even if there's little or no evidence. Paranoid delusions are a psychotic episode.'

He looked at James closely and reached for his pulse before continuing his lecture. 'You've had some disturbed nights crying out about unknown threats.'

'I know them.'

'That's the point. According to your family the threats are old age, refusal to take orders and that stubbornness common among people who've enjoyed authority in life as you did.'

James said nothing. 'This is not my main field, but I've tried it with another patient. When you feel paranoia-like symptoms coming on, just lie back and recall one pleasant memory.'

Never having had time for psycho-babble, James shifted uneasily. 'On the beach perhaps, when you were younger, maybe with your children?' The doctor sat, waiting.

With a sigh, James gave in. 'One day, I'd just finished signing five massive packets of letters from my secretary sent on from London. It was summer recess. We were on the south beach and I got ice creams for the kids but I wanted coffee. Don't know why.'

He shut his eyes. 'I felt relaxed, and said so to Elspeth, my wife, when I dropped the paper cup. The clip-on lid came off, the coffee burned my leg. I was fearful in case any constituents had seen it, how embarrassing, days before mobile phone cameras, but then I thought one of the new litter wardens trained by the Gestapo would accuse me of littering the beach.'

The doctor continued to scribble notes. 'You see, I could be seen enjoying some normal family life, but not too much. The kids had to be good. The butterfly effect was that I relaxed, dropped the coffee, got accused of littering, had it widely reported among my voters.'

'Then what?'

'I tried frantically to scoop the coffee up as it sank into the sand. It was acid, it burned my hands right off and I was waving dripping stumps at the laughing crowd.

There was silence. 'I'll mention it to Dr Frayn. Enjoy your stay at Sir Thomas More.'

He walked away, to tell Samantha and Maisie. 'Mr Ellington has a very vivid imagination. I'm sure they'll help him at Sir Thomas More.'

'He's adamant he won't go,' Samantha explained wearily.

'Oh, they all say that. Dr Frayn is a marvellous all-round medic.'

Act One, Scene 17

As if to prove his independence, the first thing James Ellington did on arrival home and the departure of his daughter and improving driver Maisie, was to book himself a place to stay.

As a ruse, he agreed to Samantha's instruction to be packed and ready when she came for him late afternoon so that he'd arrive at Sir Thomas More House in time for dinner.

His home was spoiled. No longer comfortable; packing boxes in every corner and in the kitchen just a handful of utensils left. One soft chair in the lounge – the rest was piled in his garage. This felt as much like home as a warehouse.

Booking a fortnight at the Grimaldi's Palace of Fun Holiday Camp on their out of season special rate, was the work of a three-minute phone call. Full English breakfast, a slap-up evening meal with quality international entertainment every night and accommodation in one of their elite villas, for just £35 a night. A bargain, too good to resist!

It used to be £33 but they added a £2 supplement to cover the income falls incurred during the Covid lockdowns. How long ago was that and they were still recouping their losses?

This stay would demonstrate to his loves that he was perfectly capable of making his own arrangements. Two weeks to prove he could cope. He could manage with a snack lunch if breakfast and dinner were adequate.

He wasn't bothered about the swimming pool, indoor sports or long hikes along the beach. He just wanted to make his own mind up. And sit about and read. He'd brought the Government's updated *National Risk Register* to scare himself silly with. If they knew that, the family'd be appalled.

Till he drove into the long curving approach to Grimaldi's, past the faded and lopsided clown face the size of a small house that flickered day and night to welcome visitors, he'd forgotten that the place was directly across the road from that wretched toxic tip.

He stopped up the drive to think about it. He already feared the worst. Would his staying across from the tip make them think he was provoking them? A sharp horn blast behind startled him.

It was the municipal rubbish lorry, so he continued into the site to let that through. Parking in a disabled bay, he stepped out and grabbing his stick he made his way to the Recep-ion. The T was missing. For the first time he wondered about the quality of the accommodation.

A teenage acne-covered girl with lank greasy hair was chewing behind the desk, playing a mindless low-skill game on her phone with one hand and picking her nose with the other. He half expected her name tag to read 'Imelda' but it was Joy.

Her *'welcome to Grimaldi's, have you been before, would you like a daily paper, will you sign up for sports sessions, are you vegetarian, would you like to pre-order alcohol with your evening meal and would you like a length of rope to hang yourself or did you bring your own?'* was rattled off in a deadpan monotone with no pause for an answer.

The 'elite villa' turned out to be a breeze block room warmed by a two-bar electric fire high on a wall. The facilities were in a side bathroom, modern three decades ago. There was no heating there and the bath looked as appetising as an underground Blitz bunker.

He rang Samantha first. 'Sorry love, I told you I wouldn't go to that place, so I have booked myself into a holiday palace for a fortnight.' She was livid. So was Rebecca when he rang her next, ahead of Samantha calling to vent mutual rage.

Maisie was ordered to ring him and was followed by Joseph and Emily. Henry and William made calls, though they forgot to tell him how annoying and selfish he was being as the prospect of getting a family dog was higher up their agenda.

The 'slap up' evening meal was provided in the canteen, with clown faces plastered round the walls, and a giant red nose as the feature above the hot food section. Somebody had painted a dripping green boogie emerging from one nostril.

The choice was three types of roast, cheese omelette, gammon steak or Bolognese – all with chips. He ate alone, making the best of the half plateful he'd chosen. He wondered if there'd be a different selection on offer the next night. Peering at the smeared menu taped to the wall he saw that this fare was the daily autumn, winter and spring one.

The 'quality international entertainment' was an old 'comedian' from Wales who'd once been a Redcoat at Butlins but had lived a hard life since, a pair of dancers who claimed to be from Italy till their accents dropped and a woman from Argentina who murdered a few classic songs accompanied by dodgy backing tracks.

He was one of about a dozen off-peak residents. A couple were waiting for their new house to be ready; another pair was reliving their youths when the camp had been 'something to see' and a couple of blokes were clearly some sort of businesspeople slumming it to save a few quid on their expense allowances.

The rest were contractors put up there by their boss so they'd be able to get on with the contract to build the crematorium at Sir Thomas More House. He gave them a wide berth.

Avoiding talking more than polite vagueness and platitudes to anyone who tried to engage him in conversation, James cut out and went back to the concrete cell, not requiring the bar where the contractors soon made themselves at home.

Messages telling him not to be so selfish, secretive, awkward and independent from almost his entire family including Rebecca's husband Simon plus one from Imelda at Sir Thomas More House took him awhile to plough through before he hit the sack.

Despite the moth wing-like sheets being too short, the single lumpy pillow smelling musty and the metal windows allowing in a constant draft, he fell asleep certain he'd made a terrible mistake. He didn't need the *National Risk Register.*

After a greasy fry-up breakfast – also with chips – he was convinced of it. A walk for some bracing air straight off the sea took him to the front gate, where the imagined gun turret and barbed wire made him apprehensive.

Over the road, heavy with streaming white vans and

armoured vehicles, was the pit, its contents festering away. He'd more or less decided to cut his losses and leave today – even his house would be better than this when he saw a white van leaving the camp. Both driver and passenger looked familiar; both were thugs.

Almost at the Recep-ion, he was hailed by a very old man, bent double, perched on a flaking wooden bench. Trying to read yesterday's *Eastern Daily Press*, his fingers couldn't hold the pages against the breeze.

Not seeing him as an old constituent, James recalled him last evening in the 'entertainment', making no response at all, just huddled up, nursing a mug of cheap instant coffee, as if trying to keep warm endlessly, as he was again.

'Hello, there,' the old man croaked. Are you a fellow sufferer in this ghastly place?'

'I am. How did you guess?' conceded James sitting next to him.

'It's cheaper at these winter rates than any old folks' home in town, so I stick it out. Hell on wheels. Did you know they modelled the early holiday camps on Nazi concentration camps without the gas chambers and ovens?'

'I didn't know that,' James smiled.

The old boy was deadly serious. 'I dream of spiders all over me, almost every night. I'm arachnophobic.'

'Me too,' James conceded. 'I'm also ophidiophobic, fear of snakes and chiroptophobic, fear of bats.'

'Me too,' the old boy agreed, staring into space. 'I'm also spheksophobic, fear of wasps and selachophobic, fear of sharks. If I'm honest, I'm a bit ailurophobic, fear of cats.'

James wondered whether to go on. He wasn't going to outdo this old boy with phobias, not even with fear of radiators, curvy lines or white vans.

'Have you got family?'

'Two sons and my daughter. All dead now. I have no grandchildren. I'm alone, but they do their best I suppose. Christmas is a shade less ghastly here than in a care home or hospital. When the winter ends, I'll be back in the Civic Forgotten People's Home. If I survive another summer, I'll be back here come autumn. I can hardly wait.'

'Have you ever walked over the road to that tip?'

'I can't walk. In any case when the wind is from the west, you can smell the rotting corpses. I suppose I'll join them soon. I mean, if you don't bring your own, they lend you a rope to hang yourself. Most thoughtful.'

James didn't check out at the Recep-ion. Instead he found another bench, not flaking but half broken, and sat to ring Maisie.

'My darling. Get me out of here. Tell your mother or your aunt or both. If I stay here, I'll top myself.'

'Where are you, Grandpa?'

'Grimaldi's Palace of Fun. Some palace; some fun, I can tell you.'

'You can never have too much fun, Grandpa.'

After a moment Maisie came back on, 'Mum says

tomorrow, they'll come for you and the fun will stop.'

'I know that, Maisie.'

He endured one more evening meal, a further bout of quality entertainment and went a final time to his cell to sleep and dream of spiders all over him before a last fry-up breakfast. With chips.

Act One, Scene 18

In his house, just ahead of Judy Blowers showing potential buyers round, James was served his second ultimatum. This, with the full force of THE FAMILY.

Even Judy joined in. She offered to keep showing people round and James felt less uncomfortable with her than some sharp-suited junior estate agent. Her gratitude to James still ran deep and wide.

Samantha informed him he'd need a couple of weeks to recover from the last fall at Fitzgerald or Thomas More. Even another care home was rejected firmly on the grounds that he was prevaricating and playing for time.

He produced a couple of crumpled sheets of A4 paper on which he'd scribbled phone numbers of local care agencies. Samantha glanced at it and said, 'no, Dad, too late for that. We want round-the-clock care for awhile. You could have brought more help in ages ago.'

'We'd agreed that you'd go to Rebecca for Christmas, well away from what is now your empty house, but she can't look after you with Simon's parents and a homeless woman they've taken in.'

He never cared much for Christmas anyway; just an ordeal to be got through most years, especially without Elspeth and all the constituency duties he used to do – final surgeries of the year, early morning visit to the post sorting office and 300 plus cards to sign.

Happy season in Essex would be grim, especially with both Simon's parents still alive and their homeless person could be a serial killer or a carrier of near dormant coronavirus they welcomed in. Just for a fleeting moment he wondered if Christmas in Sir Thomas More would be the lesser of two evils.

Judy Blowers walked right in. 'Hello, James, Samantha. It's fifteen minutes to the next visit, but I like to be early. One last week I understand is coming back for a second look round, so that's promising.'

Samantha gushed her thanks; James was lukewarm. 'If we accept an offer, then I'm more or less out of here for good. I'm homeless.'

'Don't be so melodramatic. You'll be in a different home. If you go to Thomas More, you can store all your precious junk in their warehouse. Anywhere else, and you'll have to live round the boxes.'

A white van pulled up outside. James froze. Samantha frowned, puzzled as to why white vans kept bothering him.

'They've come to take your stuff.' James said nothing. Judy flung wide the door and stepped outside to greet the two men who emerged. Big, burly men, dirty T-shirts, torn jeans, heavy boots. Their machine guns were probably left in the cab.

Judy pointed out their task. The lead man muttered, 'we may need two trips, lady!' Judy smiled sweetly and nodded. No expense spared if it was someone else's money.

'We've booked your arrival an hour from now, Dad.'

'He looked her in the eye. 'No reprieve, Samantha?'

'Dad, come on. Please don't make this any harder.'

As the men gripped hold of the box nearest the front door, James sidestepped them, thanked Judy and walked outside. He'd said his goodbyes to the house long ago. Even the memories of forty years of marriage and raising their girls had vanished.

Elspeth was also long gone, with the little touches of comfort she'd brought to their home. The kids' stockings and Christmas tree trinkets they loved – all boxed and destined for a charity shop. He said goodbye to Elspeth and the memories in his head. She replied that he'd be fine.

Slowly, he walked to Samantha's car like a man going to the gallows. His own car was to be borrowed by Maisie. He climbed in, buckled up and stared straight ahead.

The drive down his road to the main street was not exactly lined with tearful neighbours waving him off; but a couple did look up and watch him go. He didn't feel like talking; Samantha sensed that, so they made the distance in silence and met little traffic.

The imposing front view of Sir Thomas More House made James' heart sink even lower than before, especially as they'd dotted twinkling Christmas lights everywhere. Samantha led him to the front door and gave the quaint old dangling bell a fulsome tug.

The old wooden door rescued from a fire damaged Victorian folly in Yorkshire opened to reveal the gormless young woman staring at them through misaligned bulbous eyes, under a dead black head of nylon substitute hair as if she'd just arrived from the Planet Vacant. A ridiculous gnome hat was perched on the head, a concession to seasonal jollity.

'Morning, James Ellington is checking in.' The servant shuffled aside. The immediate reception area was still a cage, imprisoning them momentarily while they sanitised their hands and had their faces filmed and their eyes scanned for security passes, which plopped from the machine after a matter of seconds.

As a buzzer sounded, the gate swung open allowing them access to the main hallway. To James it definitely was the entrance to one of those high security American prisons with a purpose-built Death Row he'd seen in films. He didn't bother to look back at the outer gate. It was sealed, as was his fate.

The enormous foyer, the central curving staircase, rescued from an old house in Devon, was unchanged, except for a large, top heavy Christmas tree adorned with lights arranged by an idiot. The same ambient calmness recording played, to cover the anguished cries of demented inmates. No Christmas carols yet.

As the functionary stood behind the Edwardian reception desk, James wanted to shriek at her to put a light on and get screaming, choking, crying, swearing and running about like headless chickens before the Christmas music. But she did it all without his prompting.

She peered at their just issued passes and wrote them into the identical big, old-fashioned book, underneath what she'd recorded before. Right on cue, a metallic voice from a silo behind startled them. 'Thank you, Imelda 4, I'll take over now.'

It was, of course, the tall, gangly woman dressed in nurse costume, devoid of the normal human features. Her face was even more smoothed out, with tiny eye sockets, small protruding nose and a mouth that barely twitched.

'I'm Matron Mercury. Welcome to Sir Thomas More House. We hope you will be very happy here.' She turned to the skivvy. 'I said I'll take over now.'

With a scared little 'yes, Matron,' Imelda 4 curtsied clumsily and made her escape. Nurse Ratched from *One Flew Over the Cuckoo's Nest* no longer came into James' mind; this was artificial intelligence on legs.

Placing one leg down heavily after the other, Matron moved off, leaving them to follow and James to glance at his daughter who seemed to be regarding everything so far as perfectly normal and reasonable.

All that entry palaver was the curtain raiser for the rest of his life in madness. He was trapped in a cross between a circus of lunatics and an old fashioned asylum where normal people would visit on Sunday afternoons to be entertained.

Their first port of call, ushered in by the automaton, was to the former MPs' wing, down a long, wide corridor with about ten doors each side stretching ahead.

'Former Honourable Members and Members of the House of Lords who were once MPs live along this wing. Here are four day-rooms with relaxing facilities where families can visit, there is a unique state of the art medical facility here and a small dining room and a mini cafeteria.'

As they looked around, Samantha started to make appreciative noises as if she was about to move in. James kept his screaming internal. Nobody seemed to pay any regard to the fact that he'd seen all this a few days ago. This whole pantomime was being staged to try his patience.

Any minute now they'd point out the little bars that knew no licensing laws and he'd start seeing faces, dotted about, faces he'd recognise despite the ravages of the years they'd endured.

And sure enough, the one whose name he'd forgotten

but now knew was Bill Forbes, one-time Leader of the House, approached with a broad grin, grabbed his shoulder and said, 'Hello, Dad, can we play football now?' before James recoiled, wiping the spittle from his face.

In a lounge they were introduced to Lord Wyford, with his history recited by the robot. They were shown into the room recently vacated by the late Mrs Clemmy Denton that was to be his. Samantha nodded approval.

As if acting in the remake of the humans-interacting-with-robots film *Westworld*, James allowed the show to roll on around him. To the office suite of the Rt Hon Ralph Dines, MP for West Norton 1987-2019, Junior Whip, Under-Secretary for Industry, Chairman of Sir Thomas More House.

Imelda 4 was in place; the office with the Queen Anne desk and throne-like platform was empty, Dines' apologies were conveyed. Samantha studied the huge smug portrait of the man himself. In the outer office she stood taking in the pictorial map.

'It's a pretty big operation you have here,' Samantha commented, off-script.

'Yes, it is.' Matron pointed out the corridors, offices, lounges, dining rooms and cafeteria and place where the crematorium would be built. 'There's the Archives and Records store. There's a small extra fee for hiring a bay.'

'I mentioned you can put your stuff in there, Dad.'

Stabbing a finger at the map, she announced, 'we'll see the Chamber now.'

Leading to the toilets on the way to the Chamber, they passed the very same old dear being helped to swallow medicine and making more than a meal of it. James' gorge rose again.

The same old man was in his spot having his head banged on the wall as two white-coated assistants rushed to help him.

The replica Chamber was busy. A dozen or more residents were rehearsing for their annual Speech of the Year contest in the New Year. The stage lights were on – the green benches were bright. The full fantasy.

As before, he was recognised by several who waved or called out, to the irritation of Dame Winifred Carswood, gathering her vocal cords for the climax, for her peroration on the shocking treatment of the mentally unwell.

'I remember this, Dad.' Samantha muttered.

Timmy Greenwood (North Westway East) gibbered from the gallery and hung on the rail of the press area, swinging himself backwards and forwards, shrieking 'Me thinks the honourable Lady doth protest too much!' which led to Sir Gerry Manders pronouncing, 'he thinks he's an actor,' his chins wobbling.

James hoped he'd wake up any moment. He'd been forced to dream all this pantomime previously. It was surely cruel and unusual punishment to make him live through it again, verbatim.

But he was already awake. He introduced his daughter to Manders. Dame Winifred's speech had been interrupted so she was unable to continue. Presumably there never was an actual contest because all the performers just kept going round in a perpetual hellish spiral of rehearsal.

He knew when she discovered his seat that she'd say

he should be on the board. And she did. He was advised to prepare a speech for the contest. It was presumably lunch time soon.

As he turned to tread the familiar steps to the Dining Room, a new player appeared in front of him. The woman was young, by comparison with everyone around, and wore a crisp white coat, her glossy, dark hair held back by a bow behind her head.

'You must be James Ellington. I'm Dr Zoe Frayn.' He shook her hand enthusiastically delighted to break out of the nightmare for a second, unless she suddenly repeated her line as if she'd never said it.

She had a trained observer's eye and knack of focussing on whoever she was talking with, weighting up what really lay behind their actual words.

'Hello, Doctor Frayn, I'm Samantha, James' daughter.' The medic took her eyes from James to look closely at his daughter.

'Shall we walk?' She led off at the normal pace of a woman in her 30s, with all her joints functioning. 'I'm in charge of everyone's well-being and physical health. Notice I put my duties in that order. Well-being leads to better physical health.'

'I couldn't agree more,' said Samantha as the two set off arm in arm even more quickly, leaving James to limp along behind.

Before they reached the Dining Room, the women were so far ahead they could chat about his loneliness, loss of authority, self-esteem and perception, manageable physical exercises and quality social interaction with others as if they were old friends.

James was hungry enough to face lunch. But would it be identical to the previous occasion?

It was. And it wasn't.

Act One, Scene 19

Lunch got off to an almost sane and calm start. To James it seemed that the same people were in the same places at the same tables as his first visit.

Lord Wyford joined as they were being sat down, expelling nicotine breath and dandruff confetti. Ralph Dines strode in, but was over-bold. His ankle went over, stick flew away and as he fell he grabbed the lapel of a hapless waiter.

They fell together, there was a moment of shock all round before staff rushed to help Dines up. The waiter managed himself. 'Sorry, my friend,' Dines spluttered. 'Bloody ankles.'

From the table James watched. Of course, Dines stumbled and fell just as he did. Damned feet, ankles, knees. How strange that they both had the same condition.

No time to think further, Dines limped over to shake Samantha's hand warmly, look into her eyes and solemnly promise to take good care of her dear, precious, ancient father.

'He's my oldest friend in politics and I will go to the end of the earth to stop anything bad befalling him.' Samantha swallowed it,

They ordered from the identical menu, but without problems from the ambient background sound effects, no interruptions, no madmen appeared before them, including Lennie Sanders, and the meal went off without a hitch. Wyford actually ate.

Matron met them at the door. James had the impression that she'd just been parked there in the corridor in a rest position to conserve energy and now sprang to life to guide him.

'James, it's time to return to the office, sign the contract and say goodbye to your daughter. We like residents to unpack into their rooms without help so they can begin to feel at home.'

By now a certain air of inevitability had seized James, but he'd not abandon hope of an escape. Maybe prisoners facing execution cling to the image of an earthquake springing the locks or a last-minute reprieve. Perhaps he could behave badly so was asked to leave? But then, what was 'behaving badly' in a palace of lunatics?

Samantha counter-signed the admission form, agreed the fees and add-ons, took hold of the regulations about visiting and exit passes, no smoking indoors, no pets and no snacking in bedrooms and within the hour was in the hall bidding her father a fond farewell. At least she had the decency to shed a tear at what she was doing.

'Bye Dad. Rebecca and family are coming up on Saturday. We'll come and see you on Sunday and then make sure you see somebody from the family regularly. Don't fret. Try and make the most of it.'

He nodded. 'Of course. When you come bring some tunnelling equipment and take away with you a few bags of sand from my tunnel.'

She smiled, he was only half joking. Imelda appeared

to guide her through the security gates and out of the building.

Matron asked James, 'Now, would you like to start making yourself at home in your room? They've taken your luggage upstairs.'

'No, thanks, I think I'll stroll around the grounds till I feel at home, Mrs Robinson.' The allusion to the 1968 Simon and Garfunkel song was lost on the machine. The brain whirred for a second and she replied, 'Very well. It's a good day for a walk.'

And to his surprise he was not only pointed to the garden door but allowed to pass through without triggering alarms and guards rugby tackling him to the ground before hanging him up by his finger nails from the ceiling.

A full twenty minutes of slow limping, pausing to enjoy the sound of birdsong, a slight breeze rustling shrubs and trees, was his. He admired rhododendrons, geraniums, hydrangeas and forsythia without a clue as to what were their real names. Perhaps that was a metaphor for Sir Thomas More House – people's old seats and former jobs mattered more than their real names.

Except that they didn't after a decade or two or three. Feigning interest in a blackbird, or sparrow or reedwarbler (he knew birds as well as flowers) singing from an overhead branch, he avoided a cluster of inmates round a bench arguing the price of free trade and a single inmate in a self-propelled wheel chair explaining his bowel problems to his imaginary friend beside him.

Just as James was beginning to loosen up and feel a bit more human, Ralph found him. 'Ah, there you are!'

'Yes, so I am and I wasn't lost.'

'Nobody is lost here, James, nobody.'

As James continued his stroll, Ralph stepped along beside him, their limps in unison. 'I wanted to explain a couple of things. Are you religious, at all?'

'You've got files on me, you tell me.'

'Nominal Christian, of course. Well, the message is that nobody should enter church with a grudge, envy, jealousy or hatred for another believer, but must make the peace first, mmm?'

James was unsure if a response was actually needed. They clumped on, right legs and walking sticks now just out of perfect unison.

'You'll be moved by our Christmas Carols and Readings in the Chamber; it will fill you with that passionate desire to bring peace on earth and goodwill to your fellow men and women! Not to put too fine a point on it, James, old man, it's about poor old Lennie Sanders and that prisoner incident of yours.'

James stopped abruptly. 'What? I looked up the one and only prisoner in my case work. A lifer called Tommy Cross, coming to the end of his sentence, needed help settling back into his home area, that's all.'

'All? You should have done more research.'

'Did you research the background to every single case you were presented with?'

'Well, actually, yes.'

'So what's that got to do with Lennie Sanders, for crying out loud?'

'Lennie's done some crying out loud, I can tell you.' He waited, expecting James to make a connection between Tommy Cross and Lennie Sanders.

Still James could think of no link. 'Look out you two, scooter coming', yelled a man, grey hair streaming behind him, white knuckles driving a battery powered mobility scooter. He was almost on them.

Dines and James moved as sharply aside as their limps and walking sticks allowed. 'Oh, looks like the children are playing with their toys. We should keep out of the way.'

Suddenly the path and adjoining areas were thick with old people astride a range of mobility scooters. Lady Helen Fulcher was gripping the bar of a lightweight model that could be folded into a car boot; Gerrymandering, head down over the bar of a heavy-weight model, switched to its maximum 8 miles per hour.

Several nursing staff, a couple of Imeldas and a pair of maintenance men he hadn't yet met came out to watch. 'It's an idea I had to let off steam. They play in something between a dodgem car derby and a sprint. Does them a power of good.'

'Play' was the word. Like kids, a dozen or more inmates on their individual motorised wheels streaked around, tight circling, whooping for joy, bumping into each other, racing, aiming at residents who had no machines but stood or sat to watch.

Lord Wyford lost control at one point and damaged a bush as he wedged himself in, covered in petals.

'Keep right except when going east, all of you! Clockwise on Mondays, Wednesdays and Fridays; anticlockwise on other days!' yelled Dines. Then, to

James, 'I had to make rules otherwise it would be anarchy. Civil service rules, they are.'

No more could be heard above the frantic little wheels with shouts and laughter filling the air. From the corner of his eye, James noticed Lennie Sanders astride a small 50cc moped, coming straight at him.

He sidestepped; then fell to the grass, so Lennie just missed him. He stopped dead as assistants ran to get him off the moped. 'Not allowed, Lennie, you know that. Mobility scooters only.'

Lennie spat at James, 'That's what you'll get till you've made reparations for Tommy Cross.'

Opening his mouth to protest his ignorance of the Cross connection, James was hit with the moped wheel as Sanders restarted it and rode off, flourishing a middle finger gesture at James as he went.

'You see what I mean, James? Your arrival has ruffled the smooth waters of this haven. Build a bridge to Lennie Sanders and all will be well. You can never make too many peace overtures here.'

James watched him leave, noticing his limp was almost identical to his own. Well, with those feet...

In need of a rest, he sat next to Sir Ronald Hasbery who'd been watching dispassionately. During his forty years of service to Parliament culminating in the highest legal advice position of Clerk to the House, Hasbery had seen and advised on countless disagreements.

'You saw that, Ronald. I really have no idea what either Lennie Sanders or Ralph Dines is on about.'

Ronald looked at him over the top of his half moon glasses – a gesture James had watched him perform countless times at the clerks' table in front of the Speaker's Chair.

'Well, I have no idea of the particulars, either. But in my experience, James, it's wise to beware the anger of men who nurture rages over decades.'

'Lennie Sanders has done that, apparently.'

Hasbery nodded, waving his folded open copy of *The Times* crossword page. 'You need to be aware of the psychopomp, I fancy.'

When James looked puzzled at the word, Ronald explained, 'Psychopomp, someone or some thing that leads souls to the land of the dead.'

James nodded, still little the wiser. 'I have taken up a number of harmless hobbies in this place. Macramé, speed *Scrabble* and linguipotence. The mastery of weird and wonderful words, many no longer in use in the English language. Quite helpful when I wish to a) impress or b) confuse somebody, but rarely a) and b) simultaneously.'

James nodded. He too needed a few hobbies that would confuse people, especially the management, and opened his mouth to tell the man so. But Ronald hadn't finished his advice.

'However, there is another anger in men that you need to be careful of, I'd say. The person with an agenda he or she is happy to kill for. An adherent to the cult of chirocracy, government by physical force.'

'Ralph Dines?'

''I like it here. My wife died and my children are in the USA and in France now. So I live here in calm and relative comfort. I have no other plans. I suspect this will see me out. Ralph Dines is a man with an agenda that will not let him go but eats into him day and night.'

'To kill someone?'

'You don't have to actually see a thing before you know it to be true.'

James nodded. 'Could have been a direct quote from Erskine May, the Procedural Bible.' Ronald smiled indulgently.

That was confirmation that in the view of this gentle, unassuming man, Ralph Dines was the most dangerous person in his world. Apart from the A12 gang. Unless they were one and the same.

With that thought uppermost in his mind, James neither saw nor heard Sanders' moped approaching. Far from putting it away, Lennie had waited, chosen his moment.

He hit his victim from behind, sending him flying. The roar of the two-stroke engine sounded like a herd of artificial bees swarming round as he sank into oblivion, even while being carried up by staff and placed in the hospital wing.

James didn't hear someone say, 'and just before Christmas, too. Poor bloke. Good job he's signed up for the full care package.'

Act One, Scene 20

Their full care package turned out to be heavy sedation and making more of his injuries than necessary. In his conscious moments, James was told he was in the best place among so much better equipment than the local NHS could provide and, by the way, his family sent their love.

Periodically he imagined he heard angelic choirs singing Christmas music that uplifted before it was shut down mid chord. He was fed through a tube to begin with and then gradually weaned onto soft solids. Oh, and by the way, his family sent their love.

His legs were encased in thick white plaster and he lay in a hoist contraption that restricted his movements. Staff who loomed over him occasionally told him he was doing well, he'd soon be up and about, swallow this and that tablet and, by the way, his family sent their love.

Dr Zoe was a frequent visitor, staring down with her clear blue eyes and her gentle face smiling to encourage him. She didn't appear to be doing more than overseeing his treatment and was the only one not wearing a ludicrous cracker paper hat.

Samantha visited almost every day as far as he could tell and brought him little anecdotes about their family Christmas. The weather had been too bad for Rebecca and family to make the journey but they all sent their love.

Dines stumped in one morning and told him he'd

missed Christmas and the New Year festivities for which Sir Thomas More was legendary, but never mind, all that good food, lots of alcohol and sparkling entertainment and community would have been wasted on a curmudgeon like him.

'Everyone makes resolutions this time of the year, don't they, old man? Mmm? Better think about yours. Better resolve to be a bit more co-operative while you're here, a bit more sociable and understanding that people only want to help you. Mmm?'

James didn't reply. Just imagined himself as Scrooge redeemed, resolving to be a better human being. Exhibiting kindness to strangers and animals. Buying everyone a bigger turkey.

A few days into January Samantha told him that Rebecca would be coming the next day; able to talk to him in a sensible two-way conversation. Clearly the drugs were being reduced.

'I suppose they dope residents over the holiday so they save on the food bill,' James muttered. His younger daughter smiled and said, 'well, Dad, if you're back to your old cynical self, things are looking up.'

True enough, within 24 hours he'd seen all his family including the children and was asked if he'd like to have a visit from Judy Blowers. 'I'm not feeling that much better!'

With evidence of Christmas packed away, trimmings and goodwill evaporated, resolutions made and discarded like litter, the New Year Normal broke out everywhere. But after nearly three weeks, James hadn't settled in any sense. He hadn't even unpacked his things in the room he'd been given!

To encourage him, Dr Zoe accompanied him on a walk

around the building, his dressing gown flapping and his surgical boots on as slippers weren't made for his deformed feet.

Sebby Catchpole was the first of his circle he encountered. 'You're back from the krankenhaus, James, my old son! Are you properly awake?'

'I suppose I must be as I haven't woken up swimming in the toxic tip.'

'Not that again, James,' Zoe said softly but firmly.

With a break in the weather, James settled into his new routines. Finally, his things had been unpacked and put away in his wardrobe and drawers in a quite random, chaotic manner. He started eating in the cafeteria and occasionally in the Members' Dining Room when bullied into it by Dines and Wyford. Seeing nothing of Lenny Sanders was a relief.

He took to a daily meander around the grounds, attractive in rain or shine. He found he followed predictable paths, admired the same plants as the winter season moved onwards. Ever wary of a fresh outbreak of invalidity scooter madness, it was an enjoyable part of his routine.

One day leaving his room for a walk, he encountered a huddle of female cleaners gathered round an industrial sized vacuum. They were sharing something from a night out or one of the residents, with lots of giggles and smiles at each other.

The instant they spotted James, they stopped, curtsied in unison and formed a line to let him pass. 'Morning, Mr James,' one said, echoed by the others. As soon as he was round the corner the laughter resumed. Perhaps the cleaners were actual flesh and blood.

In fact, all staff and fellow inmates seemed to know his name and that he'd missed Christmas as if that was the worst outcome any human being could suffer. In short, he was accepted in a surreal sort of way. People appeared to tolerate him as part of the furniture and fittings. After all, he was no more peculiar than any of the others. He remained determined to leave at the earliest safe time.

He had his first proper weekend visits using his room, the lounge and the gardens, rather than the sick bed. Samantha and Leroy brought Maisie, Henry and William one Saturday afternoon.

Outside on a bench, Maisie listened to a little of Grandpa's description of horrors and tortures, mental battles and wacky treatments before Leroy took her off for a driving lesson and left bored Henry and William to kick a ball between them till it was lost up a tree.

Sunday, Rebecca and Simon drove from Essex bringing Joseph preoccupied counting down the days till he'd be old enough to start driving 'just like cousin Maisie' and Emily keen that her kind old Grandpa should buy her the games Father Christmas had forgotten to bring – *Women's Soccer Death Derby* and *Ten Severed Heads Sitting On the Wall*.

Heart-breaking pleas to his daughters for clemency, time off for good behaviour and hope of convalescence in either of their homes fell on deaf ears. The husbands were no better, clearly under the thumbs of their wives. Even separating off the kids and offering ready cash won him no family allies.

Judy sent a message that she personally liked the couple, a pleasant little woman with a disabled husband who'd seen his house three times and were ready to make an offer. She'd be living next door to them, after all.

He had mixed feelings about the offer. While there was an empty house to return to, he had a strong argument for release.

Within a week he'd explored every corridor he could find, made an excuse to ask the Imelda in Dines' office something to sneak a look at the pictorial map. Even to the site of the new crematorium, he ventured a glimpse.

Close by the portable facilities were parked no less than five identically dirty white vans of the A12 variety. Despite struggling for some minutes, he was unable to recall the registration number of the one he'd memorised. But that was in the tip, wasn't it?

He managed to avoid being spotted nosing around. He hoped he'd mastered the art of clumping around silently, but everyone always heard them both approaching. Dines and Ellington.

Obviously, he was being filmed constantly, but so what? Exploring wasn't against the rules; he'd read them thoroughly. He'd even looked in on the speech contest rehearsals and had penned a few lines for a contribution, though he'd not been invited to sample the acoustics yet.

He sorted his stuff into the sizeable warehouse given over to Archives and Records. It was partly disguised behind a Victorian cottage façade, presumably to acquire planning consent. Every resident was allocated a lockable area, the size of a medium public toilet.

The whole place dripped fire extinguishers and cameras. A guard was on duty 24/7, a man who turned out to be the spitting image of a gardener James had talked to occasionally, a mechanic who looked after company vehicles and one who humped in food and carted out waste. They were all called Karl, apparently.

In Westminster James had always made a point of chatting to police officers, messengers and other staff. It was an activity few other Members bothered with, he noticed. Here he tried the same, but so many were robots.

He joined a twice-weekly coach laid on to take people into East Point for winter shopping and free time. He longed for a change of scene and a bowl of Mediterranean bread and butter pudding in a little Italian kiosk in the town. Four separate people recognised him as their MP, their former MP, a minor soap opera performer or as a famous retired cricketer, so it was a small relief to arrive back at Sir Thomas More.

Avoiding Lennie Sanders, he talked with Lord Wyford over coffee, Dame Winifred Carswood in the gardens, Lady Helen Fulcher over breakfast when he failed to persuade her he wasn't her therapist and Sebastian Catchpole everywhere, out of hospital now and loving having a pal.

Sir Ronald Hasbery occasionally tagged along for a drink and a game of chess or *Go, Mahjong* or, his particular favourite, the Malaysian take on the board game *Xiangqi*. He said he liked games that required brainpower, tactics and an ultimate quar for the opponent.

'Quar, my dear fellow, means to choke or fill up. Usually applied to narrow passages and small cupboards, I like to imagine somebody's throat being filled to choking.'

It was the first time he'd heard Sir Ronald express even mildly violent feelings towards another human being. He looked at the man with new eyes after that, and resisted his normal instinct to feel he spoke too slowly and wondering if he should finish his sentences for him.

Hasbery was a walking fount of wisdom. Little pearls of knowledge and common sense plus shrewd observations joined apt quotations which equalled gravitas to what naturally slipped into quite juvenile antics whenever MPs were gathered together.

Timmy Greenwood often put in wild-eyed, manic-haired appearances to declaim mutilated Shakespeare. One he got right was 'thou damned and luxurious mountain goat' which puzzled everyone except Sir Ronald who declared it 'from *Henry V*, if I'm not mistaken.'

Matron Mercury was never far from any scene, and after a day it occurred to James that Matrons were available in every corridor because all those robots had been created in the one stereotypical nurse image. He imagined a rogue Matron robot ripping the limbs off inmates, like a brat might pull the legs off a spider.

One afternoon, he planned for a pretend stomach ache that evening that would necessitate a hospital stay from which he could discharge himself and hitch-hike to Essex where he'd throw himself on the mercy of Simon, his son-in-law who worked for a Christian charity so would surely take him in.

A previously unexplored door at the back of the main building caught his eye. Karl was humping food boxes in and empty crates out. Rations were arriving. Perhaps he could hide in the van and be driven out?

Inside was gloomy, against the tepid winter afternoon sunshine outside. There were loud voices as two Karls lugged stuff around. He hid hastily behind a pile of boxes before cutting through a door into a storeroom and then another. He was soon lost.

Embarrassed to show himself to a Karl and ask for

direction, he moved on, ignoring that old political adage about 'stop digging when you're in a hole.'

There were definite footsteps behind as someone shadowed him. He waited a moment. Nothing. As he stepped forward, imagining a door into the house or Dining Room ahead, with a banshee wailing Lennie Sanders ran at him, a meat cleaver held aloft, whistling as it was swung from side to side.

Mouth white-flecked, Sanders raised the cleaver in his right hand and fumbled around with his left to hold James' lambs-wool jumper, As a door ahead was flung open and a familiar voice barked, 'what the fuck are you doing?' there was a flash of light to help Sanders take aim.

It was only stepping back an inch that caused James' foot to catch a dropped plastic box which sent him reeling away, his life saved. The deadly cleaver took his finger top off rather than his head.

James howled with pain and scuttled back; Sanders smelt blood and lunged forward. Dines was just in time to hit the attacker across the back of his head with an empty wooden crate which splintered; Sander's head stayed intact.

Dines stood between them, warning Sanders with his upright palm-out hand. James struggled to his feet. Assistants appeared with a first aid box and the bleeding was staunched. 'Find the finger, they can sew it back on', screeched James, breathing hard, almost crying in pain and anger.

'You clearly have not made it up with Lennie, James. I'm disappointed. You've been here since just before Christmas. Next time it *will* be your head.'

'Is nobody calling the ambulance for my finger and the police to section Lennie Lunatic Sanders? Bag the cleaver for evidence.'

'This is what you get for befriending a convicted murderer, James, I tried to warn you.' He gestured and Sanders was led to Matron who produced a needle for his arm.

'Get the police and medical help for me, Dines, Now!' James yelled, panicking from his attack and that nobody was doing a thing to help him. Time was of the essence in sewing back severed limbs, he knew.

'I think, James, this is one we can handle in-house. Dr Frayn will look at your finger. Our mental health team will assess Sanders.' He was calm and quiet.

'That's not good enough! I need to escape from here or my only way out will be in a body bag for that bloody crematorium you're building.'

'Keep your voice down, James; you're making a spectacle of yourself. You're not on the stage. Co-operate, make friends not enemies. DO YOU HEAR ME?' he shouted, shaking James violently.

James deliberately calmed his breathing, his middle finger upright to ease the bleeding. His face almost touching Dines', he released a horror film, scared-stiff, utter mad scream for as long as he had breath – 11 seconds.

As he stopped he realised that Dines had matched him with a similar scream which went on for a further four seconds after James has stopped to draw breath.

'You can never be too mad, Ralph, can you?'

'I don't know, James. Can't you?'

Before either man could repeat the demented screaming, Dr Zoe Frayn appeared, dressed in a loose white coat over an up-market pink jumper and jangly golden necklace, a midi-skirt that showed off her legs without being obvious. Cool in her thirties, James guessed, she was just the Florence Nightingale he needed at that moment.

'Small cut on the finger, Zoe,' Dines snapped, clearly irritated by the whole incident.

'Come on James, come to the medical room. Sorry we haven't had a chance for a good long chinwag before this. We've been so busy. We must be due for a second Halloween with so much barking and baying at the moon!'

She was bright, friendly and kept him moving at a cracking pace, aware they were leaving a blood trail. Since he kept whining about the finger tip that must be on the floor, she sent an assistant back to look for it.

In her room, she gave him an injection that calmed him. Feeling so much better so quickly he knew he and Dr Zoe Frayn would be great friends. She might even release him on medical and/or compassionate grounds.

'Now tell me what happened. I gather Lennie Sanders went for you with a meat cleaver?'

Needing no second invitation, James told her all he knew about Lennie Sanders in Sir Thomas More, when they were in the House and about his visit to Tommy Cross in prison where the man was on the point of release. He spoke avidly with continuing bursts of anger, but it took his mind off her working on his finger.

The assistant returned to report no found fingertip, so she sewed him up, bandaged the wound and nodded and smiled at his tale.

'I can help you, James. I'll find out what the Lennie Sanders problem is. You just relax and come back in the morning so I can dress the wound.'

'No hospital?'

'No need.'

Ralph Dines appeared, calm, reasonable with a professionally caring expression across his pale face. 'How are you, James, old soldier? I was so worried.' It was if the mutual face screaming had never happened, as if Dines had not even seen it. As if he was a different man.

'I'm talking sternly to Lennie Sanders, be assured. Whatever his grievance against you, that's no way to settle differences.'

James was disappointed. 'No police?'

'No need. Give him something to knock him out for the night, Zoe. He'll be right as sixpence by breakfast.'

'He's already had pain killers, Ralph. He doesn't need anything more.'

'I said give him something to knock him out, he's upsetting everyone,' he hissed.

'And I said no, he's had enough,' she spoke softly but smiled, too.

Groggy as he was, James noted that this young, female doctor had refused a direct order from the mighty, alpha Ralph Dines, her boss.

Perhaps she could be trusted after all.

Act One, Scene 21

Before his probationary 'first month' was quite over and he'd paid the bill, he was offered a further contract, this time for five years. He'd hoped to be able to take his leave and go.

His finger still throbbed like hell, but Dr Frayn took care of it with happy pills and made sure the wound was closing over. He'd always be a little short on that digit, but given his age, it 'hardly mattered.'

He'd talked to his girls about the offer they'd received on his house. After a debate they decided to push a little harder and early in the morning, Rebecca had called to say it'd been accepted. So, was he good to go?

Wrapped up warm, walking outside, thinking deeply, picturing the house as it used to be when Elspeth was there and their girls were little, there was no way he'd shut all that down.

Then the A12 van problem, the changes in the locality, Judy becoming too grateful for her vanished youth problem, different people moving into their neighbourhood, ugly extensions made to some attractive dwellings and Elspeth no longer making the house a home. No, it *was* time to let all that go.

He called them to confirm and both said they'd ring the solicitor with a view to completion before Easter. He asked them to thank Judy Blowers for her invaluable help and concern.

Easter? Blimey, James could remember the day when a house could be bought and sold within a month. Nowadays they blamed long-Covid, the debilitating illness left behind by the coronavirus.

That only left his decision about where to live. He fancied a drive out to think. Then he remembered he'd loaned Maisie his car; she'd just passed her driving test and was inseparable from it. There was no coach trip to town, but he could always take a taxi.

As he walked, he heard more than one old Member rehearsing his or her speech aloud. Two were practising to each other, armed with a glass each of something soothing for their throats they'd carried from a bar.

He sat on a bench and took his own scribbled notes from his jacket pocket. It was turning chilly, too early in the year to sit about for long, but he'd decided he might as well have a go at speaking again.

After a few minutes he returned indoors where in the lounge a pair of residents sat doing a jigsaw featuring what looked from the box lid like a sewage works, despite most pieces being too small and flimsy for arthritic fingers. All seemed to be going well until one sneezed, her dental plate flying out, which scattered the pieces.

Another pair played chess, one clearly clueless about the rules thinking it was draughts, which led to a bout of swearing and finger stabbing, which swiftly led to replaying an old skirmish about an amendment to a Finance Bill forty odd years ago that still rankled.

James turned down an invitation to join Bill Forbes in a game of *Scrabble,* at a pound a point, not being confident the man could spell any word longer than three letters now. Constant pressure to join, be sociable was what James had baulked at all along; the real cost of a care home was total loss of independence. He was watched, needing permission to do anything.

While management blotted out cries of pain, howls of anguish and bays of insanity through a range of pleasant background music, they could do nothing about the stench.

It hung over every room where residents gathered. People got used to it, but occasionally it was particularly bad. Piss from catheters leaking into clothing, disinfectant from cleaning spillages, belches from the food that kept on giving for several hours after digestion. And the flatulence!

Once one started, it set off others. Several in a row squeezed their faces up as if gurning or entered in a *Name That Tune* contest. Then he recognised it. *The Hallelujah Chorus* was clearly distinguishable in the emissions from a dozen backsides. Nobody else noticed.

Gagging, James had to get out. The bloody tune wouldn't leave his brain for hours. Not in fact till later, in the afternoon, when Samantha turned up unexpectedly with the boys.

They'd just been picked up from school. Exhausted and monosyllabic at best, they sat with him in his room while Henry played on his phone as if he'd just been given it and William watched an adult movie on his without his mother noticing.

'Dad, I just want to be sure before you sign on the dotted line, that you're really OK to let the house go. It's not what it was, is it?'

'That's true. Far from it. Samantha, I've given it endless thought and I know you and Rebecca are right. No, I'll sign it off.' He paused. 'Yes, absolutely.'

'And you'll stay here for a bit longer?'

'I don't want to; I still don't want to. Look, I lost Christmas, New Year and half my hand so far, what next?' He held up his heavily bandaged finger.

William paused the movie and came over. 'Not the whole hand, is it Grandpa? Can I see?' He'd expressed an interest in medicine and wanted to look closely at the stitches, bruising and congealed blood.

'If Doctor Frayn sends for me for a new dressing, you can come with me.'

'We never got the full story on how that happened, Dad.'

Already James' mind was merging the mobility scooter event with Sanders' attacks by moped and cleaver – 'well, a bunch of residents had a mobility scooter race. I fell and then – '

'You fell? Again?'

'It was nothing.'

'Nothing but a finger?'

It was a mistake to admit he'd fallen, but he launched into an exaggerated account of the mobility scooter circus omitting mention of Lennie Sanders and the meat cleaver.

'Are you sure you're safe here?'

'Oh no, I'm not but Dr Frayn is very caring. Some of the robots are half decent. A few of the former MPs and Lords are harmlessly dotty; some are full scale insane. They usually look after us all, wrapping us in cotton wool.

Except when they don't, and we are assaulted by maniacs.'

'And are all your papers and stuff securely locked in that storehouse now?'

'Yes, that's one good thing. They realise we all need a place to keep our memories. I imagine more than one of us is writing a memoir.'

'Are you?'

'No. Not yet. I might do. In meantime I've been writing my speech for the contest.'

'That's brilliant, Dad! I've counted more positives than negatives so far.'

'Can we hear it, Grandpa?' asked Henry, no longer fully engrossed in his game.

'Oh, it's just notes so far.' They looked at him. They'd keep on till he gave them something. 'Mr Speaker, I'm honoured as a new resident to be following in what I understand has been a tradition here in this annual contest at Sir Thomas More House and am delighted to be called first to speak after the front benches.'

They were listening. He had them. He wasn't sure he'd hold the inmates as easily. 'If any of us is serious about considering the real state of mental health in this country, one only has to lift the stone that is a famous place in East Anglia, not a million miles from here.'

Samantha saw where this was going. He pressed on, enjoying himself, 'this house, masquerading as a care home is a glorified crematorium with a sideline in care and nursing. It's what any decent playwright would describe as an asylum run by lunatics. Only one man stands against what has become an unconscionable tyranny.'

He looked up. Henry had resumed his game; William his movie. Samantha shook her head.

A nurse assistant entered to inform him that Dr Frayn was running late after an assessment in the dementia ward came up for review; she'd dress his finger in the morning.

His mother put her arm round her son. 'Well, William, you can't see the wound now. Maisie will be home soon; she's got some 6th form presentation tonight, so she'll want to eat quickly. Leroy should have prepared the lasagne and salad. So, we'll see you at the weekend.'

They embraced goodbye. 'The speech is likely to be more coherent than most, Dad, but you know there's a red line around sarcasm and self-parody. You shouldn't cross it.'

And they left, secure in the knowledge that Dad/Grandpa was more than halfway institutionalised and would settle effectively from then on.

The next morning, he took what had become his after breakfast habit of a walk in the grounds, despite the drizzle and enough wind to shake every leafless tree. He had to tread carefully on slippery leaves, his stick sliding about. He should get a new rubber ferrule from somebody.

The problem with a habit is that people can be found easily. Those in danger of assassination were advised to establish no patterns. Special Branch had visited them when he was first elected and told Elspeth to walk the girls to school a different way each day. In fact, there were just two ways they could take.

Ralph Dines, wrapped warm in his very smart long dark overcoat, rather like the one James had bought for funerals and Remembrance Day parades, found him.

'Ah there you are, James.'

'I wasn't lost, Ralph. I told you, nobody is ever lost here. Now, I wanted to touch on the Lennie Sanders matter. I know we thought we'd sorted it, but Lennie needs something, even a parsimonious compensation package. I understand that he'll settle for a regular payment to help defray his expenses on a five-year deal. What do you say?'

'Ralph, till I know what Lennie Sanders is on about with me and a constituent I helped, I say, fuck off. The lot of you.'

'Not a constituent. A convicted murderer.' James said nothing.

'We've been friends since before we got into the House. You remember that trip to the former East Germany, before the Berlin Wall came down, courtesy of the Konrad Adenauer Stiftung for candidates they thought would go places?'

'Of course, I remember it. We enjoyed it. Gave us a head start in making friends once we got in.'

'The Dresden Group we called ourselves. Raised a few eyebrows, naturally!'

They smiled and sat, recalling the visits in quest of knowledge and understanding about international affairs.

'But, James, let me take you back eighteen months before that. Do you remember the selection process that took you from a humble agent, former teacher to the giddy heights of prospective Parliamentary candidate?'

'How can I forget that battle! Several thought I was getting above my station, a corporal trying to become a general. But I had many friends who supported me and helped me get selected and then elected.'

'The shortlist, dear boy, the final four. You remember?'

'Yes, there was Constance Fleming, Billy Harvey and –

'And me. Yes, I was there with a chance of a winnable seat before you stole it from me and I had to wait six months till I found another winnable one!'

'I did no such thing. It was a fair and square contest, based on speeches and glad-handing, plus in my case, local knowledge.'

'Yes, speaking. You could do that. James, that's why I've withdrawn your speech from the contest. You ought not to win first time in.'

James was astonished. Was Lennie Sanders' hostility really Dines' by proxy?

A phone in Ralph's pocket rang; he answered with monosyllables. 'Got to go. Think about the offer of a thousand a month extra to help Lennie Sanders out, which in turn will help me to forget the past and concentrate on the good things of knowing you. Such as they are.'

As he walked off, he crossed paths with Maisie, just visiting before college. After greeting her effusively he pushed on to the house.

'Nice man, Grandpa,' she said, bending to kiss him.

'Yes, if you think psychopaths are nice men. How did your presentation go at college?'

'Oh, you know. Fine. I like performing, get that from you I suppose. No, I just wanted to thank you again for the use of the car and to make sure you're OK after Mum said you lost an arm and a leg...'

'Half a finger.' He showed her the bandaged digit. She smiled and hugged him.

At that moment the bushes parted and out leapt Lennie Sanders, again under-dressed for the weather and with a wild horror film look about him that spelt danger to James, who was caught off guard.

Leaving Maisie on the bench, Sanders hauled James by the lapel and, kicking both feet in a little dance, rolled him towards the pond. They called it a lake in the house, but really it was a large pond.

Maisie stood to defend her old grandfather as Sanders sat on James' back, his own feet in the water to get a firm purchase as he pushed and held James' head under the surface. He kept an iron grip and a firm saddle while James thrashed, his head fully submerged.

Maisie yelled and waved madly for help, just as two assistants led by Dr Frayn sprinted towards them, hauled Sanders off and dragged James to the bank. Dr Frayn hauled him up so he could cough water and draw fresh air, while yet again, Sanders was taken off for an injection.

Once he'd recovered a little and shivering before the full quaking set in, and as Dines was spotted striding towards them, Maisie said, 'You can't stay here, Grandpa. They're trying to kill you.'

'Nonsense, a little disagreement, mostly in James' mind,' Dines barked, coming up and looking closely at James. 'I believe James has agreed to pay compensation to Lennie for damages done years ago. Lennie doesn't know that yet, that's all.'

'Come with me, James, I'll check you over and looks like that finger took a bashing.' Blood stained the bandage.

As he let Dr Frayn lead him to the house he mouthed the word 'help' at his granddaughter, who nodded. Dines refrained from giving Zoe orders concerning James Ellington, but he disliked the way she seemed on his side somehow.

In politics you can never have too many sides, but his 'tame' doctor didn't appear to be on his.

Act One, Scene 22

A week later Dr Frayn gave him the once over, confirmed he was no worse physically, but how was he coping emotionally and mentally?

'Well, it's not exactly the paradise on earth I was led to believe. I feel under constant attack, quite literally. And I'm not sure who I can trust here anyway.'

'I hope you can trust me.'

'I hope so, too. I recall on my first day in Parliament I went into the Chamber to listen to the proceedings. The end of an empty row was occupied by Ian Paisley, formidable Northern Ireland loyalist politician. He beckoned me across his lap to take an empty space. He wasn't moving anywhere. So, I did that, climbed over him, and as I drew level with his face, I said *'I didn't realise you chaps sat on our side*. I meant the Conservative side.'

She sat and smiled as she listened. 'He replied in that rich brogue which I can't copy, *Never mistake sitting on your side for being on your side*. It was a powerful lesson then and it still applies, especially here.'

'That's a lovely story. Are you going to use it in your speech?' She was making mental notes.

'No, I've used it before. Some of them might remember.'

'Would make no difference to most. Many don't remember what they did three minutes ago. People like to hear familiar things, especially if they think they said them.'

She finished re-bandaging his finger in a friendly, comfortable silence. People at ease don't have to fill every second with words. 'It's coming on nicely now, healing well. But I think we need to schedule some time to talk honestly about what's really behind how you feel here. Do you still want to leave us?'

It was the personalisation, the 'us' that made him mumble, 'I'm thinking about that.'

He walked to her office window as if to think. One of the ubiquitous dirty white vans was parked nearer the house than normal, but still close to the crematorium. A dreadfully familiar contractor was unlocking the back doors. After a moment he stepped back holding what looked like a petrol can.

It was clearly full, as he walked lopsided with it. Blimey, were they going to set fire to the bodies using petrol? Or was he going to incinerate the whole building so Dines could claim on the insurance?

The man met Ralph Dines coming from the crematorium. They exchanged a few words and James watched the boss pat the worker on the shoulder and nod approval or permission.

Permission for what?

Was the man going beyond the crematorium and to the rear of the Archives and Records? Were there matches or a lighter in his pocket? Would the Archives become an inferno in the next few minutes?

If so, why? James wondered about their intention to kill

off residents. Why? They'd lose money, surely? Weren't residents too old to possess saleable body parts? Unless people had already made a bequest and so it was all a scam? Or were their actions simply to turn borderline eccentrics into raving lunatics?

Fearful for his own precious papers in the Archives, he moved to the door. She watched. For a moment he'd forgotten she was in the room with him.

Something drew him to return to the window. Dines stood alone in the middle of the footpath, staring at the house. James pictured a mobility scooter coming from behind while another approached from the front. They collided head on just where Dines stood, breaking every bone in his odious body.

James relived that time when a minor reshuffle had been expected all day and Dines had been like a cat on a hot roof. James expected nothing for himself and was equally unconvinced Dines would get anything. They agreed to meet for a cafeteria dinner.

But when he didn't show, James ate alone and then wandered into the Chamber to see what was going on. To his horror, there at the end of the front bench nearest the Speaker's chair sat a preening Ralph Dines.

He'd been made a junior whip!

Appointments took instant effect, so suddenly with one phone call from Downing Street, his Honourable Friend now clung to the first rung of the ladder ready to lord it over rank and file Members.

James sidled along the second bench, leaned over to the front bench and whispered congratulations through gritted teeth, hoping Dines wasn't going to be the East Anglian Whip, in charge of James himself. He was. And he'd have sight of the Black Book of rebellious thoughts, government misgivings and treacherous dreams by James and others.

He sighed. Even now, Dines was in charge of him. It ought to have stiffened his backbone to leave. But it made him consider staying in order to resist Dines' authority.

She interrupted his thoughts. 'James, are you keeping a diary these days?'

'What? No, I used to keep one. My Westminster years, of course. Since then, no, well yes, though I wondered if I should write my dairies into a biography. For my grandchildren? Why do you ask?"

"You should feel free to write one, but do give yourself time and space. Diaries help people in all sorts of ways and if you feel a bit threatened in here, it might help you to put things into some perspective.'

'You can never have too many people reading your private thoughts, hey?'

'Exactly so!'

Bidding Dr Frayn farewell he made for the door. 'Oh by the way, James, I nearly forgot. I've found out why Lennie Sanders wants to kill you.'

James spun round, almost fell and grabbed the door handle. 'Your prisoner, Tommy Cross, the publican who murdered his wife in a jealous fit...'

'Yes, what of him?'

'The wife was called Ellen, Ellen Cross. Maiden name Sanders, Ellen Sanders. She was Lennie's daughter.

Apparently he had no grudge with you being the MP, but when you helped her killer, you went too far.'

He considered it. 'Thank you, Doctor. Be so good as to inform Ralph Dines when you next talk, that I've decided to stay. I'm not being pushed around by anyone, Sanders, Dines or whoever.'

It was that same stubborn determination that led him to refuse to support the Government on issues affecting his constituents despite the Whips' emotional, personal and blackmailing pressure.

Like a man suddenly seeing the light of heavenly revelation he was now certain beyond doubt he'd stay and fight.

He'd crossed the threshold. Dines now had a real opponent in his camp.

Act Two, Scene 1

Through that dreary winter, time in Sir Thomas More House was a strange mix of spot-on routine for feeding and medicines which left hours, gaping chasms of emptiness and chaos to fall into and go doolally in amidst the mad illogicality that elderly people often cause.

James opened a diary, deciding to be as forthright as Zoe had intimated. He wrote rude but witty, shrewd but whimsical observations about residents, the staff, the routines and events, in his own opinion.

Not really believing in coincidences, the topic of a diary came up after he mentioned Zoe's enthusiasm for diaries to Dame Henrietta Bolsome. They'd got on in their Parliamentary days. She was a Deputy Speaker and an unlikely holder of a Conservative seat amidst a sea of Labour strongholds in the Midlands.

Now she was forced to stagger slowly on a walking frame, refusing to consider a wheelchair and seemed to have retained a handful of wits about her. She'd bought a little table that stayed in the lounge and that she returned to every so often to have another go at the laid out jigsaw.

The edges were done along with a single patch in the middle. Occasionally people would fetch up beside the table and position a few pieces to help her out, regardless of whether they fitted or not. What struck James was that nobody noticed the puzzle was upside down.

Unfailingly polite – she called him 'a nice boy' – he understood that her eccentricities were ancient and fundamental to her upbringing in a minor northern stately home, raised in a family of impoverished nobility. She'd been a commanding presence in the Chamber; now she was three quarters batty and deaf with it.

They sat in the lounge, he enjoying a coffee, she a cup of very weak tea without milk. Nearby a woman nodded and drooled at him, a little checked blanket covering the space where her legs would have been if diabetes hadn't stolen them.

Henrietta's red-raw scalp had almost won the battle to devour her wispy hair; there was more on her chin these days. But she kept a kindly twinkle as she appraised him through NHS glasses held together by sticking plaster across the bridge of her nose, much like a grandmother might gaze dotingly on a naughty but favoured grandson.

'I've never told anyone this before, but in 1979 I was in...' This was her invariable opening to any conversation. She had told thousands of people that news. She informed James that she was keeping a diary of her time in Thomas More.

He said that Dr Zoe had suggested he should do the same. 'But you must! You owe it to posterity. And the taxman.' He nodded, only a little puzzled. 'And Winnie Carswood keeps one, swears by it, full of her naughty thoughts and how to kill off her enemies.'

'Ha, ha. I doubt Winnie Carswood has many enemies, Henrietta!'

'You can never have too many enemies in politics. They keep you on your toes.'

'Well, not mine, I haven't any serviceable toes,' he

muttered, instinctively folding his legs under the seat. She smiled but hadn't followed him.

He confessed that his Westminster diaries were invaluable for reminding him of events, people and facts as he'd perceived them at the time. A diary of his care home incarceration would be interesting; perhaps his grandchildren would publish it once he was gone.

And maybe they'd feel a tiny bit guilty for having stitched him up to imprison him with no parole. *In the Badlands of Lunacy*, he liked; *Idiots' Twilight Zone* he liked more. But he finally settled on *The Threshold of Madness* and as he made a note to open it with the Bible quote with which Dines had greeted him weeks ago, he shared it with Dame Henrietta.

'Am I so short of madmen that you have to bring this fellow here to carry on like this?' 1 *Samuel 21*. Entirely appropriate. You can never have too many mad men and women.

It was just at that moment that Sir Ronald walked past, slowly, unobtrusively, clutching a novel, reading glasses and a scarf, heading for the gardens. He stopped, waited for James to complete the quotation, and said, *'when dealing with the insane, it's best to pretend to be sane.* I do believe that is attributed to the German writer, Hermann Hesse.'

He smiled and stepped forward, only to wheel back to them again. 'Before I go to sample the rawky weather – that's wet, foggy or cold – you might enjoy Edgar Allan Poe's line*, I don't suffer from insanity, but enjoy every minute of it!'* Leaving them to make what they would of it, he resumed his journey to the great outdoors.

One morning, just ahead of lunch, as James walked through one of the 'smoking rooms' though the habit was banned, Lady Helen Fulcher caught his eye, putting down her oracle of all wisdom, *The Daily Torygraph*. 'James, have you heard about old Skein?'

James straightened a faded print of a politician on a soapbox, which immediately fell lopsided again the moment he turned from it. 'No, what about him? Is he here?' James was still coming across former colleagues he thought had died decades ago.

'He's just died. Not here. In some nursing home in Northamptonshire, it says here.'

Sir Bob Skein was old when James had entered Parliament and he hung on, year after year, becoming more of an institution than a national treasure. James was only astonished he'd lived this long.

'Received and read his 100-year birthday telegram from His Majesty and just faced the wall and went to sleep, apparently. That was it.' She folded her newspaper, 'I'll cut this out and stick it on the wall in Obituary Corner.'

James shared a reminiscence. 'I was in the Commons Library one evening when Skein walked through. You know how old people fart a lot without realising it? Well, he farted on every step of the dozen or more paces he took across the library. He didn't bat an eyelid. Somebody said, 'thank you, Sir Bob.'

She smiled, not at that memory which wasn't hers and she hadn't heard properly, but others with and around Skein. 'Quite a legacy, hey, James? He helped pass laws on road safety, clean air and military housing and is best remembered for his repertoire of farts.'

James was about to share the *Hallelujah Chorus* moment with her when there was a kerfuffle in the near distance. Timmy Greenwood was always audible some distance ahead, so James looked away to avoid engaging eye contact as the man gibbered mangled Shakespeare while being injected by something that calmed him for an increasingly short time.

Other days he talked and walked with Dame Winifred Carswell, a pair of slow coaches hobbling around chatting. They talked about diary styles, the Whips' black book and how she had always wanted to be a Deputy Speaker, but 'wasn't nice enough.'

James protested she was the nicest person he knew in politics, but she brushed it aside. 'Wait till I'm a customer for the new crematorium, and my life may come out. Then you'll see.'

He managed to avoid Lenny Sanders completely apart from a murderous look across the garden one afternoon while he grabbed a bit of fresh, East Anglian January wind to clear his head.

Gerry Manders, Douglas Gardener, Lady Helen Fulcher, Dame Henrietta Bolsome and Lord Wyford conscientiously manufactured illusions of pleasure at seeing him about the place. Sir Ronald Hasbery was excellent company at any time. James enjoyed his slightly sarcastic, clever wit and self-deprecation.

When he heard that Sebastian Catchpole was back in hospital, he realised that he'd missed his endless, long-winded, fully detailed tales. There was always Dame Henrietta Bolsome to make up for him, 'I've never told anyone this before...'

He watched Ralph Dines being whisked away in a big black car on three occasions, wearing his long dark overcoat. What a busy man he was; how important he had to be seen to be.

An unexpected encounter with Sir Michael Michaelson was a not entirely welcome surprise. It came in the corridor housing rooms occupied by civil servants and similar who could afford it and who wished to maintain the pretence of high importance.

Michaelson was of noble origins, he always asserted, and had made a living being a party Agent for several decades. Right up to his retirement he'd been James' own Agent, responsible for running the local party organisation, fundraising, all elections, ministers' tours and hobnobbing. In their part of the world it was common for agents to be elected as councillors.

Michaelson served five terms on the County Council but was best remembered for discovering his title by accident. One Christmas, a relative sent a round-robin, an all-purpose newsletter inside a card, which informed him that a distant cousin had passed away childless. Michaelson put two and two together, roughed out his family tree and grasped that he was next in line.

The baronetcy eventually came his way after months of copious enquiries by the honours system. He loved it. It suited him. He was born to swan around with his late 'Lady' wife on his arm. He was dismayed at the demise of forelock tugging as a mark of respect among the junior classes.

From a military background, Michaelson had run the Association with a firm smack of discipline, a gift for kicking new ideas into the long grass and as time went on a visceral dislike of James Ellington whom he saw as a jumped up nobody, son of a shopkeeper and with a poor sense of judgement as if he himself was blessed with the wisdom of Solomon.

'Our oldest resident, Sir Michael Michaelson, survived two bouts of Covid,' Matron Mercury informed James as he approached the frail, wheelchair-bound prehistoric husk, a drool-sodden bib round his neck. His head sagged forward and when he looked up, James guessed that the watery blue eyes saw little.

Matron politely, but pointlessly, had introduced James to their oldest resident, but there was no conversation. Nothing could be communicated, which suited James nicely. He wasn't in the mood to relive their shared campaigns, their disagreements when James had put himself forward to be the candidate and the hideous unpleasantness after his election.

He was relieved when Matron wheeled the old man away. If he'd signed over a substantial bequest to the company, then he was on his way to the crematorium.

The only people he looked forward to seeing were his family. True to their word and plan, Samantha visited twice each week, once alone and the second time with Leroy and the kids after school. Rebecca and children and often Simon too made the trip from Essex every other weekend.

Maisie's calls were irregular and occurred whenever she had a moment or his car needed a repair, or mechanical check up or the insurance was due. One weekend the whole family came for a buffet lunch at Samantha's and Leroy's.

Judy Blowers was invited and told him that the couple in his house were not a patch on him and Elspeth. They were noisier, messier and less caring about the locality. Their five children she'd neglected to mention before they mysteriously vanished, leaving only the poor husband nobody saw and the small, old woman, 'pure poison.' It actually pleased James.

Another Sunday a special lunch was laid on in the

boardroom of Sir Thomas More House. Dines claimed it was a tradition enjoyed by new residents on their first Sunday and it was a pity they'd had to wait so long for his because he'd missed Christmas, as if it was his fault.

'No family. No speeches. No toasts. Just a few of your friends in Sir Thomas More. We are your new family.'

Dines made the selection of guests as James 'was not capable of it just yet.' Besides himself at the head of the table, he brought in Lord Wyford, Dr Frayn, Winnie Carswood, Gerry Manders, Sebby Catchpole, Douglas Gardener, Helen Fulcher, Henrietta Bolsome, Kenny Sloan, Ronald Hasbery and two old buffers he'd never seen before.

Timmy Greenwood was not asked along, 'we don't need any Shakespeare today, thanks,' while Lenny Sanders was invited to make himself scarce. Sir Michael Michaelson was 'unwell', which James took as code for his appointment at the crematorium.

There were neither speeches nor toasts, as promised, no madhouse noises piped in and no problems for James, other than trying not to stare hatred at Kenny Sloan.

Dines ordered soup, full roast beef dinner and dessert. Everyone tucked in, mouths full and remembering to thank James when they noticed him at the foot of the table. For geriatrics gradually losing their everyday functions, it was remarkable how the ability to devour food and drink was the last to go.

Only when his end of the month invoice arrived, did James look back on his 'welcome' lunch with less than fondness. He was charged for every meal and drink, the whole lot, including hire of the boardroom and the time that Dines spent with them.

Some sort of winter virus went round, despite everyone having flu and corona virus jabs in the autumn and staff taking great care to isolate those who so much as sneezed. James recorded in his dairy that he didn't dread getting the bug, only being ill with it in the house.

However, it didn't appear unduly fatal as the number of bodies wheeled out stayed around the same, one or two a week. But Dr Zoe ordered everyone to mingle less, keep distant, eat alone with spaces between and the Chamber closed and sealed off for a deep clean.

As a consequence, the annual New Year Speech competition was postponed till late spring which everyone seemed to think was an outrage and that rules shouldn't apply to them. Some even tried to hold an informal session of 'Parliament' by tabling an Emergency Question to Ralph Dines on the matter.

His response was to order staff to clear the entire corridor leading to the Chamber, having taken the 'very best scientific advice.' The Doctor and her assistants took to wearing protective masks, dishing them out to any resident who asked. James requested a box of them to give him some privacy.

Robots clearly didn't need masks, so it was a strange assortment of the masked mute and the normally silent, the hard of hearing and the partially confused never quite communicating effectively.

There was some debate about stopping family visits for a time, but one afternoon in mid February, Samantha visited alone with an hour before picking up William from school.

James wanted to ask her about her childhood memories while he was carving out his political career.

Several of his fellow inmates spoke often of their families now and then, when they used to be so busy.

'Well, it was hard, Dad, but you know that.'

'I know, Samantha, love, I just wanted to understand a bit more from your perspective.'

'It was purgatory at school, you know that too. A teenager with her dad in your position was an excuse for most of the teachers to lay into me, as if I was to blame and keep making sarcastic digs and comments. Not all the time and not all of them.'

'I did it ...'

'Don't say you did it for us, so we could have good holidays and outings and a standard of life ... '

'No, I know that. I did it for me. I was focused on it totally. The most important election is always the next one, which starts as the last one ends. Everything might be a photo opportunity. Every utterance might be picked up.'

'We never went out without you in your suit. Any place we went you were looking for people to greet or avoid.'

'Same here in this hell hole.'

'This isn't a hell hole. I'm just glad it didn't happen in the age of social media or I don't know how we'd have stood it.'

'I'm sorry, Samantha.'

'No you're not, Dad. How can you be?

Act Two, Scene 2

From the gloomy corridor devoted to old dears that the management of Sir Thomas More House helped in an impressive spirit of public benevolence, another who'd given up the struggle was wheeled out to be the first customer at the now finished site crematorium.

His mortal coil shuffled off, a widower with a name and a former constituency that rang no bells to James, his Union Flag covered box on a gurney was trundled around the interior of the House, the Chamber, the dining room and the lounges. The bars momentarily stopped serving as a mark or respect.

Most residents recognised the coffin for what it was – an intimation of what was to come. A couple raised a glass in toast to old what's 'is name or 'er name as he or she passed. The little bars resumed business.

Three residents made a beeline for the deceased's room the moment the coast was clear to secure first dibs on his possessions – this was an occasion that usually led to full scale squabbles and fisticuffs. To their irritation, the room had been stripped; decorators' equipment was already in the corner.

As the procession arrived outdoors, word sped round that there were 'technical difficulties' and so the dearly departed would be laid to rest in the traditional way after all and the family and ancient friends were chivvied into waiting cars.

Knowing that you couldn't just rock up with a body on the roof and have it buried in the civic cemetery without proper paperwork, James assumed they were all going to the toxic tip.

He pictured the sad scene, mourners gathered round in the mud as the box was crane-lowered into a fetid, steaming pond of stench that bubbled and frothed in delight at receiving something else to gobble up.

The pall bearers, a collection of differently-heighted men and strong women, were clearly jarred off having to replace the coffin in the hearse. From his position by the door, James heard one mutter to all and sundry, 'they could have saved us all this extra work.'

Sir Ronald Hasbury was just a few mourners away, and he sidled through to stand next to him and intone, 'this was a nyctophobic, James, did you know?' Seeing that James neither knew he was nyctophobic nor what it meant, he was told, 'it's an irrational, sometimes extreme fear of darkness. Well, he's through that now, poor man.'

James looked at him and asked, 'but how do you know where he's gone? He might be in eternal darkness now.'

'I'm a believer, an optimistic follower of the Light, Jesus of course. And you?'

'I hope I am.' He had never been a vociferous believer nor the devotee of regular Sunday mornings of singing, praying and listening that Elspeth had been. But he had seen the point of the glad-handing afterwards.

Ralph Dines stood out amongst the increasing crowd, immaculate in a dark suit, black tie and that long dark overcoat. James hadn't seen him for awhile. He looked no less unpleasant, but treated James to a cheery wave and grin that would have looked at home across a partying crowd.

To cap off the total inappropriateness of his behaviour, Dines yelled across the space to James, 'Morning, old cock, and fine one for the sad business we're about, hey!' Nobody responded; after nodding James looked to the ground to escape further eye contact.

Unexpectedly the voice of Sebastian Catchpole boomed at him from three people away, 'James, we must stop meeting like this!' He bellowed in laughter; most people shuffled in embarrassment.

James was back at the funeral of a young lad who'd helped both of them during one election campaign, putting himself about as the 'young presence' of supporters in school debates and public spaces where they expected to come across young voters.

Victim of the most appalling black dog depression, the lad had overdosed later; the whole affair was tragic, dark and crushing. James had wondered why Sebby and some MPs couldn't stop themselves grandstanding at any opportunity as if people would be impressed. Five MPs attended that funeral; four played to the gallery.

Determinedly staring ahead to avoid further words from other residents, James squinted to see more clearly, half recognising the man in charge of the carriers. Long-distance sight had improved as he grew older, but was now deteriorating again. James must get an eye test, he reminded himself.

Yes. That was... the name escaped him. But he couldn't forget the face of the sad constituent who had wept across the desk at one of his surgeries. Older now, of course, this was the man who'd lost his son in an accident on an offshore gas platform and nobody cared.

After the inquest, the company had apparently offered peanuts by way of compensation to the family. It was a derisory insult. Is that all a 21-year old man's life was worth? He'd sue them. The directors should be locked up after a public flogging.

Nodding agreement, James had exuded sympathy. He genuinely felt the family had had a rough deal, so he wrote to ministers, to the company bosses and to the press to secure better compensation. He did all he could. He got nowhere with a dollop of nothing.

The man returned to a surgery six months later to say that he'd been offered employment by one of the directors. He didn't know who and the job was to take on a variable amount of lifting, carrying, loading and driving as he possessed a van driving licence.

White vans came to James' mind. He bet the job offer had come from Dines; Dines would be a director of a North Sea exploration company. Of course Dines would.

He looked over at the man himself, stood beside Wyford, both their heads bowed as if paying sincere respects. They'd be a bit short of income this week, thought James. Then he recalled the small print of the contract that decreed in the event of death, residents agreed to pay a month's fees in lieu of notice.

With the toxic pit now back in mind, James edged closer to Dines and Wyford to ask about it, but the hearse sped off and the crowd at once thinned. Who was that person who died? Which constituency was it? Nobody remembered at that moment; nobody tried to remember later.

'Ah, there you are, James!' Dines slapped him on the back, delighted to have skipped a tedious trip to a funeral.

'So I am, I wondered where I'd got to,' James acknowledged, standing facing Wyford who was beginning to shiver in the keen wind without an overcoat while Dines who had wedged himself on his walking stick was rock steady and warm.

'Off to the toxic pit, are they, to bury that poor old bugger?'

Wyford looked surprised, Dines laughed loudly. 'Ah, James, not lost your biting sense of humour and irony. The toxic tip? Yeah, that would solve the problem. Perhaps we should suggest it to the government and say that those who decline cremation shall be disposed off in a closed toxic tip.'

Wyford added, 'I can see that one going down well.'

Looking directly at Dines, James asked, 'Do you own the toxic tip, Ralph?'

Dines laughed; Wyford frowned, making a pantomime spread of hands to his boss. 'How would I own the toxic tip, James, old man? More to the point, why would I?'

Wyford added, 'or why would anybody else?'

'I just thought you might be using it for disposing of things that you want never to see the light again.'

'Good idea, James, perhaps I'll look into it and see if the local authority will accept a cash offer to be rid of what I imagine is a huge financial millstone.'

Wyford cleared his throat as a warning to Dines, having seen Lenny Sanders heading for them. 'Ah, Lenny, my dear fellow, happy belated New Year to you and yours...'

Dines stopped Sanders' progress with the upright hand facing him. Sanders, dressed merely in a faded blue shirt one size too small with open neck, frayed sleeves unbuttoned and flapping, spluttered, pointing at James, screwing his shirt into a ball near his stomach. 'Steady, old man,' Dines spoke softly.

James stepped back, careful not to fall over his stick in case Sanders did a flying jump and landed on top of him.

'This business of your daughter still not sorted, Lenny? You remember we went through all this?' Dines demanded, glowering at James. 'You haven't paid reparations, James?'

James stayed stock still, defying Dines to make him do anything. Wyford took a nod from Dines and moved Sanders aside, a big avuncular arm round his shoulders. His fist was like a side of ham and despite being pudgy was known to have been toughened in a youth spent boxing and a year rodeo riding in the USA.

'Steady now, calm down, Lenny. Ralph is on it for you.'

'Listen, James,' hissed Dines putting his thinner arm round James' neck and squeezing while pulling him towards the ground. 'Listen, I can't have this anymore. I asked you, I threatened you. Now I'm insisting on a deal.'

James could only hand gesture that he was listening. 'When I let you go, nod agreement to me, eye to eye and then shake Lennie's hand. Tell him you're sorry and that you will underwrite his monthly fees for five years. I will adjust his bill accordingly.'

James stopped struggling. No way. James had paid enough. 'And none of your family will make an unscheduled visit to the toxic tip.' At least, that's what Dines' mutter sounded like to James.

He'd been bullied by experts - whips, low-life criminals and political opponents - but had never received that kind of threat. Too stunned to digest it quickly, he was released, looked Dines in the eye, had his head made to nod with a chuck under the chin and wheeled round to face Sanders.

For his part, Sanders was stunned from what he thought Lord Wyford had whispered into his ear that his son, his only remaining child, was in trouble financially and people he owed money to had asked Ralph Dines to sort the lad out and if Lennie didn't accept the peace offering from James Ellington, he'd be visiting his boy in the toxic tip.'

The pair was guided into a handshake and Dines gave James the words to speak, like a vicar in a wedding, 'repeat after me'.

'I'm so sorry, Lennie, that my ignorance about the tragic and unforgivable death of your daughter led me to support and help the murderer who killed her. I will gladly subsidise your monthly fees for five years to show how sorry I am. Let's shake on it.'

Their hands shook, a quick up and down. Dines and Wyford grinned broadly, slapped both on the backs and pushed James towards the house and Sanders towards the front garden. Job done; the peace had to be seen to be believed. For the third time, Dines had made James agree to his demands.

'You can never have too much peace and harmony in a place like this,' Dines intoned.

The subsidy was added to James' monthly bill 'until further notice'. Lenny's invoice was reduced by the same amount 'until further notice' and he was informed by the small print that in the event of Ellington failing to make a monthly payment, Dines would sell some of the Sanders' family business shares he'd been given authority over years back when he'd bailed Sanders out of a local fiscal difficulty.

'You can never have too many assets,' Wyford smiled at Dines, who bowed his head in full agreement.

Act Two, Scene 3

After three months, new residents were deemed to have settled. Accepted their lot. Resigned themselves to incarceration till the show closed.

James still slept badly. It was the night-vision cameras that stared at him, unblinking, recording his every movement that made sleep for more than an hour at a time quite impossible.

Central heating turned itself off at 10,30pm and the room was cold in the winter nights. Yet he felt sweaty when he woke, Limping barefoot, furniture-walking to the tiny ensuite for his three or four pees a night chilled him deeply. Yet as soon as he drifted off, he knew he'd wake in a sweat again.

After a particularly bad night when he had driven a bullet-ridden car at breakneck speed over California's Tioga Pass into the Yosemite National Park pursued by a mafia family with his toddler daughter Samantha clinging to the roof rack, everyone said he looked terrific. The place must be agreeing with him.

His daily walk took him ever closer to the boundary, where stood, temptingly, the road stretching to freedom beyond, down a country lane. But he didn't need to see the machine gun turrets looming over him to know he'd not get far. The electrified barbed wire fence was well-hidden among hedgerows, but could still inflict a nasty shock.

The sign facing drivers exiting the gate, read: *Thank you for visiting. Please come again. Drive safely.* James read it as: *Warning. Inmates may try to stowaway in your vehicle.*

One Friday as he turned back to the house, expecting to see an Imelda or a Karl approaching to talk him back from the exit, he noticed someone gesturing from an upstairs window. Too far out to see if the person was waving or drowning; somebody half sane or Timmy Greenwood shrieking behind the glass, 'want-wits, you're such want-wits,' misquoting *The Merchant of Venice.*

Waving back as he stepped closer to the house, he realised it was Dr Zoe Frayn indicating he should come in and upstairs to her office. With a tap on her wrist he remembered his appointment with her, which he'd been looking forward to, provided she saw him alone.

He 'dashed' in, 'rushed' up the stairs and 'fled' along the corridor to her office with all the agility of a man unable to walk more than three paces without pain. Nobody waylaid him with a fatuous comment or piece of news he really didn't need.

Her door stood open, so he clumped straight in to her broad grin as she tucked her long dark hair from her face behind her ear.

Brushing aside his breathless apology for lateness, she closed the door as she asked how he felt, physically. Standard stuff. She noted his aches and pains and nodded when he acknowledged they were the normal consequences of reaching his mid-70s. 'How are you sleeping?'

'Like a baby.'

'Really?'

'Yes, I wake every couple of hours for a feed and a nappy change.'

'What about your mental, health, James?'

'Ah, that's a more difficult one, Doctor. I feel a tile might fall off the roof and decapitate me, or one of my grandchildren gets gangrene from a paper cut and loses an arm.'

'Standard anxieties, they happen a lot when you're not entirely sure you made the right choice coming here and, from what you've told me, you're not new to a range of fears and worries. Tell me more about your medical condition.'

He sipped the coffee she'd placed in front of him. 'This is decaff, isn't it?'

'You shouldn't drink so much caffeine.'

'CMT. Charcot Marie Tooth disease, a deformity of the hands and feet, or just the feet in my case. Neurotic thing, I know.'

'I know the medical aspects. I wanted to know about how you've coped with it all your life.'

'You're writing a book on it?'

'Why do you think I'm writing a book?'

'So you *are* writing a book!'

With a smile, she said, 'Just tell me.'

'It was never going stop me doing what I wanted. The performing arts or its close cousin, politics. I've clumped, staggered and fallen my way through the years and the challenges. I live with it. And still do. My old diaries are full of it, the pain; the frustration. These surgical boots are terrific, but I'm not able to balance in them as well as I could.'

'I've noted your walking is less secure than it was.'

'Good way of putting it. Less secure. You can never have too much security in your walking, Doctor.'

'Do you think you have succeeded in life despite your condition or because of it, James?'

'Despite it, I think. Yet, maybe, I don't know. Because of it I am the determined, stubborn old bastard, so that helped in getting into politics and then surviving a decade in it. It's not a trade for the faint hearted, you know.'

'Oh, yes, I've been here long enough to learn that!'

'I don't know how a bright young woman like you can stand it here.'

'What, among a lot of old politicos?'

'Partly. But I meant working under Ralph Dines and his henchmen.'

'I'm not here forever. I'll use my skills in another field later on.'

'Unless you get married?'

'How do you know I'm not married?'

''Just a hunch. I always felt with my lovely wife, Elspeth, she could have done so much more if she hadn't chosen to be my support, sidekick, soul-mate and invaluable Godsend...'

'Any more troubles with or from Lennie Sanders?'

'No, we're best mates now, Dines' orders.'

'Good.' They both waited; she had something on her mind.

'You know when you told me about your drive up the A12 and the incident with the dead bodies in the tip?'

He looked more closely at her, 'of course.'

'Do dead bodies feature more in your anxieties than anything else?'

'Besides the dread of my loved ones being dead bodies? I used to fear that Elspeth would be killed, strangled, chopped, sliced, poisoned, hanged, kidnapped, crushed, suffocated, burned, drowned or lost in a mysterious mist from the swamps.'

'What did she die from?'

'Breast cancer. And then with my two daughters, I feared the worst for them. And as each grandchild came along, it got worse. But I know I have to live with it. I deal with it. I keep it in perspective.'

'I have notes on the tip. And I have notes on Lenny Sanders' daughter incident. Any more fears involving death?'

'Not today. I am afraid, Zoe. Truly dreading that bad things will happen to my loves – hell, I used to feel the same about my calling when I was MP for this constituency which I love with a passion. Now, I just fear growing old, helpless, forgotten, finishing my days in this nuthouse being made to revisit my past with equally unhinged loonies and frothing morons.'

'You don't feel you all share that common experience, given to few people in a lifetime, yet have all lived such different lives outside politics that you enrich each other?'

'No. That's veering towards psychobabble.'

'And in all this now feeling, there is one enemy, one person responsible?'

'Oh yes, I don't blame my family or grandkids. I get that I'm a menace to myself if left on my own. I blame Ralph Dines and all his minions and all his works and I suppose I have done ever since I first met him a year before were elected.'

'You feel he is a real danger to you personally?'

'He is. I know he is. He'll bleed me dry here, get me to sign away all my assets and my soul and then one day I'll be wheeled to his bloody crematorium and he will go on exercising mindless power over everything he touches.'

'Mmm.' She made notes. 'He's not God, you know.'

'No, he's not. But he thinks he is and has persuaded others to think it, so in a sense he is.'

'Well, I can't talk about him. I'm going to give you advice.'

'No medication?'

'No medication. It's not uncommon in people who have enjoyed a degree of power, authority, the ability to make things happen in life, to find in old age they are frustrated, impotent and darkly disappointed.'

'I like that. Darkly disappointed. Title of your book?'

'You are suffering PPD, political power delusion, in a very mild form. Others here have it quite strongly. It's related to the Napoleon Complex, often experienced by small men surrounded by tall, powerful, non-compliant women.'

'Several MPs have that. I suppose I can see it in me, a bit.'

'Exactly. Unfit people, physically I mean, often feel it when compared to fitter people. But remember, the fittest mental person in old age may be a frail doddering incompetent physically.'

'And everybody's the same size in bed, I know. Thanks, that's comforting.'

'Your CMT neuropathy on top of aging and the work you once did and loved which ended at the hands of the voters not by you, has been a big challenge and achievement. Don't let them get you down. You are as meaningful, competent and as good company as most and certainly as a handful.'

'Will you help me cut Ralph Dines down to size?'

She offered her small, gentle hand to indicate the discussion was over. For now.

Act Two, Scene 4

While Sebastian Catchpole enjoyed yet another stay in hospital, James neither missed him nor, in truth, realised he was gone. But his former colleague made a beeline for James almost as soon as the ambulance brought him back.

He caught him in the cafeteria housed in a restored barn, attached to the House by a modern throughway of glass and brick. Visitors were often taken there by residents and sometimes locals from the village were authorised to enjoy meals amidst agreeable surroundings.

A recording of country and western ballads played softly. James finished reading his local weekly newspaper, the habit of most of his adult life, and picked up his diary to add a thought.

'Ah, there you are, old thing!' Catchpole boomed moving towards James, sat at a table for two. He repeated it, louder as he neared James.

Several old dears looked up at the unnecessary volume. He exchanged elaborate waves with several. An old woman was slurping liquid through a straw in a closed cup. James knew she had no teeth, not even the dentures freely lying around.

Another inmate grinned at him but then, he grinned at everyone: a Lord of the Realm who no longer knew his elbow from Tuesday, if he ever did.

'I wasn't lost,' James protested, realising that even Catchpole had caught Dines' way of speaking.

As Catchpole approached his table, none too steady on his feet, James stood to move an empty cup and saucer from danger on the edge of the adjacent table.

'Just back, James, and glad I've found you. I'll have a pot of tea, builders will do, and a couple of slices of white, toasted with a little pot of that strawberry jam,' he yelled across the space to a girl waiting behind the counter who curtsied on receipt of his order.

'Remind me, Sebastian, where have you been?'

Catchpole released a roar of laughter, banging the table. 'You were always funny, James, you could have done stand-up, at one time in your life.'

'Isn't that what we did, both of us?'

'Yes, indeed. I've been in hospital again. Same tests to come to the same conclusion – I'm good for a few years yet. Same bloody bed, I think. Same nurses but there was a very attractive girl from Asia I should say. Out of bounds, of course.'

'Some things don't change, hey, Seb?'

Smiling sadly, he asked, 'has anything changed here?'

'No, I don't think so. A couple of deaths. No surprise there. I should think we are way above the national average. And you know they cancelled the Speech contest?'

'I heard it is merely postponed. But yes, yes. I was gutted, as they say. Like a cod. How have you coped without me to listen to?'

'I've just about survived. I like to keep myself to myself,

you know that.'

'How's the family? You're a lucky bastard with grandchildren. I think that's my one regret, nobody but you and one or two others to carry on my legacy.'

'The family's fine, as far as I know. But I only know what they tell me and what I read between the lines. None has been murdered, yet. Have you put all your papers and files in their Archive here?'

'Of course, but I don't trust anyone to keep them safe. When I go, I imagine my papers will burn in the crematorium that reduces me to ashes.'

That fear hadn't occurred to James yet, not to any great depth. Now it did. All his papers gone; his memory wiped.

'You live as long as anybody remembers you. It's an old Russian proverb, I think.'

'Very true. I remember my grandmother on my father's side. She was born in the 1880s, so we leave behind a long line of memories,' Sebastian offered, with a full yellow false-teethed smile at the girl as she arrived with his order on a tray.

'Tea Room breakfast, do you remember, James? Many a man made a breakfast from tea, two slices of white, toasted with a pot of jam.'

'Yes, but I always had coffee.'

Someone changed the music mid-song to northern brass band favourites; the men remained silent. Catchpole spread his toast with jam, and the table and floor with crumbs. Only when his mouth was full of the first bite, second slice, did he resume talking, which accelerated the dispersal of toast crumbs far and wide.

'Can you remember that Scottish bloke? What was his name? Large, overweight, looked like something you'd go fishing with. He always came up to the newspaper rack near where we sat, looked us up and down and snarled, 'have either of you Tory scum got the *Torygraph*?'

'He probably guessed that we sat on the copies of all the main papers till we'd read them!'

'He should have come in a little bit earlier of a morning.'

'I once had a nightmare about him.'

'I should think most of the House did and all the staff.'

'He's not here, is he?' James was alarmed.

'No, he's gone. Couple of years back. Overindulgence of haggis, amber liquid and women. Gone to that great Chamber in the sky where he can bore as long as he likes.'

Laughing, neither heard nor saw Ralph Dines sliding up. 'Morning, gentlemen!'

Sebastian finished his toast and picked up the plate to lick it clean, looking at Dines. James held on to his chair and clenched the side of the table.

'Gentleman, I'm sorry to interrupt the reminiscing, but there's work to do. I was wondering if you'd like to give me a hand, sometime today. A man's work is never done in this place. Many old, gnarled hands make light work, mmm? Do you think you could go round and check on the well-being of Honourable Members? We have our annual inspection coming up soon.'

'Me? You want me to talk to lots of other inmates?'

'Yes, and if you call them that, it may push some over the edge, and they are very near it.'

He smiled at Seb. 'And you, too, old Seb. Go round together, the Laurel and Hardy, Morecambe and Wise, Mutt and Jeff of East Anglia in a reprise of that old double act you used to do to raise a few smiles.'

Seb spluttered agreement; James nodded likewise. He was back on that snowy mountain in East Germany before they were elected when he'd been on the candidates' visit to that area some years ahead of German reunification. He'd slipped and stumbled as they left the restaurant en route to their coach that had been unable to take them to the top where the restaurant sat on the edge.

It afforded lovely views when it was daylight and without mist. Dines had grabbed his arm, while somebody else took the other and they had frogmarched him to the bus. It was a nightmare again, but he got there without further falls. Even then Dines had sported a stick, so it was a surprise that he was able to help James practically.

But really, James knew, nothing about Dines should surprise him in the past, present or future.

Act Two, Scene 5

The only place James felt safe enough to talk freely with any of his family was in the gardens. But even here, he spotted microphones and cameras cleverly disguised on tree branches, amidst the foliage of bushes and plants. Even attached to some inmates, he reckoned.

Truly, nobody is ever alone in Sir Thomas More House.

He couldn't always be in the gardens. Family rang at times to suit themselves, of course. So, the consensus in the family was that he talked fairly freely in the gardens; but said little of value if he was indoors.

They decided that on the first mild day of late winter that came along and Samantha was free, she'd take him off site and let him talk.

He had an hour's warning and wondered when his daughter had actually applied for the permit to take him out for a couple of hours. No matter, an hour was more than enough to get ready and wait by the exit.

She picked him up just inside the gate and drove almost back to the house before making a reasonable five point turn. They got away without raising any alarms or being shot from behind.

'Well, thanks for the escape, Samantha, my love.' he started off, tangling the seat belt around his stick which he held upright against his chest rather than putting it on the back seat. 'If we get a move on now we can be in the Channel Tunnel before they realise I haven't returned.'

'Anywhere particular, Dad?' she asked, ignoring his point.

'Wherever the car goes, Samantha. The open road. It's just so good to feel the wind in my absent hair, the sand between my twisted toes...'

'You seem to be settling in, now, Dad.' It was a statement, not a question.

'Yes, like a rat in a cage settles down.'

'You coping with so many people from the past, all a lot older now?'

'And even more mad than they were. Samantha, it's a jungle in there. Not unlike how it was in Parliament, so they have been successful in recreating much of that stab-in-the-back atmosphere controlled by a handful of puppet masters under the evil mind of one man.'

'Sounds like a film plot,' she smiled.

'It is, in many ways,' he replied seriously.

She told him what the family was up to – all the usuals of school, home, friends, leisure activities, hopes and dreams and growing pains.

She told him how Maisie loved his car but that all her siblings and cousins now expected he'd buy them one when their time came.

With a smile, he said, 'well, I'll be dead by then so they can buy their own from what I leave them in my will. If there's any left after the fees and extras here.' She shook her head, but had to smile, too.

They drove in silence for awhile, Samantha wondering if he was going to open up about the issues that bothered him; he weighing up how much to share with her.

They reached the town and she just slowly cruised up and down the prom and beach area, then down the old High Street, finally out to Gibbet Broad to park where the Suffolk and Norfolk Broads meet the North Sea.

As she looked for a parking space he fished his Disabled Parking badge and cardboard clock from his pocket. She smiled and pulled into a nice wide bay near the park entrance, so he was able to get out simply and quickly. In the near distance a traffic warden dressed like a paramilitary inspected badges and parking tickets.

Their walk was slow and measured, she holding his left arm, he clutching the trusty stick, given by a grateful family he'd helped when he was forcibly retired from his political career.

A weak sun tried its best to come out. While there was a definite sense of spring coming, the stiff breeze reminded everyone there were a few weeks yet before it fully bloomed. They were fully wrapped up, scarves and gloves, the lot. They were still needed.

'Do you want to tell me the truth about what happened to your finger? How is it by the way?'

'It's covering up. A shorter digit isn't the end of the world. If he'd carved a piece off my toes, I'd be seriously affected by that.'

'Who did it, Dad, truthfully?'

'It was Lennie Sanders, as I said at the time.'

'Yes, but why?'

'Because he's as mad as a box of frogs, that's why.'

'I vaguely remember his name, from years ago.'

'Yes, he was just a colleague, there at the same time as me, no more than that. I helped somebody who'd done something bad to his wife who turns out to have been Lennie's daughter!'

'That's why you were looking for notes about a prison visit when we cleared out your house?' She sensed he'd be happy to rest, so steered him towards a park bench, overlooking the broad lapping under the safety barrier near their feet. To their side a toddler was having a meltdown because he'd wanted to climb over the metal barrier and his mother had scooped him out of danger.

'Nah, get the fuck away from that, Corona,' the woman snapped. Some people had named their offspring from words common in the great global pandemic of 2020-22, as if it was to be celebrated, with over 3 million deaths and untold economic and mental health damage.

He turned away from the touching scene of model parenting.

'It's OK, I just avoid Sanders if I see him coming. There's some sort of deal whereby I compensate him for his loss, I go along with it, and the place runs smoothly. But I'm not demented enough to be numbed by it all, my love. Mentally I'm too well for that kind of care.'

'You can never have too much care, Dad. Physical problems trump mental. You can survive and enjoy some of it, surely? You are being looked after.'

'Not with Ralph Dines in charge. There's never a safe moment for relaxation with that man watching the security cameras.'

'He seemed very nice to us and he said you were his oldest friend.'

James merely shook his head. 'Al Capone or Heinrich Himmler would have made better friends. Dines is a smooth talking, Machiavellian bastard with an agenda of power and wealth and I'm just a stooge. Well, I would be if I wasn't determined to resist him.'

'And we thought you were in a safe place, Dad!'

'Safe as death, Samantha.'

As she was thinking of a suitable response, a sudden short sharp shower of icy early spring rain sent them shuffling back to the car.

She expected no more from him on that subject as they set off for The Royal, overlooking the sea, where she'd booked an early lunch.

Act Two, Scene 6

A three-line whip is an instruction to all members of a given party on their business for the following week that they MUST attend on pain of torture and death to vote with the Government or against in the case of the opposition members.

It was underlined three times, hence the title. Severe illness was no excuse – he'd seen Members wheeled in from ambulances to vote, though that had been stopped more recently. Death itself was usually grudgingly accepted as a reason to get off a three-liner.

A two-line whip was attendance required unless a Member was officially paired with one of the opposition or had special dispensation to be absent. James was once tricked by being approached by a Labour MP and offered a pairing arrangement for a night of heavy voting. He accepted with thanks.

Not till the next day of checking the numbers and chasing up the absentees did the Whips realise what had happened. That Labour MP had told three Government MPs that he'd pair with them. It could have meant losing a vote that actually mattered.

James and the two other hapless victims were told they should have known, should have checked. And they should have registered the pair in the Whips' office. With a big government majority, there weren't enough opposition members to go round, of course.

A one-line whip was voluntary attendance and was designated on Fridays, when Private Members' bills were considered and on local election days. They also had it on St Andrew's, St Patrick's and St David's Days as sops to members from those parts of the United Kingdom.

St George's Day was never afforded the same treatment.

If the government took against a particular Private Members' bill it was not unknown for a two or three-liner to be issued to crush it before it got too far through its electoral journey.

Generally it was a system for running business that was long hallowed by time. Most Sunday evenings at tea, James had addressed his wife and daughters when they were young in the style and pompous tones of the Chief Whip announcing the whipping at the weekly backbench gathering, the '1922' committee.

'The family business for next week is as follows. On Monday I shall be carrying out constituency visits and meetings before driving back to London late afternoon. Your mother will be shopping before lunch at the Ladies' Club. Samantha will have school followed by choir practice and Rebecca will also have school followed by helping with the setting up of chairs and tables for the Women's Night at the church.'

So, no inmate at Sir Thomas More House batted an eyelid when a three-line whip circulated that all Hon. Members and Lords desirous of entering the rescheduled annual speech competition should attend a running rehearsal in the Chamber throughout the next day.

During the morning discontent was expressed in the form of muted mutterings in Lord Wyford's ear about the importance of the Bridge Club, Tai Chi in the gardens and family visits already arranged for that time.

Deaf in alternating ears, Wyford would indicate which ear a supplicant should whisper in. The working one if that person was in favour; the deaf if he or she was out.

When James stuck his nose in the Chamber, skirting round an old fool asking the messenger for a pinch of snuff -- an ancient tradition upheld in Westminster that had not travelled to Thomas More.

James smiled to himself – the old man was already a martyr to hayfever. Why on earth did he want to force himself to sneeze with snuff?

Inside, Wyford filled the chair. Sir Ronald was in the Clerks' place in front of the Speaker's Chair exercising that habit he'd perfected over decades in the House of appearing to follow spoken drivel from MPs while doing a crossword on his lap and being crafty, occasionally nodding wisely.

Douglas Gardener, Winnie Carswood and Sebastian Catchpole were holding up Lady Helen Fulcher, propped on the bench without her legs, in full flow having drawn 'Is there a future for democracy?' as her unprepared speech, at least for this practice. They clustered around her in what was called 'doughnutting,' an art of making the Chamber looked packed around whoever was speaking dating from the start of TV broadcasting from the Chamber in 1988.

Lennie Sanders, looking furtively round for Ellington and Timmy Greenwood muttering 'I will leave you now to your gossip-like humour' from *Much Ado About Nothing,* had positioned themselves on the opposition benches to heckle and interrupt Lady Fulcher.

They weren't Opposition members and never had been, but a few of the awkward squad always sat opposite to enjoy more legroom and there were no life and death divisions of the House here.

'So, Mr Speaker, China is even more of a surveillance society than the UK, and they hold more data on their citizens and those of other nations than God himself.' She was enjoying herself. 'And don't forget they started Covid 19!'

A pity not even the doughnut looked interested on her side, but opposite Timmy Greenwood shouted out, without making it a formal intervention, 'who watches the watchers, then? Tell me that!'

Ignoring him, Lady Fulcher pressed on, anxious not to lose her train of thought. 'They scrape data from social media, they hack. They influence the media and companies, they are accelerating AI, so that they can mock the democratic world for some perceived hiccup and declare that dictatorship works better than democracy.'

Lennie Sanders decided it was time he was heard, so he stood and asked her to give way, which she did reluctantly. 'I'm following most careful what the Hon Lady is saying, but is China really relevant to a debate about the future of democracy?'

He plonked himself down again. She snapped, 'Of course it is for the reasons I have just mentioned. And if the honourable gentleman cares to look at Russia which is racing to out-dictate their people, China and the rest of us, he will agree with me.'

Lennie had lost interest and moved, sliding along the green benches, putting his trousers in danger of a shining. A handful of others stood at the Bar, not a drinks outlet but the line that marked the beginning and end of the chamber. Cross it, and Parliamentary rules applied.

'North Korea. Iran. Venezuela. The fully Islamic states. And the European Union, all rogue states as far as we judge and all against democracy....'

Douglas Gardener was on his feet on a spurious point of order. 'Mr Deputy Speaker, is the Honourable Lady calling the European Union a rogue state!' He seemed genuinely outraged.

'I most certainly am! As far as democracy is concerned their track record is lamentable....'

The rest of her comment was lost in the sort of baying that is peculiar to the Commons. Nobody could be heard. Wyford stopped dreaming of a nicotine fix and attempted to restore order. Without success.

James slipped out, realising that his own rehearsal time would vanish at this rate and not minding over much. He came up against Ralph Dines, hand ready up and facing him, 'What, sidling out, old boy? I've had lunch put back half an hour so you should get your little rehearsal in.'

'Don't think I'll bother. The House is a bit heated, just now.'

'Ah Dr Zoe,' Dines beamed, spotting her over James' shoulder. 'Injections all round in here, I think, my dear. Calm some of the old buggers down.'

'You know I don't administer drugs to keep patients in a state of permanent catatonia, Mr Dines.'

He looked at her. 'I was joking, dear Doctor, just jesting.'

'Shouldn't a joke make people laugh, make them amused?'

He smiled coldly. James sensed the hatred building, neither having any time for the other. The relationship was crumbling fast, manners all but gone.

Why would Dines fall out with his young doctor?

Act Two, Scene 7

Sir Ronald Hasbery poured hot water from a little pot into the matching one that contained his tea. He left it a moment before he poured himself a third cup, with a dash of semi-skimmed milk, no sugar.

'I used to drink only coffee, like you,' he informed James who'd drained his mug of Ethiopian coffee. 'Then one day I woke up to the more subtle taste of quality tea. I found I was becoming a bit of a pulsiloge, a pendulum of heart movement from the caffeine.'

'In fact, I'd go so far as to admit, 'Hasbery continued with a twinkle, 'I was experiencing eructations, a belching forth of gases from my alimentary tract.'

'I can scarcely believe that of you, Ronald. I always thought you defused your farts.'

They'd been discussing madness, after James had invited him to consider the topic in relation to power and Members of Parliament, using Timmy Greenwood as the intro, but really wanting to turn it towards Ralph Dines without being over obvious.

'As you know, there is a handful of obstacles to standing as an MP, under the Disqualification Act 1975, as amended. Much of it followed on from the Marriage of Lunatics Act, 1811.'

'I suppose much depends on how you define lunacy?'

'Not really. There are quite specific definitions about mental capacity. Many cast in stone in the Mental Health

Act 1983, as amended. A Member loses his or her seat if detained under this Act for over six months.'

'And being a power hungry, self-obsessed maniac doesn't qualify?'

'Not on its own. Or we'd have had to lock up almost all the great achievers of the past.' He paused to gauge James' thinking. 'Not quite what you wanted to know, James?'

'Well, Ronald, I'm not entirely sure what I want to know. Obviously, people can come in and out of degrees of madness and one man's madness is another man's genius....'

'That's poetic terminology. In *Parker's Law and Conduct of Elections*, the Bible of these matters, I think it's section 5.6, idiots are disqualified from election to Parliament and lunatics disqualified in their non-lucid intervals.'

James nodded, 'so we have idiots and lunatics.'

'And maniacs, mental cripples, deranged, demented, psychotic, crazy, eccentric, loopy and crackpot. The full range is exhibited here, wouldn't you say, including us?'

'Yes. Not the full shilling, a sandwich short of the picnic, off your trolley, barking and out to lunch, including us.'

'Poetic terminology again,' Hasbery waved his hand in dismissal. 'I don't think I can say with absolute certainty, but I suspect that we display more than the average examples of a long line of different behaviours, but about the average for people who have spent many years in public life, frequently believing their own hype.'

'Many show signs of mental exhaustion, withering away of the mind's faculties, decayed to a high degree. In fact many are, you may conclude, actually fully marcid.'

As if on cue, one of the more eccentric examples rolled up. 'Good morning gentleman, might I join you?' Sebastian Catchpole boomed.

'Of course, Seb, but we're almost done.'

Catchpole shouted, 'I've never let anybody's agendas get in the way of my own!'

'That's what we love about you, Sebastian!'

A girl followed, carrying Catchpole's tea tray and toasted tea cakes to the table, which rocked as he sat. He buttered them, cut them into manageable pieces and began to munch heartily, spraying crumbs over the whole table and down his front as normal.

And all the while talking with little or no pause.

'I've just been talking to one of the Karls to see if I can be fixed up with some company. Gets very tedious at times here, when we've all run out of things to say to each other. Not that I don't admire you all tremendously and earnestly, I must say. And I thought to myself that an hour or two of company not drawn from the cast list of oddities we have collected in this mausoleum, would suit me down to the ground, what do they call it these days, looking after my mental well-being? Yes, and it would take care of other well-beings as well. Of course, I'll want to be more discrete than old Douggie Gardener who has got into a spot of bother over trying to sort out his well-being, so I hear, have you heard?'

If a drama student had been looking for a monologue to perform on stage, this might have been a good one.

Pauses were short and insufficient for interruption, the eating offered splendid opportunities for physicality and it was designed to grandstand for the benefit of the whole cafeteria.

After a few minutes of polite listening and not blinking as crumbs sprayed him, Hasbery feigned a sneeze. James knew it was fake. But he carried it off brilliantly, pulling a perfectly white, crisp handkerchief from his pocket and saying, 'Excuse me a moment, gentlemen."

It left the impression that he'd be back very soon to listen to more wisdom from Catchpole, but James knew he wouldn't.

'QED, "*quod erat demonstrandu,* point demonstrated, James,' and he made good his getaway.

'What point is demonstrated, James?'

'Oh, we were talking about how different we all are, one from another, with just certain memories and experiences in common.'

Catchpole snapped his fingers in the direction of the counter, whereupon a girl who'd been staring into space came across. 'My dear, another of your excellent toasted teacakes, if I may be so bold. James, it's the memories and experiences that bind us together, covering the cracks and gaps between us.'

'Do you really think so?' James wondered, absently.

'Have you forgotten how hard the long and winding road is to getting elected? All the people you had to win over, the toes you had to stand on, the arses you had to lick, pompous people you had to elbow aside, the backs you had to stab, the pavements you walked, the doors you knocked on, the questions you had to answer, the doubters and faint hearts you had to persuade?'

'No, of course not.'

'That bonds us, my friend. However strange we might seem, we all had to win that war every time. And we did. We joined what is a very small group in this country, ex-MPs. I reckon about 2,000 of us, tops, still alive.'

Knowing it was a figure plucked from the ether, it helped James recall vividly the hard grind that his first election had been, but oh that euphoria on the night, the cheers, the media, the joy of his supporters and his opponents who slunk away.

He'd loved the feeling as a police officer escorted them to their car. And then the second election, so much harder because few thought he or the party could win. But they did. He won and that so sweet joy of raising his and Elspeth's hand to the cheers of his people. And being escorted to their car again.

What a contrast to his third run. Nobody thought he or the party would win. He was dead man walking alone often, with just a driver on his minibus who used it to do errands for his business while James tramped streets, knocked on doors and put on a good face to hide the screaming pains in his knees and feet.

Results night. Tables holding the votes of his opponent groaned under the weight of ballot papers. He scanned around hoping they'd put aside more for him. By the time of the declaration, he had few supporters left in the hall. And the only people who escorted him to his car were a handful of jeering jubilants from the victorious side.

'I have to go to the toilet, Sebastian. Excuse me.'

James stood up as the first mouthful of his freshly arrived second tea cake went into Catchpole's mouth, a few moments before a fresh torrent of crumbs and flakes sprayed out.

Act Two, Scene 8

'So, Maisie, what are you instructed to grill me about today?' He opened the conversation once she'd pulled clear of the internment camp and they were beyond sight of it in the rear view mirror.

'I'm under no instructions, Grandpa. Just deliver you fifty miles down the road to meet Aunt Rebecca and cousins to give you a change of scene.'

'Take the back roads, not past the tip.'

'Why not?'

'I mean that ridiculous fun house holiday camp you had to rescue me from.'

'You often clam up about the tip. What's there? Or was there?'

He gave his reply a moment's thought. 'I can't tell you, Maisie.'

'Why not?'

'I saw something truly terrifying there. I'm not going to spoil your dreams with images. Leave it at that?'

Glancing at him, she pushed up into top gear once they hit the dual carriageway and proceeded to chatter about the 6th form, progress towards exams, her wonderful freedom in his car and the impossibility of living with her mum always 'on her case.'

Besides one panic moment when a car cut her up by undertaking on a fast stretch and James' life flashed before his eyes picturing the road closed for seven hours to clear the debris and bodies, it was a good journey. He was pleased with how she was improving as a driver.

'You need petrol, Maisie,' he told her, glancing at the dial in front of her.

'Oh yes.' She drove another mile before sweeping into a service station, parking not quite square to the self-service pump. He was relieved they were safe, having imagined a grinding to a halt out of petrol in the fast lane with all sorts of pile up consequences.

She filled up. He walked in to pay. A bloke threw him a very funny look as he walked outside to a white van which he drove off with one hand, as his other clamped a mobile phone to his head.

They arrived at East Bergholt Farm, south of Ipswich in good shape and Maisie pulled into a disabled space near the main gate. He put his disabled parking badge on her dashboard.

The Farm was a new development built into what had been a working farm which had gone bust. They'd laid out a range of ancient rusting farmyard equipment and called it a rural life museum. Rare British plants were cultivated and seeds were sold. They'd installed kiddies' areas with animals and games. People could ride on a trailer pulled by a vintage tractor. Depending on the weather, they ran animal and birds of prey displays, dog shows, sheep contests, domestic pets' days and staged an East Anglian version of a rodeo once a year.

They'd built a mini village of stalls selling handicrafts,

fairground attractions such as hoopla and a coconut shy. A bearded lady occupied one tent while fortunes were told in another. A 'floating match' in a booth turned out to be a giant safety match lying in a tin bath of cold water.

And there were acres of different foods, some cooked on outdoor fires, some baked in stone kilns, all fresh and locally sourced. Their homemade ice cream was to die for. They brewed cider and an experiment with wine from their own vineyard looked promising.

Just off the main A12 by less than a mile, it had become hugely popular, as a mix of garden centre, heritage farm, mini theme park, parkland, fairground, village fete, old-fashioned retail opportunities and recreational gardens. It was conveniently about half way between Rebecca's house and where Samantha and family lived, and James.

Emily spotted them first from her slouch against a wooden fence across the car park from the far side. 'Hi, Maisie; hello Grandpa.'

'My darling, Emily.' James embraced her and then punched fists with Joseph who came up to them. The boy turned his eyes enviously to Grandpa's old car now very obviously Maisie's pride and joy.

'Hello, Dad, Maisie,' Rebecca smiled, embracing both.

Maisie extracted herself and asked Joseph, 'how's it going, Joseph?'

'School? Same old, same old. Exams! Teachers are obsessed and starting to make us very nervous.'

'Wait till you start A-Levels!'

'How's Grandpa's car? Do you think he'll buy me one when I'm 17?

'He didn't buy me this; he gave it when he stopped driving. But you might be lucky.'

James overheard without responding as he reached out a hand to Simon who arrived carrying a winter coat for Rebecca and her handbag. The two men shook hands warmly.

'Hey, James, you look good. Daily square meals, exercise, fresh air and lots of human beings to communicate with – the stuff of life, hey?'

'Variable food, exercise to escape others, a constant chill wind, nightmares, a murderous, controlling management and a new crematorium on site if I don't obey orders.'

They laughed; Grandpa off on his hobby horse again.

It was the signal to move into the site to share quality family time. As they walked, Joseph told Maisie, 'I'm not supposed to know but my parents have booked me driving lessons to start on my 17th birthday next month.'

'It will transform your life.'

Simon and James chatted about his work, his problems with one particular over-ambitious member of his team. Rebecca attempted to get her father to be honest about life at Sir Thomas More. Emily decided she was too old at 14 to ride anything, watch anything, eat anything or communicate with her embarrassing family.

They walked around knowing that James couldn't go too far. They swallowed indifferent coffees in paper cups with freshly made donuts. James ate the donut but poured out the filthy coffee. Soon they decided it was past lunch time, so bought beef salad baguettes and fresh apple juice from the orchard.

A couple of hours in, with Rebecca wrapped in the coat her husband had carried and the teenagers off riding go-karts on the far side of the park, so as not to make it too noisy for most visitors, James sat on a bench between Rebecca and Simon.

'Samantha says you're still worried about lots of things, Dad?' It was a question but also a statement.

'My hand. I lost half of it.'

'Yeah, how is it recovering?'

'I'm getting there on my permanently short hand, as if I've had my hand chopped off for crimes against the state.'

'It's part of a finger. How are you coping mentally?'

'They say that almost 99% of care home residents struggle to settle properly. It can take up to 18 months, they say,' Simon chipped in.

'Do they, Simon, is that what they say?'

'Samantha told me about the white vans. Is it that you think someone is trying to kill you off?'

'Exactly. I don't think; I know it. And that's besides all sorts of dark and nefarious activities going on it that place. It's just a front for a criminal empire with poison links across the world.'

'You have proof of this, Dad?'

'If I live long enough, I'll have proof.'

Simon was puzzled. 'But why would they want to kill off their paying customers? Makes no sense.'

James replied, 'the fees are not enough. They want everyone to leave them a bequest – that's the real income stream.'

There was really no answer to that and they didn't have to come up with one, as the teenagers returned, buzzing from their go-kart rides. It was getting windier and chillier from all directions. A natural point at which to say goodbye, hug all round and return to their cars.

To his amazement, James relaxed enough on the return journey to fall asleep, his head lolling against the car window. Smiling, Maisie drove to the legal maximum, putting the lights on as it grew darker.

The engine being turned off roused him; he expected to see the institution outside. Instead, he was at Samantha's and she was opening the door to let him out.

'Hello, Dad. We thought you'd have some tea here with us. Maisie can take you back later on.'

'Oh, I thought for a minute I was being freed.'

'Mum, I have that rehearsal at 7, remember?'

'I'll drive Grandpa home, then. No problem.'

'Home. That's a thought.'

'Come on, Dad. Are you hungry?'

Indoors, young William was slowly, reluctantly, setting the dining room table with places for six. 'Grandpa, can you help me set this table?'

'Terrible pain in my wrist, William, sorry!'

Henry came downstairs. 'Hi Grandpa. We're just doing the lead up to the First World War in history. What was it like living in East Point in those days?'

'Cheeky young pup,' James grinned reaching for the lad, who nimbly stepped aside. Maisie disappeared upstairs to get ready to go out again.

Leroy offered James a beer, but he declined. 'I'm fine, thanks, Leroy. Just a coffee after the food. Smells good, what is it?'

'Chicken pieces wrapped in bacon with two cheeses, salad and jacket potatoes. Samantha's turn to cook.'

The family gathered, ready for Samantha's call from the kitchen. James wandered through. It was clear that Rebecca had already reported on the day with their father.

'Gathering proof, are you, Dad, at Sir Thomas More?'

'You spoke to Rebecca while we were coming back. Of course, you did.'

Leroy looked in, 'How did Maisie drive, James?'

'Like Stirling Moss.'

The analogy was lost on them both. 'No, she did it very well. She's been taught by a master driver!'

Just as they sat down a mobile phone rang. Samantha, Leroy, Maisie, Henry and William fished their phones from their pockets. Then they looked at James.

'It's yours, grandpa. Well done for charging it up.'

He fumbled around and turned it the right way up, as it kept ringing. He slid the phone symbol across as they'd shown him. 'Hello?'

'Ah there you are, James, my good friend. It's Ralph!'

They could all hear clearly. 'Are you alright? We've been a tad worried.'

'I'm fine Ralph, why wouldn't I be? What did you expect? A crash on the A12? A trip to the tip?'

'Very droll, James, old man, where are you?'

'I'm at my daughter's, actually, if it's alright with you. I didn't ...'

'Still in Essex?'

'No, Samantha and family.'

'Good. Excellent. It's just that you missed dinner tonight and we were concerned.'

'No need. I'll be back in my cell in a while.'

'Shall I send a car?'

'No, thanks,' retorted James, picturing a hearse with a cavalcade of white vans following. 'Samantha is bringing me.'

'We'll see you soon, James. Over and out.'

'You can never have too much stalking,' James muttered, suddenly not hungry enough to face chicken pieces wrapped in bacon with two cheeses, salad and jacket potatoes.

Act Two, Scene 9

James was aware that it was Ralph Dines' voice he could hear round the corner in the admin corridor. The man was either addressing someone or talking on a phone.

He guessed the mobile. 'Yes, that's right, that's what I said. We've had requests to rent out a couple of corpses. One from a medical school, one from a film company.'

James stayed still, shoulder against the wall, crouched down and pretended to tie his surgical boot laces. Dines continued, 'I really don't know. I imagine in both cases that normally they use simulation but for reasons that needn't concern us want the real things... shock value perhaps?'

Constantly looking behind to make sure nobody was approaching; James listened a little longer. 'And you know we put in for planning consent for our new cemetery? It will sit on ten acres of Butterfield's farm we just bought. Extends our grounds nicely and should be a useful revenue stream. Wyford suggested a modest rising scale of fees with big hikes every five years.'

Dines laughed. 'Well, they can dig 'em up and put 'em somewhere else, can't they. What? Oh no, we stopped using that once we'd got the crematorium open.'

James knew that Dines took the American film approach to ending phone calls – he just hung up, without bothering about farewell niceties. He might therefore walk past any second.

James stood, felt momentarily dizzy and reached for

the wall rail. He missed and ended up on the floor, biting back the pain in his knee that had twisted.

'No need to prostrate yourself in front of me, James, my dear chap. Keeping your payments up to date is sufficient homage.' Without waiting to help James up or see that he got himself up, Dines slow-marched away, his stick thumping the ground, whistling *'Amazing Grace.'*

Using the stout rail, James managed to haul himself up, pausing a moment to let the blood flow back into his legs. Walking gingerly, he made his way out to the garden for his exercise and fresh air.

He came straight back in as the wind took hold of the door and pushed him aside. It was far too cold out there; he needed his warm coat. And his scarf, gloves and woolly hat that several residents found amusing, probably because they didn't possess such functional equipment.

Lord Wyford bore down on him, directly and with a clear purpose on his fat face as he stuffed his mobile into his jacket pocket.

'Ah, James, glad I caught you. Time for a coffee?' He took hold of James' arm, the one that was holding his stick and they moved awkwardly towards the nearest lounge.

He parked James and snapped fingers at two girls chatting behind the coffee counter. With a wave at himself and James he mimed two coffees and plonked himself heavily down beside James, not across from him, releasing waves of stale nicotine and rancid body odour.

'I gather you may have overheard news about our new cemetery plans, James, my man. We'd be grateful if you'll keep that under your funny woolly hat, at least till it reaches the media. Commercial confidentiality and all that.'

'Of course, no doubts about that, Ronnie.'

'That's the spirit. Be very helpful, your sealed lips, old man, just what we need.' He smiled, showing half a row of blackened, stubby teeth, his face creasing like folded parchment.

'Who am I going to talk to anyway?'

'Well, if you mention a new cemetery to most of our guests, they'll fly into a panic. Could even hasten one or two into the facility!' His mouth released the familiar mirthless saw that Dines had perfected. 'We have a really powerful slogan for the new cemetery, by the way, you'll appreciate it.'

As James said nothing, he smiled and announced, *'Join us in the Sir Thomas More Cemetery and Gardens - we know where the bodies are buried!'*

Still James made no response. Was that really their advertising slogan?

The coffee arrived on a little tray and the girl poured them each a cup. Wyford tipped the entire contents of two milk pods into his; James took a little from one with a few brown sugar grains which he stirred with a steady eye on Wyford.

'You know what they say about graveyards, James?'

'They're full of people who thought they were indispensable?'

'That and they're full of all the secrets those people took with them.'

It was an unsubtly veiled threat, as James saw it. He thought again about how a crematorium and a cemetery on site really helped fund the lifestyles of Dines, Wyford, the staff and any others James didn't know about. Besides providing another disposal point for the departed who'd crossed the criminals Dines clearly associated with.

James sipped his coffee; Wyford slurped his while maintaining a stream of chatter about development plans they had for the land. With Butterfield's Farm now secured and an old school bought just yesterday, they were planning luxury residential homes.

Chiropodists, florist, hairdressers, disability aids, hearing aids, opticians, geriatric gym and a high-class dentist, were also on their drawing board.

'Now remember,' he wagged a podgy finger at James, 'no telling your friends Sebby Catchpole or Lennie Sanders what we've just talked about.'

'Wouldn't dream of it, Ronnie. And they're not my friends.'

'We're all friends here, James, all of us. Nothing of interest or importance you think we should know?' James gave it a moment's thought and shook his head.

It was later that evening, after dinner and half an hour before 'curfew', that James bumped into Dines again, either by chance or design. All main lights were dimmed at 10pm, so from 8pm staff administered medicines and helped prepare for bed those who could no longer manage themselves or resist it.

Residents were allowed to stay up, wander about as much as they wished, though night-lit corridors and stairs were prohibited for those suffering mobility issues, including James. Most bars stayed open till around midnight.

'Come and have a nightcap, my dear old thing.'

Dines was completely different from straight after his phone call earlier in the day. He was relaxed, affable even, and they walked slowly besides each other, sticks thumping in near unison on the carpeted corridor.

They went into his office, not to a bar, Imelda away from her reception desk, and James was pointed to a comfy old leather armchair by the grand table perched on carved, grubby gilded legs. Three very expensive lamps restfully lit the room in gentle pools of warmth.

'What's your poison these days?'

'I don't ... '

'Oh hell, James, still teetotal? Didn't you give it up when the blessed Margaret ascended her throne? Well, you can embrace it again, now she's no longer with us!'

'More's the pity. We need her steely determination at this time.'

'I couldn't agree more. Anything you think we should know about? Any news, views, gossip you've picked up?'

It was what Wyford had demanded. 'Besides the plan to build a cemetery, nothing at all.'

'I thought you told Ronnie Wyford you were going to forget that?' He took a deep slug of whiskey and looked at James over the rim. James sipped his sparkling water and returned the look.

'You know in here, with our replica Chamber and our

amusing, even whimsical traditions, we have given a sense of belonging to the old club that so many former Members miss. People don't understand.'

'You had to have been elected or elevated there for anyone to understand.'

'Exactly. What sticks in your mind most of all?'

'Being in two places simultaneously in many ways, constituency and Westminster. Remember that night I was trapped in the lift behind the Speaker's Chair?'

'Oh yes. How long were you there? A week?' He treated James to another peal of false laughter.

'It felt like forever, but was only a few minutes. I was afraid I'd miss the wind up to the debate as I'd contributed and you know how much fuss they made if you didn't listen to the front bench winding up speeches.'

Dines nodded. 'You know, I think that apart from the ability to relate to people, persuade them, carry them with you, speak in public, deal with thousands of complaints, problems and moans, be an expert in many fields, store copious amounts of information in your head, the main thing you need is stamina.'

Warming to Dines' more open attitude, James nodded. 'You're right. Stamina. Without that, you go under and very quickly. It's like in teaching, if teenagers smell weakness in a teacher, he or she is doomed.'

'We don't do it for the glory or the money, though some public think otherwise, so what is it? Altruism?'

'Partly, yes. I once sent a twenty-pound note anonymously to a constituent who came to see me with a credible story about trying to feed his kids after his wife had died. I couldn't do it all the time, but that man moved me.'

'More than Lennie Sanders' suffering over his daughter's murder while you helped her killer?'

'The knowledge of that came too recent to be relevant to our time in the House. Only once did I ask for police protection at a surgery, when some maniac threatened me over government policy.'

'Oh, I always had one or two close by.'

'Would a few coppers nearby have saved David Amess, I wonder.' Both men pondered the assassination of the MP for Southend in 2021, stabbed to death at a constituency surgery.

Dines moved it on. 'I occasionally wondered what I was doing. I only wanted to be a minister. I think I'd have handled the top job, you know?' James agreed Dines would have done, in the same way that a born thug could rise to the top of a mafia gang.

'Some of our colleagues used it to explore their sexual drives. Straight sex, abnormal sex, all sorts. The one who died with a pair of woman's tights round his neck and an orange stuffed in his mouth. Remember him?'

'You had the benefit of the Whip's Black Book, Ralph.'

'The little Black Book which officially never existed!'

Dines helped himself to another drink and topped up James' glass with water. They revisited names, faces and quirks of several MPs and Lords of their era, enjoying the trip down Memory Lane. Many were residents in Sir Thomas More now and James heard things he'd forgotten and a few happenings he'd known nothing about.

As the clock ticked, time passed and a sense of being all alone in this great house descended; with sleep beckoning, Dines suddenly changed the mood again.

'You seem to be very weary at times, James. Not sleeping properly? Guilty conscience? Unfulfilled ambitions? In fact, you come over as very nervous as you go about the place. Is that fair?'

'No, it's not fair, Ralph. Where do you draw the line between caring for all us inmates and meddling in every aspect of our lives and personalities?'

'I'm not sure there is a line. It's all one and the same.'

'But it shouldn't be. Right, thank you for the drink. I bid you goodnight.' James stood and took hold of his stick.

'Sit down, Ellington!' Dines suddenly barked.

'No, I will not. I will not jump through every hoop you hold up.'

Dines laughed again. 'Just testing. You switch from affable to angry in a second. You slide from remembering all to forgetting, selectively. You seem very nervous. And you show signs of paranoia. I'll get Zoe Frayn to look at you again. She will be interested in why you've started writing a diary in here.'

'I'm fine thanks, and if I'm a little bit paranoid, just a tad nervous, think about why in this house with all that goes on, people dying off, men in white vans, a crematorium and a hierarchy below you trying to control me.'

'You can never be too paranoid, James. Don't worry about it. Better to be a little paranoid than be barking bonkers like Timmy Greenwood, hey?'

'At least he doesn't know he's completely round the bend,' James said.

'You know, I don't think he does. No paranoia or bad dreams for old Timmy, hey?'

James, still standing but leg wedged against the settee, leaned forward and straightened the coasters and glasses. Without a word, Dines did likewise, but his straight was not the same as James'.

The old men spent the next minute in a chess-like game of 'straightening' the coasters and glasses, both giving each other the evil eye between moves.

Suddenly James was bored, having expected Dines to tire first. As he limped out of the office, past Dines' desk, he noticed in the gloom a well-thumbed *National Risk Register* and a copy of *How to Control People and Situations* on the edge.

Act Two, Scene 10

Next morning James watched as Ralph Dines displayed alarming signs of a weak grip on his sanity.

James had seen it before but the Dress Rehearsal of the annual Speech event provided proof positive for everyone to witness - a directly contradictory side of Ralph from their almost friendly chat the previous evening.

Dines was in the Speaker's Chair and everyone addressed him as Mr Speaker, a position he'd craved at one point in his Parliamentary career.

Short tempered with everyone, he kept urging honourable members to get a move on, arrive at their point, stay focused on the topic and not to play to the gallery. He was on his feet calling members to order and mouthing his displeasure for longer than the average member stood to make his or her speech, playing to the gallery himself.

One House rule they'd transposed to this pantomime was how to indicate a wish to speak. Members had to stand up in the hope of 'catching the Speaker's eye' and thus be called. A concession was made to those who couldn't stand in which they were allowed to speak from a sedentary position.

Wheelchair members could only wave their single sheet order papers in lieu of standing; for some reason this irritated Dines on this occasion. A Speaker could often be weary, impatient and out of sorts, of course, but this was a particular display of sour temper.

Sir Gerry Manders was on his feet pontificating about the mindless behaviour and attitudes of everybody under 30, all those aged 31-70 and the 71 to 100s, excluding himself with particular venom for the very old. It was the kind of rant a disappointed, disillusioned and jealous old person might spew against the world.

Dines had had enough, reminding everyone that the topic the honourable Manders had drawn was actually *The Future of School-Based Education in a Post-Democratic World.*

A handful of members still awake mumbled the 'yah-yah' sound, familiar to watchers of the Parliamentary channels. It was actually an elision of 'hear, hear' which originally meant, 'listen here, this fellow is talking sense.' Several members stood to raise Points of Order; there was an outbreak of finger pointing across the Chamber.

The familiar sound encouraged Dines to go to town. If he had called on the Clerk to produce a copy of the Riot Act 1714, as amended, and had read out the preamble about 'rebellious riots and tumults', nobody would have been surprised.

Of course, it was nothing out of the ordinary in a Parliamentary moment. The Riot Act as such would never have been read as the House had its own procedures for dealing with persistent trouble-makers.

Nobody was doing anything wrong. It was just that Dines was in a bad mood. He swept his arms about, a cross between a windmill and a man in a hurricane trying to stay upright. He criticised all members for every little thing he could come up with and threatened to name them all!

When the Speaker 'named' a member it didn't mean calling him or her to speak but to trigger the Standing

Order relating to MP suspension. It was the disciplinary procedure which meant a temporary banning from the Chamber after MPs had voted on it.

James had heard enough. Dines was getting carried away with his power. There was no way he'd expel any members from the annual Speech contest, as family and friends of inmates were invited to attend and watch and contribute to some great charitable cause Dines had chosen.

As Manders resumed his seat, the hubbub died as quickly as it arose. 'Point of Order, Mr Speaker', James alone stood, wobbled and addressed the chair.

Dines glowered at him. He repeated his request. Dines glowered even more, but sat and nodded, 'Point of Order, Mr Ellington, and I hope it is a genuine Point of Order for me and not some expression of personal opinion.'

'Indeed, Mr Speaker. It is a Point of Order about whether an honourable Member may be flexible in interpreting his or her insights into a topic that he or she has been given. Is not the flexibility, ingenuity and point of view entirely a matter of creativity so therefore cannot be subject to reprimands from the chair?'

He sat. Dines rose. 'That is a spurious Point of Order, which the Honourable Gentleman has raised, despite my warning him in advance. The occupant of the Chair interprets what is relevant, pertinent and creative, particularly in the annual contest and always in the light of custom and precedence of this House.'

He sat. James rose, briefly enjoying the return to Parliamentary ways. 'Further to that Point of Order, Mr Speaker...'

Dines waved him down and stood up smartly. 'There is

no further to that Point of Order since the Honourable Gentleman did not raise a Point of Order. The Honourable Gentleman will resume his place.'

'Mr Speaker, I just don't feel like being reprimanded just for ...' At this Sir Ronald Hasbery looked up from his knitting under the Clerks' table and watched James over his half glasses.

'What the Honourable Gentleman feels or not is of no consequence to the House. Now, resume your place as I am on my feet.'

Of course, it was good theatre; a show steeped in ancient tradition that was continued by people with different moods, attitudes and tolerance levels. If that scene was replayed to the visiting audience on the Contest night, they'd all feel they'd had a good night out.

Perhaps that was what they meant by Dress Rehearsal and it would be part of the show. James sat and Manders was called on to reach his peroration as swiftly as possible. Since everyone present including Manders had forgotten what he'd been droning about, he obliged so that Douglas Gardener could be called to entertain the House on the merits of 3D printing in the NHS.

As Hasbery resumed his surreptitious knitting, James took that opportunity to slip out of the benches, almost tripping over somebody's foot across the gangway. pausing to bow his head at the Chair and move away, he could only wonder what was wrong with Dines? Was it just that every so often he needed to exert his authority? Or was he merely unstable?

He didn't get far. A hubbub arose in the Chamber and he heard the words 'lie and liar' amongst the noise. This was worth returning for.

'The Honourable Gentlemen is familiar with the long standing prohibitions on that word or any variant of it.' Standing at the bar of the House again, it wasn't clear who had called whom a monger of untruths, a distorter of factual reality or a devotee of being economical with the actual truth.

But Dines didn't let that stop him as vitriol and bile flowed from his mouth at both sides of the House in equal measure. It was a worthy performance and James rewarded it with a slow clap. Eyes turned to him and Dines stared daggers.

Nobody else joined in, so James clapped without bringing his hands together, a step up from a one-hand clap. Dines indicated that the debate should continue.

Hasbery scribbled on a piece of paper which he passed back to Dines. The great man took it, peered at it and then decided to read it out. 'The English writer Thomas Hardy once said, *the foundation of all morality is to have done, once and for all, with lying.*' And I am in full agreement with those sentiments, so listen and learn!'

Standing beside him enjoying the performance, Dame Winnie whispered loudly enough to be heard, 'And Dame Winifred Carswell once said one man's lie is another man's perceived truth!'

Later that same evening, James was dragooned into dinner in the Members' Dining Room as Sebastian Catchpole wanted to tell him about his latest hare-brained scheme to set up a company that provided advice to film companies on any of their films that mentioned Parliament, law-making or the civil service machine.

Unwilling to commit an entire evening to it, James was ready to dismiss the plan as 'too late, too small a potential market and too easy to deride at their age' but thought better of it when Catchpole offered to stand him starters and a dessert.

They were reaching the end of soup with fresh bread rolls, when Ralph Dines swept into the room, pointed at a vacant table for four, ignoring, as usual, the custom about filling up seats on one of the big tables.

Nodding exaggeratedly at James and Sebastian, he pointed to the pair following him to join him. It was the former Agent, Sir Michael Michaelson, James' former agent no less, with Kenny Sloan in tow.

His hackles rose at once. Why was the former Member of the European Parliament (MEP) from the days when the UK sent members to that pointless institution, having dinner with Dines? And the pair of them with Michaelson who as a Party official could only eat in this room as a guest of a former Member?

Sloan had been a paying member of James' Association back in the day, during his first term of office and just into his second. Living comfortably, he seemed to have lots of free time, couldn't do enough for James and offered to make sure Elspeth and the children were well while James was away in London.

They'd known each other at Grammar School – Sloan was a year older – and James was well aware of his reputation, even then, as a girl's worst nightmare. Love 'em and leave 'em. That was Sloan.

He'd made himself indispensable during James' first and second election campaigns, driving the van frequently, organising pub and club visits, smoothing the paths, shaking the right hands along the way.

He was highly regarded in business circles and in the local political world. He even got his daughter, born while he was at school and never known about by his wife, into the office as a secretary without admitting the connection. She had a different surname. She lasted six months before being caught searching through constituents' files for information she didn't need to know to do her job.

One day Sloan had admitted to James after an event and they were clearing up that his ambition was to be an MEP. He wanted nothing less. He wasn't comfortable with James' anti-EU views and felt that the EU was the future.

They'd discussed it and he needed James' approval to go forward for selection as a candidate. James gave it but added a footnote to the effect that he was signing from constituency loyalty, not because he thought Sloan would be any good.

Despite that, Sloan was selected and shifted his attention to a Euro seat in the Midlands with less time to help James. As if he knew what James had done, he began to drop little criticism into the ears of the party faithful. He twisted minor truths into doubtful lies.

After an unsuccessful pass at Elspeth, James had it out with him in a row in his own garden. Sloan turned ugly. James seemed to remember shouting at Sloan that if he ever set eyes on him again it would be too soon.

Now, on calm reflection in Sir Thomas More House, James realised that Sloan and Dines had much in common; eating dinner together now made perfect sense.

Sloan's final stab had been hinting to several that James' younger children were not his; Elspeth was of questionable morals. It was the slur too far for James who reported to an informal meeting of his executive officers and it was settled that the Chairman would invite Sloan to resign.

The decision made James nervous, yet in the end Sloan went quietly but never lost an opportunity to stir up constituents to write critical letters to the local paper and to attend James' surgeries in anger and hatred.

In due course, Sloan was elected an MEP; he moved to Coventry. James thought little more of him – out of sight, out of mind - and the matter brought him and Elspeth closer.

Dessert and coffee done, James and Catchpole were getting up to move to the lounge, when Sloan rushed across to him. 'James, nobody told me you were here! What a lovely surprise. Ralph was telling me all about you. We must have a drink soon to talk over old times, what do you say?'

Catchpole shook his hand. Dines and Michaelson joined them, blocking the waiters' passage to and fro. 'And how is that lovely wife of yours, James? Elizabeth? Eliza?'

'Elspeth passed away. That's why I'm stuck here in Colditz.'

Everyone laughed as if he was the funniest fellow in the place. Noticing a waitress struggling to carry plates round them, Catchpole said, 'we're in the way of this lovely young lady, gentlemen.'

With effusive and embarrassing apologies, Dines returned to his table with his guests, Sebastian led James out to the lounge. James took one final look back at Dines and company and was rewarded with twisted, demonic faces, eyes in different directions and what looked like fleck at their mouths as he glared at James.

He forced himself to walk from the room slowly, head held high while he really wanted to rush out screaming, calling silently on his daughters to save him by getting him out.

   Now. Or even sooner than that.

Act Two, Scene 11

After a typically East Anglian winter – more icy wind than ice, more rain than snow – a run of decent early spring weather came as a blessing to all at Sir Thomas More House.

In the hour before his family were due to visit, James sat outside reading the daily paper but really bagging a trestle table and seven garden chairs. Dr Frayn found him and sat down beside him, waving as she did so at some old dear struggling with her false teeth plate in and out, trying to get it right.

'Hello, James, how are you today?'

'Oh, Dr Frayn. Zoe. I'm good today, just a little back ache, a few creaky knee joints, pain in the soles of my feet where the nerves still function and some numbing on my fingertips as my neuropathy advances. My anxiety is under full control. A good 4 out of 10 today.'

'I'm delighted to hear it. That's better than many.' She sounded as if she really meant it. 'And how are you sleeping?'

'Oh pretty good. You know. The night before last I dreamed I was in the kitchen and my grandkids were still toddlers. One of them reached up and pulled a pan of boiling water off the stove all over his head. Apart from that, I'm doing fine.'

'And how do you feel about some of the key people in this institution?'

'Nothing has changed.'

'So, no worse, then? I mean about them and white vans and plans to do away with the residents to inherit their generous bequests?' She asked it seriously; she wasn't making a joke of it. Nor of him.

'I know what I know, Zoe. But I can't prove anything. I'm getting used to it, keeping my eyes open, especially those in the back of my head.'

'That's what all you politicos must do, isn't it? Constantly watch your backs.'

'Of course. That's also why we back slap each other – to find the best place to insert the dagger.'

They paused while he traced a crack in the tabletop with his finger. 'Can I get you some tea or something?'

'No thanks, James. You'll be having tea with your family soon. How are you with Ralph now?'

'I've known him a long time. No, I mean I knew him a long time ago. Since then, he has become more dangerous, more successful and more ruthless. His love of power has grown, that's obvious. He was a notorious womanizer then; he's maybe too old for that now. I have noticed a couple of occasions when you've clashed swords with him.'

'Have you? Mmmm. Well, there are ways of speaking to staff and of speaking to women. I mean, a woman who could save his life one day if he has a heart attack.'

'Power. He sees women as objects to reinforce his ego and that hasn't changed. I remember the House secretary of one of our colleagues... but never mind that now. Did you say he could have a heart attack? Now, that's a thought!'

'Does what you know make him a criminal, in your view?'

'Criminals come in many shapes and disguises. They always say a person with a briefcase of secrets can be more effective than a man with a gun.'

'Well, I'm not an expert but I learned that people commit crimes, outrages against society for five reasons. One, from desperate need; two, from insatiable greed. Three, from ideological conviction, like terrorists. Four, from fear that others may control them so they must control others.'

She gave him a moment to consider that. 'And the fifth?'

'From madness, like a psychopath.'

'And which is Ralph Dines?'

'You tell me!'

'Insatiable greed. Conviction of his absolute right. Must control others. Yes, he's a psychopath. So, he's all five. You should write him up in a medical paper!'

Suddenly she stood, looking around to see if anyone had overheard her unprofessional talk. 'James, I must go. I have people to see. Enjoy your family visit. Who's coming?'

And in the distance she spotted Rebecca and Simon with Joseph and Emily approaching, the kids looking at their phones as they walked.

'Ah yes, your Essex family.' And she was gone as he struggled to standing position to welcome his loved ones. A hug and a kiss with Rebecca, handshake with Simon and a 'hi, Grandpa' from the kids.

'How are you?'

He replied without running through the list he'd give the doctor, 'I'm fine. How are all of you?' The conversation continued on a script played by all residents and visiting families. It was a game, reading behind the mask that hid the real pain, unless he or she was so far gone there was no pain inside. And nothing else, either.

He noted that both Rebecca and Simon avoided asking him about his fears, about white vans, about Ralph Dines particularly and waited for him to talk about other residents and what they did or what their danger was to him now.

Tea, crustless pate and salad sandwiches, biscuits and cream cakes arrived – James had ordered them earlier. These were tastefully laid out on a white cloth on the table; the wobbly leg was propped up with a folded paper napkin and the adults made appreciative noises.

Joseph broke off from his game to look with disapproval at the table. Another waitress appeared carrying a bowl of fresh chips and tomato ketchup which brightened him up no end. Emily asked for two diet colas, please, before helping herself to a couple of his chips.

Rebecca, smiling at her kids, rummaged and pulled a folder from her capacious handbag. 'Rebecca, I wish you'd be more careful with that bag. Anybody could snatch your purse, pass your cards down a line of criminal hands to the forger and before you know where you are your account is emptied like a suction has been in it.'

Ignoring what was after all a well-rehearsed old worry, she told him, 'Dad, this is the summary of the house sale details, costs and balance. Samantha had it from the solicitor, so I've brought your copy.'

Nodding thanks, he left the document lying on the table. His house was sold, gone forever. Could he still buy another and live away from here with help coming in?

Simon explained, 'James, they've put the proceeds into a fund which will pay the monthly fees here and you can top up if there're extras from your own account in the usual way.'

So, no, he couldn't buy another house. He'd had to agree to the investment to pay his fees for up to twenty years. He was locked in till the day he died or the twenty years was up. Rebecca poured the tea. 'They didn't bring you any coffee, Dad.'

'Tea is fine today. It's cheaper.'

'Dad, for goodness' sake!'

Sebastian Catchpole chose that moment to fetch up at their table and bestow on them a broad, yellow-toothed grin. James happened to know that his teeth were in fact ancient dentures in need of updating or cleaning.

As Catchpole's eyes took in the table of food, James had an image of crumbs and cake flakes spraying over them, but fortunately Sebby realised there was insufficient for him to barge in and share.

Instead, he stayed standing and asked the family if James had told them about Dines' outburst over un-parliamentary language of somebody 'lying.' They looked blank; James muttered, 'no, not yet Sebby, more to talk about than Ralph Dines' insanity problems.'

'Well, you'll like this. I often used it in my speeches in my constituency. A man was out walking and saw a board outside a house with the legend TALKING DOG FOR SALE, ONLY £10.'

James groaned inwardly. He'd heard it dozens of times – a Parliamentary hazard, hearing the same things as if on a loop. The adults paid Sebby polite attention; the kids rediscovered their phones.

'Well, the walker stopped outside the house and interrupted the dog's owner who was gardening. 'Talking dog? How is that possible?'

The man said, 'well, he's round the back, go and talk to him for yourself.'

So he did. And sure enough, there was a cute little Yorkshire terrier looking at him. 'Yes, I'm the talking dog.'

'Hell, you can talk! And he's selling you for just £10!'

'Oh he's a terrible man. Listen, I can read. I've been round the world, serving on the Royal Yacht Britannia, I fought rebels in Afghanistan. I worked at Sandringham for HM The Queen. I helped in operating theatres. I trained soldiers and saved a child from a burning building and he thinks I'm worth a mere tenner!'

'Wow!' The walker goes back to the front garden and asks, 'why are you selling such a talented, clever and heroic dog for just ten pounds?'

'Why? Because he's a bloody liar, that's why!'

James smiled and nodded, Rebecca and Simon laughed a little while the kids made no response beyond a grunt, a cough and a whistle. But that was because of what they saw on their phones.

Ralph Dines appeared from within a big laurel as if he'd been listening. Perhaps he had. 'Not telling you his Walter Mitty life is he, old Sebby?'

Everyone looked at Dines who positioned himself centre stage. 'Oh yes, Sebastian, before he entered the House was in the SAS, he was in the witness protection programme and worked under deep cover for Scotland Yard. I can't remember what else he was, but that's Sebby Catchpole, forgettable.'

Sebby roared approval; he loved a bit of banter. 'Well, Sebby, Ralph, if you'll excuse us, we have family business to discuss...' James noticed Timmy Greenwood approaching and abandoned hope of meaningful family time.

But the prime lunatic simply shouted across, 'Good Enough is the enemy of The Best, everyone, take note of that!' Timmy was acknowledged by waves and grins, before being distracted by another family of visitors and went to tell them to 'go thou and fill another room in Hell' from *Richard II*.

Sebby made his excuses and drifted off in search of sustenance, leaving Dines to greet James' four visitors by name and turned to the man himself.

'Hello, James, how are you today?'

'Oh, Ralph. I'm good today, just a little back ache, a few creaky knee joints, pain in the soles of my feet where the nerves still function and some numbing on my fingertips as my neuropathy advances. My anxiety is under full control. A good 4 out of 10 today.'

'Splendid! I'm delighted to hear it.' Of course, he didn't mean it. 'And how are you sleeping?'

'Oh pretty good. You know. The night before last I dreamed I was in the woods over there and disturbed a man axing up a couple of tied and gagged victims but they refused to die quietly. Apart from that, I'm doing fine.'

Emily muttered, 'Grandpa, is that true?'

Joseph offered a thumbs-up, with 'Nice one, Grandpa!'

Simon's contribution was, 'We pray for you, James, every night.'

'Thank you, Simon. Pray I don't wake up dead one of these fine mornings.'

Dines treated them to his mirthless cackle.' Very droll, James, ever the card. We can't have you popping your clogs till we've finalised the details of the very generous bequest you're thinking of leaving Sit Thomas More, can we?'

'What's this, Dad?' demanded Rebecca, thinking of the future of her children.

'We're a charity, here, Rebecca. We're a bit like a stately home. We must maximise our revenue streams to keep everything at such a high standard. We have the crematorium now and soon we'll have a cemetery, a garden of remembrance.'

They nodded.

'We are considering plans for the manufacture of incontinence aids on the west side, plenty of land for that. And we're opening optical and dental surgeries soon to provide a cost-effective service for our treasured residents. Oh, and we're starting a Suicide Survivors Club in the old dairy. Quite a demand for that, I understand.'

Simon helped himself to the last cream horn. 'That sounds very enterprising, Mr Dines, using your talents and assets to the full.'

'I'm glad you approve! But of course, we do rely heavily on the generous bequests our grateful residents leave us when they move on. So, think about it, would you? Lovely to chat to you.'

And he moved away to smooth-talk others, stick thumping on the lawn, manicured to within an inch of its life so he wouldn't stumble on any rough patch, and neither would James.

Rebecca put her plate down, the slice of malt loaf unfinished, 'Have we thought of a bequest here?' She looked concerned if not actually shocked.

'No, and nor will we,' James told her firmly. 'As soon as he knows I've left them money, I'm a dead man walking.'

Joseph, who'd been only half listening, said. "Nice one, Grandpa!'

Act Two, Scene 12

James rarely looked at his mobile phone. It was kept charged at the request of his family in case they needed to call him urgently. But late evening in the calm quiet of his room as he was getting ready for bed, he heard the ping of a message arriving.

After a search through his jacket pockets, the table and the bedside cabinet, he discovered his phone under a copy of yesterday's *Daily Torygraph*. He began to shake as he keyed the passcode in, found messages and opened the latest one. Surely a grandchild had been run over in a hit and run, his son in law was erroneously arrested for fraud or both his daughters were stabbed to death in a bloodbath in the back of a white van.

It was from Dr Zoe. Rather than wonder why she'd be sending him a text at this late hour, he read it twice and reversed his undressing ritual, ready to leave.

'James, sorry so late, come at once to the staff accommodation block. Urgent. Make no noise. Come now. Please.'

Arousing no suspicions in James, it excited his curiosity. Checking the clear corridor in both directions, he did his comic version of a tiptoe from the room, his stick gently thumping the carpet, down the corridor and staircase, keeping to the edges, listening carefully.

Only the strangulated moans of the tortured and/or crazed emerged from two rooms in the distance. Two Karls were closing one of the bars, washing glasses, draping towels over the beer handles.

There was a sudden scream from the dementia ward, a cross between a banshee and sound effect in a horror movie. He was glad he'd put his dressing gown over his pyjamas and pulled it round him with his free hand. It wasn't there. He'd forgotten to bring it, along with his phone.

Too late now, so, bravely, he pressed on. The entrance to the staff rooms was blocked by four Karls, one up a ladder changing a lightbulb, the others holding the base steady. How many Karls does it take to change a light bulb?

With no way James could slide past unseen, he veered off down the corridor to the kitchens, thinking there must be another way to reach the staff area.

He turned a corner and bumped straight into Ralph Dines, who grinned at him like they were a couple of kids on a school jape out to cause mischief. He put his finger to his lips and indicated James should follow him, as if they were in a pantomime.

They turned into a store area, a giant pantry, not unlike the one where James had been almost murdered by Lennie Sanders, so he gripped his stick firmly and slowed to put three paces between Dines and himself.

Dines unlocked a door which led to an old staircase that was clearly the servants' access up and down when the old house had been a significant gentleman's residence.

At the top, both men breathing heavily, James was led into a Spartan bedroom in dull utilitarian wallpaper and a stained mattress on a single bed besides a rickety side cabinet with a lopsided lamp, one fifth-hand garden chair and a battered, badly painted, wobbly tallboy that could have belonged to anybody.

'I sent the text, James. You wouldn't have come if I'd asked you to,' Dines whispered in James' face, a cloud of halitosis making him recoil.

'Too bloody true I wouldn't. What am I doing here and why the fuck are we whispering?' James demanded, getting angry now, a) at being tricked and b) that Dines had imposed his will on him yet again.

Without replying, Dines approached the wall carefully. Moving aside a painting of a headless chicken, painted in the late 1960s with a large palette knife by someone out of his or her head, he put his eye to the wall, squinting awkwardly through a peep hole into the room next door.

'Look,' Dines grabbed James by his pyjama jacket lapel to push him to the hole. Once he'd adjusted his varifocals to the right angle, he saw Dr Zoe Frayn, white coat, blue surgical gloves and a serious look on her face treating a man on a bed.

Young, dressed in casual clothes, he was not a member of staff that James had noticed before. But whoever he was, he sported a nasty bleeding gash along his bare arm, which Dr Zoe was cleaning before reaching for her needle.

Squeamish at the best of times, James pulled back to avoid watching the man receive stitches, only to have his head returned to the wall, hurting his face where the glasses pressed into him. Dines kept his hand on the back of James' head.

Mercifully, she moved round for a better grip on his tattooed arm so her body masked what she was doing. The man grunted, gripped his mouth closed and was clearly in pain.

After a moment, James was allowed to move from the

wall. Dines put the bedside lamp on and sat heavily on the only chair, indicating the bed that James could sit on. Or lie on if he felt that bad.

'Now, I expect you're wondering? Well, Dr Frayn is patching up one of my men from our special projects division who had a bit of altercation with somebody brandishing a serrated knife.'

If he weren't shivering from the cold and the fear, James would have thought he was having a severe nightmare. The door opened; in came Dr Zoe, having peeled off her gloves. 'Good evening, James.'

She was followed by the patient, a man James saw was about forty, muscular, heavily built, brutally-cropped hair and a badly shaven chin, probably a fan of working out. He smiled at James and revealed a few blackened teeth, damaged either by drugs or excessive fighting.

James' spine ran even colder. He knew the man. He was one of the ruffians from the A12 van incident. This was a member of Dines' hired killers and the doctor had just patched him up to kill again. Perhaps he was to kill James this time.

Keeping his eye on the man, he saw from the corner of his eye Dines take an envelope from his jacket pocket which he passed to Zoe. 'The usual fee, my dear Doctor. And Mum's the word, as always.'

She took the envelope, stuffed it into her white coat pocket without checking it and ushered the patient out. 'Follow me, I'll give you some antibiotics and painkillers before you go. Good night, James. Do you need something to help you sleep, you look very pale?'

'No thanks, Dr Zoe. I'll never sleep again.'

'I doubt that, James. Nobody can stay awake forever,' Dines told him. The ruffian smiled again, thinking that no, nobody would avoid the eternal sleep.

And they were gone. James relaxed a little, but at any point from here to his room the thug could grab him.

'Ralph, what sort of game is this?'

'James, I wanted to show you the kind, considerate side to my nature and the enterprise I run here. You have a bad image of us, quite unjustified, but you are paranoid. I wanted you to see that I paid for one of my team to be looked after quietly, no fuss, no plaudits and the good Doctor earned a few extra quid.'

'What do you want, a fucking medal?'

'I just want you, James, to modify your low opinion of me and this House.' He brought his face close to James again and to avoid another poison cloud of bad breath, James managed, 'I'll do my best, Ralph.'

The door opened again and, tensed up, James wheeled to see an Imelda who bowed to Dines.' They're ready now, Mr Dines.'

'Thank you, Imelda. Now James, if you'd be so good as to look through the spy-hole once again. You will see another side to my personality to remind you what you will get if you don't start to think well of me and all I do in this place.'

There were noises from next door, an anxious female voice, a chair falling over. He looked again, imagining he'd see an inmate being roughed up. But it was Zoe.

The man she'd just patched up and another, identical moron from the white van incident were slapping her round the face, one after the other, a choreographed sequence. They exchanged slaps for punches, one took hold of her hair; the other punched her in the stomach. She doubled over and vomited near the man's feet.

James looked away and opened his mouth to protest, but Dines had him by the back of the neck and proceeded to push his face into the wall once, twice, three times, a little harder each time.

James lost his glasses and his grip on his standing place. His stick had vanished. His eye was back at the hole, a glimpse of Zoe being strangled and shaken so her cries for help were silenced was all he saw before he was pulled away again.

Dines, showing enormous upper body strength, forced James onto the bed where he sat astride him, hands reaching for his throat to replicate what Zoe was suffering next door. James fought back, kicking and yelling.

Then he was seeing it from a distance. He was above the scene, below the scene. He was inside his head, looking through cracked eyeballs. He was floating above as a black cloud slowly enveloped his mind.

Neck deep in treacle, he was stuck in a fudge-like bog of blood and human remains. Lights, blurred at the edges, flashed on and off. There was music, a distorted opera aria he couldn't place. He was walking with his father who'd been dead for forty years who just said, 'go back' but he might also have said 'come on.'

Clouds of what seemed like fluffy pink marshmallow floated gently from above, suffocating him, holding his arms round him. He was spinning, swirling, he lost all sense of up and down.

Act Two, Scene 13

When he woke, he was in his own room where the clock read 6am and if they'd played Sonny and Cher's *I Got You Babe,* he'd not have been surprised.

An assistant nurse with jerky arm and hand movements was attempting to tidy his bedding with him still lying on top. Maintaining a stony face as she worked, she showed neither surprise nor irritation.

'You might want to have a bath, Mr Ellington, so I can make your bed. Doctor's orders are to calm down. Your blood pressure is too high. The doctor will see you soon. Clean up and rest. No walking about till the Doctor gives you the all-clear.'

These orders were given in a monotone, clear and unfeeling. Which doctor was she running on about? Surely not Zoe Frayn? She'd be in no state to resume her duties any time soon. If ever.

A bath sounded and smelt like a good idea judging by the stench from his armpits, but his head still swirled somewhat. Gingerly, he stood from the bed, furniture-walked through to the now-ready bath. The nurse had poured in soothing foam bubbles and set out clean clothes for him.

After trying the bath with a finger to rule out acid, he lowered himself in, using the rails and supports provided, carefully, glad of his upper body strength. He relived the fight, the attack on Zoe and the whole Ralph Dines' mental situation.

He just couldn't fathom what the patching up of the hoodlum was and why was Zoe beaten like that? After what seemed like a mere minute, the assistant nurse woke him.

The bath was cold, the bubbles had gone. He lay in what was rapidly looking like a slime pit. He brushed her aside when she tried to help him out. He could manage. He dried himself, thinking more clearly now and made a plan of sorts.

Dressed, he limped into the bedroom to demand that the nurse took him to whoever was in charge. It was empty.

Sitting on the now made bed, he picked up the house phone and demanded of whoever answered that he wanted to be taken to whoever was in charge. Now. No, not in a minute because everyone was busy. Now. And if he didn't get taken now, he'd press the fire alarm.

A clutch of assistants arrived sharply, flooding into his room. 'Good morning, I wish to be taken to whoever is in charge of this madhouse!'

One held a syringe, but put it behind her when he noticed. He was lifted up, the stick put in his hand and was walked out of the bedroom and down the corridor. One led the way, two flanked him and one brought up the rear. If he tired, presumably they'd all lift him up a few inches off the ground and convey him that way.

Downstairs, ignoring good mornings and the same old dear still being helped to her medicine, they arrived at Dines' office and entered without ceremony. Imelda nodded at the inner door but said nothing.

James was back in the command centre. Sat at the raised desk was Lord Wyford, swallowing his liquid breakfast. He waved James over.

'You want to speak to whoever is in charge? You know who that is, James, what's all the fuss about, hey? Ralph Dines is in charge, and as his deputy I'm temporarily in charge as he had to rush off to an important meeting in London about the humane disposal of the departed.'

'Ronnie, you're his sidekick so I don't think I can trust you, but perhaps you don't know what Dines is doing here? How he's having people beaten up, some killed, disposing of bodies, he's not merely a madman but he's dangerous. Nobody is safe. We're all puppets in his game.'

'I'm no medic, James, but I'd say, judging by what I've seen in others of our paying guests, you have a little bit of CHD, Care Home Delusion, not uncommon among residents in their first year or two.'

'Don't try to analyse me as if you have a fucking clue what you're talking about. I shouldn't have mentioned a thing to you, should have waited for Dines to get back.'

Wyford came round from behind the desk, stepped carefully off the platform to stand directly in front of James and took hold of his wrist, fumbling for his pulse. The door suddenly swung open to admit Ralph Dines, clumping loudly, beaming broadly.

'James, my dear old fellow, you should have said last evening you wanted to have breakfast with me. No need to raise a panic code and make a lot of work for everybody. James, you know Ronnie, Lord Wyford, don't you? He's my right-hand man, or person, as we have to say these days.'

'Of course, I know him. And I know you. I know what you're up to. You kill people, you manipulate, you lie, you twist the truth...'

'Care Home Delusion, stage 1, I'd say, wouldn't you, Ronnie?'

'Just what I told him, Ralph!'

'Dr Zoe will be here in a moment. She'll have a soothing injection for you, I'm sure, calm you down.'

Anger rising as the absurdity of the situation weighed heavily on his chest, he drew breath with difficulty. The room began to spin around him, like last night.

He was vaguely aware that Dr Zoe entered, sat him down on the couch, felt his brow and took his pulse. She gave no injection, but smiled sadly at him.'

'Zoe, how can you be alright? After last night?'

Ralph replied. 'Last night? You must be even worse than we thought, James, old man. I gather you've raised the question, who is in charge? Well, it's like the Midlothian Question, who rules the UK? But rest in peace that I'm in charge and all is well in Sir Thomas More.'

'Dr Zoe, James can lie there for a while. I can see you've not given him a shot to calm him. Why don't you carry out company protocols? Oh well. By the way, James, this might be a good time to give you a heads up that we've had to increase the fees by a tad, a smidgeon, as costs are rising so swiftly. In two month's time, is that alright?'

'It damned well isn't! I'm not staying. Take this as my notice to leave.'

'Increase will be deferred for all residents making a generous bequest to the House in their wills.'

'I said I'm going!'

'I'm afraid we'll need your daughters to set that in motion, but I don't think they'll be happy, do you, now your house is sold.'

'For my sanity and my well-being I'm not staying here, Ralph, so get that into your head.'

'Oh, I do hate the baseness of threats. I don't think when your family receive the latest medical assessment that Dr Frayn will write today about your delusions, they'll want you to cut short your treatment. And if you tell them, I'm sorry to say they will have to be shown the video.'

'What video?'

'The one of you watching through a peephole while a member of staff was beaten up and you doing nothing to stop it. In fact, it looks as if you're enjoying it!' He sat behind his desk, pleased with himself.

'Zoe? Dr Zoe? What the hell is going on here?'

'I'll talk to you later, James. All will be well.' To James she sounded like a robot.

Act Two, Scene 14

James wasn't surprised that his door was locked from the outside after he was escorted back. Presumably they'd bring him food and if there was a fire nearby, someone would rescue him. Or not.

He dozed but dreamed of being a doormat for myriad giant scorpions, any of one of which would sting him if he moved at all. He jerked awake, sweating, looked out of his window and sat in the armchair, determined not to doze again.

When the door was unlocked he knew it was too early for lunch. It was Dr Zoe, looking perfectly normal and no worse for her attack ordeal.

'How are you feeling now, James?'

'I'm fine. How are *you* feeling now, Dr Zoe?'

'I'm fine. Why do you ask in that way?'

'Well, after that beating up I saw...'

'What beating up?'

I saw you through the wall. I was made to watch. He pushed my head against the wall.'

She sat on the bed, facing him, searching his face closely. 'Through the wall?'

'I mean, there was a peep hole drilled through the wall, so I saw what was done to you. It was grotesque.' He described what he saw of the attack. Her expression didn't change as she watched him.

'There was no attack. Look at me. I'm fine. James, I'm not sure how to say this but, was it real? Did you imagine it because you fear it happening to me after what you've seen of Dines and me? Or what you feared would happen to you?'

He considered it. He stood to pour a glass of water from the English sparkling bottle left on his table.

'What do you think, Zoe?'

'I think it's a bit of both. You have fears, you have imaginative delusions.'

'But?'

'But I go along with what Ralph Dines demands of me almost all the time. Just occasionally, it sticks in my gullet, I must rebel. Up to a point. Oh, I can't explain, not really.'

He moved to the ensuite and switched the sink taps on, the bath taps on full, got the shower working and flushed the toilet. He waved her in, and whispered, 'try to explain, please.'

'He has information about my father and his business dealings going back years. He has that over me. He helped me through med school and in return I agreed to work for him. He insisted I did both a straight medical training course and extra hours studying psychology and psychiatry. I like the job, a bit of general practice, lots of mental health work. I sign death certificates.'

'Ah yes, death certificates. So, he planned to have you work here all along?' He stood close to her, holding the door jamb for support so they could whisper.

'I agreed because my father is in such a state, totally enslaved by him, living in trembling fear of being exposed and my mother finding out, he adores her, she looks up to him.'

'Why are you telling me this?'

'Because you remind me of him. The same sort of irrational fears. You touched me, quite unintentionally.' He didn't know what to say.

She went on, 'there was no attack on me. It was all staged to push you closer to the edge. We must do all kinds of horrible things to make patients question their sanity. I often wonder why Dines didn't want me to go to drama college as well.'

'How is this going to end?'

'When somebody exposes him, gets on top of his plans and he stands in the dock. But he's a powerful man. He owns so much, shares in so many businesses and activities. He literally owns people. Me.'

'All enterprises are finally betrayed from within, Zoe. He must have a weak spot?'

'At first I thought he'd want me to perform sex for him and his chosen men, but he has others for that. I'm not his type.' James thought that any woman with two legs and a pair of breasts was Dines' type but didn't say it.

'Let's start to gather evidence. Let's get proper chapter and verse, in writing and find people prepared to testify against him.'

'We'll take him down a peg or two.'

'We'll kill him and dispose of him in the crematorium.'

'All except his head, which we'll bury in the graveyard.'

'And before that we'll roll the lawnmower over him.'

'And we'll make him eat shit because he's so hungry so he knows what it's like for others...'

'And we'll chain him down in the workshops and make a deep cut on his body every day, so gradually he bleeds out with too many cuts to heal properly.'

'And we'll ...' they kept adding extreme tortures and deaths for Ralph Dines, beginning to find them funny in their impossible ridiculousness and soon they were laughing aloud, released from earlier tension.

She reached into the shower, held a few drops of water and flung them at him, laughing at his shocked response.

He grabbed the toothbrush glass, filled it and flung cold water at her. Like kids, they had a great time, forgetting their situation. Giggles became infectious and then the door opened in the bedroom.

They tried to stop the noise, exaggerated 'shh' sounds to each other, holding their mouths to keep in the mirth. It was Lennie Sanders, dressed in a shiny, dark suit, white shirt with well-worn collar and a black tie decorated with some of his breakfast.

Sobered instantly, she left the ensuite, 'Lennie? Should you be in here?'

James followed her, keeping his distance from Sanders, who watched his enemy, but without the madness and killer instinct James had received previously.

Standing stock still in the centre of the floor space, James was poised for a getaway if Sanders suddenly produced a weapon from inside his jacket. Zoe stood by the door, ready to get out and raise the alarm, if necessary.

But Lennie Sanders was a broken man. 'You will not know this, Ellington, but today is the anniversary of the day my world collapsed. Thirty two years today, my darling little girl, Ellen, was murdered by that bastard Tommy Cross, and you helped him!'

'We've been through all this and I thought we'd moved past it.'

'Did you? When I wake up every day and realise my daughter is gone and you think we're past it? I will never be past it, Ellington, never.'

'I agreed to pay...'

'You think it's about money? You're a shallow man, you really are. This is about blood being thicker than water, deeper than money.' His lip curled in contempt as he looked James up and down.

'Listen, Lennie, the man came to my surgery. You know this. I did not know about your daughter. How could I? Hell, you and I hadn't met till I was elected so I knew nothing of your family! When he came to ask for some assistance as he'd almost served his time, I did what any MP would do. I helped.'

'Served his time. My time is a literal life sentence.'

'Yes, I get that, but I was only...'

'What doing your job? Don't give me that shite.'

'I was doing my job as an MP. How could I think there'd be a connection with a fellow MP who'd never mentioned to me that his late daughter had been murdered in my constituency years before I was elected?'

'Just doing your job? The excuse of the Nazis after the war. I was just carrying out orders. Just running the death camps. Now can we move on? No, we can't. Ever.'

Act Two, Scene 15

It had been a filthy day of endless drizzle, heavy dark skies and a chill. Towards the end of the afternoon, it dried, the sun came out, the breeze dropped. It was pleasant enough for James to take his stroll, avoiding those 'walking' on their mobility scooters.

Dines found him by the woods, talking quietly to himself. 'Ah, there you are!'

'I've told you before, I'm not lost.'

'I thought you were asking yourself the way because you were lost!'

Dines pointed at a bench, still wet but nicely out of sight of the main house. James sat beside him, immediately feeling the wet on his trousers, looking for the cameras and microphones that had to be there.

Dines parked his stick between them, resting on the bench; James kept a tight hold of his. 'James, when are you next due to have a drive out with your delightful granddaughter, Maisie?'

'I don't know. Why?'

'I need you to do a little job for me.' He waited, but James said nothing. 'Get Maisie to drive you to Broadland one morning soon, say you want to visit an old friend who's fallen on hard times. I will give you the address and timings, of course.'

'Haven't you got enough errand boys on the payroll?'

'This is special work, needs your sensitivity. Make sure Maisie stays sitting in the car, you'll only be ten minutes, tops.'

'Are you asking me or telling me?'

'I was going to ask Lennie to do it, but he's not reliable in the mouth-shut department. Timmy Greenwood is... well, you know. A woman wouldn't look right. Catchpole would get distracted. Kenny Sloan has too big an axe to grind. Douglas has enough to worry about this week having been caught on an internet porn site. Gerry wouldn't understand his instructions. You get the drift.'

'So, that's why me? What makes you think I'll jump to it?'

'Because, my dear fellow, I was browsing through my copy of the Whip's Black Book...'

'The book that doesn't exist?'

'It never has. But it reminded me of the peccadilloes that so many of our former colleagues thought they were keeping to themselves! For instance,' he unfolded a wad of scribbled notes from his pocket, 'there was the man who had his wallet stolen from the red light district in Ipswich and came up with some fantastic tale...'

'That certainly wasn't me. I never...'

'I didn't say it was you! The police file says who it is. The reports from roadside cameras have placed this man at several red lights in London, Soho, Streatham, Whitechapel, Paddington, Kings Cross...'

'Why are you accusing me?'

'I'm not. The man claimed it was those false plates

someone put on his car. Anyway, that was then. More recently we have accounts from Tide Investments, where money certainly flows in and out! We have an assassination on the A12, in a lay-by off the road and reports of body disposals at the old tip...am I ringing any bells?'

'This is outrageous! I've done nothing wrong, despite what you claim...'

'Memory is a funny thing. We can forget what we want, James. That's why reports, files, photos, videos are so useful.'

'You sound like the bloody East German Stasi.'

'Ah yes. Think what they could have achieved if the digital era had come earlier!' he said, wistfully.

'Anyway, I must go. A small gift-wrapped package will be in your room tonight. It's for the man you are to visit. Leave it with him after you have explained that while there is no honour among thieves, he can do the honourable thing.'

James stared hard at Dines. 'What's the gift?'

'A handgun and one bullet. Don't open it, don't touch it, don't accept a drink or anything. Just in and out. The gift is from me, tell him. He'll understand. His family will be safe.'

'You want him to shoot himself?'

'It will solve several problems. The parcel will carry fingerprints from someone who's already dead. Pretend to Maisie you got some mild skin infection on your hands and Dr Zoe has prescribed not exposing them to the air for a week so you must wear gloves.'

If he'd heard it correctly, if he'd understood it, Dines was inviting him to contribute to an illegal act. At last, proof he could use. He couldn't wait to be alone to record it in his diary.

With a cheery, 'I'm obliged to you, James,' Dines clumped off, looking around warily. Taking out his diary, James scribbled the gist of what had just occurred. If he could find what he knew would be a recording of that conversation before Dines deleted it, he'd be on solid ground to go to the cops.

It was getting dark, but he decided he'd put the diary in his locker, just for a bit. Of course, they could open it and look, but if he put it there for a day, then in his bedroom for a day, then ask Dr Zoe to look after it for a day, he'd keep it safe.

He clumped over to the warehouse where everyone's precious papers and memories were stored. He slipped once on a modest mound of leaves that was invisible in the gloom, but pressed on.

As he reached the Archives building, security lamps flashed on to light his way. A Karl watched him silently from the far end of the building. Another appeared to open the double doors for him.

'Evening, Karl.'

'It *is* evening, Mr Ellington, I can confirm that.' Then the man reached into his overalls to produce a phone on which he texted a message before closing the doors behind James.

Inside was warm, oppressively so. Probably just the contrast with the chill of gathering night outside. Knowing the whole place bristled with cameras, he still looked around furtively.

Pulling a key from the chain round his neck, he opened the key console, retrieved his actual key, pressed in his passcode on the door before inserting the key and turning the handle in an anticlockwise, counter-intuitive way.

His private, personal storage area was completely empty! Not a box left, not a file, not any evidence of his years in the House and his career before and since. He no longer existed.

Leaning against the plain, smooth walls, he stood a moment gulping in air and trying to process what he saw. If his records were gone, he definitely had ceased to exist.

From a short distance outside his area, he heard a baying sound, like a lunatic howling at the moon. It was joined by others in varying distances from it. He stepped out of the area, fearing that if he was locked inside, he'd never be seen again.

Footsteps, magnified on metal staircases and corridors ran towards him. There was maniacal laughter, some hysterical screaming, he pressed himself to the wall, legs apart to stand as firmly as he could and gripped the stick to use as a weapon.

The noises never got any closer, so he slid carefully along the wall to the end of the row. In what served as a foyer with several staircases leading up to mezzanine and higher floors, he'd burst into some kind of damned play. Or among literal, hellish demons. It was a site-specific theatre piece of demented vileness; it was a carnival of the resurrected from somebody's nightmare.

He recognised Timmy Greenwood, dressed as jester, conducting all the players like instruments. Dames Winnie Carswood and Henrietta Bolsome were being hoisted into a harness which lifted them up, swinging dangerously.

Three Imeldas, two Karls, two Matrons, Ronnie Wyford, Douglas Gardener and Ronald Hasbery danced past, wearing carnival or Commedia dell'Arte full masks, yet he knew who they were. Lady Helen Fulcher uncoiled a rope which she used to whip Kenny Sloan and Gerry Manders who seemed to be enjoying themselves.

Lenny Sanders kept putting the rope round his neck and jumping off stools over and over. Looking closer he realised that it was actually he on the stool and Sanders was tying the rope end to a wall hook.

When he spoke, James was under putrid mud, his hands clawing at the landslide, trying to get out. But they all spoke above him, over him, across him, each one with a needle in the centre of his or her forehead.

They knew who he was; they laughed at him, yet he couldn't communicate. And the word, the only word was 'hated' which came to mind and he knew with an illogical certainty that everyone hated him. Perhaps the gun he was to deliver to Dines' old friend was actually for him?

With a crashing, raucous metallic explosion, the freaks vanished. He was standing in his private area, looking for a box in which to hide his diary. Safe, safe among his other valuables now back in the bay, just where and how he'd supervised their placing when he'd arrived at the asylum.

Act Two, Scene 16

For candidates and their troops, paid and voluntary, General Election campaigns follow a certain set of traditional patterns. Late afternoons and early evenings are out for door-knocking as that's teatime and TV news time. Big mass popular television programmes are also avoided.

Some years new technological developments are born, such as wider use of social media. There are also societal changes – many people won't open their doors late evening, or even at all as soon as word spreads of electioneering in the neighbourhood.

Loud-hailing from a loaned vehicle, walking through shopping areas, buying little things in shops being careful not to be accused of bribery, meetings with voters, making a handful of speeches, fabricating photo opportunities and following national news closely for local angles and the party machine on the day of helpers, drivers and tellers – all are common in every election.

But there are different perspectives. James had experienced all three.

The first and preferred option is when things go so well one's opponents are in such disarray that they know the game is up before it finishes. This was James' first standing, where he was generally well received on doorsteps and in meetings and walked with a confident air about him, even using a stick.

The second is when the outcome is touch and go, the media and one's own team start to call it for the other side. For James in his second campaign many of his people got cold feet, everyone thought he was out but didn't say so.

When Prime Minister John Major got out his soapbox and appealed to the crowds he surprised everyone with a convincing win, carrying James in with him. Then, of course, all the helpers and supporters knew all along that James was going to defy the odds.

James found the third type on his third appeal to the electorate. The soapbox, warnings about the imminent Armageddon that the opposition would unleash and the successes from the record were all beach sand during a surge tide. The party was wiped out, James with them, stick and all.

The final campaign was an absence of helpers, embarrassed shuffles on doorsteps, nobody engaging him in the eye. Stilted, awkward conversations. People knew he'd soon be yesterday's man. And when it was all over and his triumphant opponent strutted his stuff, James became invisible except to a few family and friends.

He felt bereavement, as if someone had died; well, someone had. James had died. He'd so longed to be the MP after working so hard to make it and keep it. Then it was gone. You live by the ballot box; you die by it.

Voters had spoken. He didn't blame them; he pointed the finger at his government and leaders who had made such a hash of the issues he cared about for his constituency. But as he was invisible, his pointing finger went unseen.

He had been the job; the job was him. So, when it was stripped out of him, he took a very long time to recover and move on in any meaningful way.

Escaping from the deserted Archives building as rapidly as he could, he stumbled several times before finding a spot in the gardens to crouch against a wall and collect his thoughts. That period had been the second lowest point of his life.

Shaking, chilled to the bone, he turned the crouch into a sit down on the cold, damp soil. His knuckles clung to his stick – it was a reflex action he'd learned ever since he acquired it, to ensure he always had to hand a means of getting up and/or fighting off attackers.

'Elspeth, it was not credible, a horror circus, really, I don't know now what was real and what I was meant to feel. It was a set up. What're they doing to me? Elspeth, can you see? Can you help?'

Elspeth made no reply, of course.

'What was it all for, all those years? It's come to this, cold, afraid and in real danger. Hiding in a garden. A fugitive. Did I sacrifice family time for this? Did I give my all to help people and make a difference in Westminster and here? You know I did. But now it counts for nothing. Elspeth?'

Still Elspeth made no response.

'I've really hurt my ankle and my knee again. Need to see Dr Zoe. Yes, now. Dr Zoe, did you see that? You said you help them do things that fool people? Are you part of the evil that's going on here? Are you making me crazy?'

Dr Zoe made no reply.

'I don't know if I can make you understand, Zoe. When I was first elected to the district council, I took my seat round the central table. It felt so good, so right. But when I first sat on those green benches in Westminster, I knew I'd come home to where I truly belonged.'

'You remember that, Rebecca, Samantha. I told you. I'm so sorry that it mattered so much to me, not that you didn't matter, but I told myself I was doing it to give us all a good life style with a sense of achievement.'

Neither Rebecca nor Samantha replied.

He shook his head to clear it. It was the wall! Realising he'd been talking to a wall, he struggled up, felt an overpowering need to pee so stood precariously one hand against the wall and relieved himself.

James returned to his room, avoiding dining room noises on the way. Everyone was enjoying dinner and drinks afterwards. In the lounge, there was a game of bridge and a round of Scrabble between two old folks who could neither spell nor grasp the rules. Two nurses were preparing the medicine round which usually went through the chosen inmates ahead of cocoa or hot milk.

It was a joy to put his head down on the pillows. The sheets had been changed that morning, so he slipped away, slightly amused that he'd been talking to a wall. Was he really losing it?

The next time he opened eyes, after what felt like ten minutes, it was to blue flashing lights, as three police cars and an ambulance pulled up outside the house. He blinked, stretched his left arm which had gone numb, felt the sore spot on his face where he scraped against the wall as he dozed off.

Convinced he'd gone back to the house, it was now plain that he hadn't. Why hadn't Elspeth, Zoe, Samantha or Rebecca warned him?

Feeling an overpowering need to pee, he stood precariously one hand against the wall and relieved himself. Surely he'd just done that?

He walked closer to the house to find about a dozen inmates frantically dashing about in circles, flapping, in a tizzy. Dame Henrietta Bolsome braked her wheelchair in front of him, 'Oh James, Dr Zoe is dead!'

His first thought was that this was another display of theatricals laid on by Ralph Dines, Esquire, for his and others' entertainment. But there was genuine weeping and wailing and real terror from several people not normally given to histrionics.

Could she really be dead? And by the hand of which of these sick people?

Protesting loudly, Sebastian Catchpole was being led by two youngsters dressed as police officers. Timmy Greenwood treated everyone to a verse or two of, 'Oh fie is me, oh fie is you!' in a tune he recognised in his brain.

Lennie Sanders made a run for it to the rhododendron bushes but was rugby tackled from behind by an actor dressed as a policewoman. Wyford and Dines were nowhere to be seen while the handful of pretend officers assisted by five Karls did their best to herd cats, get everyone else inside.

James was caught up and led to the house and told to go to his room and await further instructions.

'Is it true that Dr Zoe is dead?' James demanded.

'I'm not at liberty to say, sir. Now if you'd just step inside and go to your room, thank you.'

'It's a simple enough question!'

'And my reply was simple enough.' The man fidgeted with a pair of handcuffs dangling from his belt. James complied.

On his way indoors, passing several fellow inmates he was offered instant suggestions about what had happened. She was dead, she was half alive, she'd committed suicide by hanging, poison or jumping off the roof; she'd been taken away in a strait jacket or it wasn't her at all, but Timmy Greenwood or Sir Michael Michaelson who'd gone berserk.

Legion were the rumours, the gossip; few had been caught up in such excitement for decades. Perhaps as far back as their first election wins. Nobody knew any actual facts; those that did were saying nothing.

James looked down from his bedroom window, watching as residents who'd been persuaded indoors were emerging outside again. Bedlam. Chaos.

If this was a staged event, the management had really pulled out all the stops this morning. But why? What was to be achieved?

Was Zoe really hurt this time or playing dead somewhere?

And what about lunch? At this rate nobody would be able to go down for food and he'd missed his breakfast as it was.

Would there be a panic soon that James Ellington had perished from starvation?

Act Two, Scene 17

The police, if police they were, made a slow and somewhat ham-fisted job of conducting their interviews of the inmates. At least, that was James' view of proceedings.

During a couple of forced hours of room confinement, he received only a coffee and a little china plate of homemade wheat biscuits so hard they had to be dunked to get over his dental plates to substitute for his missed breakfast.

He bathed and put on clean clothes and kept returning to the window, but apart from one sighting of Douglas Gardener being led back indoors by a young policewoman he'd been trying to chat up, he saw nothing.

And opening his surprisingly unlocked door to the corridor produced no unusual or different sounds to inform him of what was going on.

What worried away at his mind were the ideas of unintended consequences, chain reactions and butterfly effects. It was a matter that frequently topped his daily worry list.

He was certain that after he and Zoe'd talked in the garden last night, she was fine, even if he wasn't. She must have returned indoors, her mind full of the problems he was engulfed by, and been attacked in the corridor. Or had a bag pulled over her head when she confronted Dines and she was murdered on his office floor on a sheet of clear plastic.

Or she was taken by the hoods in their white van. No, there must be a body or they wouldn't know she was dead. Or was she dead? Was it all part of the extravagant games that seemed to be absorbing Dines more and more?

Questions, questions; no answers.

While he was in the throes of talking to himself, Dines crept in, startling James who jumped to Dines' great amusement.

'Ah, my dear fellow. Here you are all cooped up in your room and wondering about your meals, I dare say. Especially as you missed your breakfast, they tell me.'

Dines knew that much. Must have been looking at the CCTV monitors.

'Now listen, old chap, sorry about the little bit of unexpected kerfuffle this morning. Poor Dr Frayn, hey, who'd have thought it?'

'What's supposed to have happened to her?'

'My lips are sealed, old chap. Not my story to tell. And that's not important.'

'Not important? What about Zoe?'

'What's important, James, is that you get your story straight. They're going to be interviewing you after lunch, I believe. They'll find it very suspicious if you appear to be clueless, as usual.'

'What am I supposed to know? What story is straight?'

'Well, that you were the last person to see Zoe alive, last night, that's all!'

'But I wasn't. If she was really there, she left me and went indoors. If she wasn't real, then I didn't see her anyway.'

'Blimey riley, James, old fellow, you're in a bad way.'

'No, you are. I know that attack on her through the peephole was entirely fiction. So, therefore, it's no stretch of the imagination to say that her death is as well. Why on earth, what the hell you are playing at, it's an entirely different matter. And there we have it, m'lud, I'm at a loss to offer any explanation.'

Dines shook his head sadly. 'James, James, delusions are gripping you. Come back to the real world, even if it's to say goodbye. I can't bear to see you so far gone already.'

'I'm reporting that thug who beat her up, when the police talk to me.'

'I told you already, there was no thug who beat her up.' The door opened to reveal an Imelda, who apologised for interrupting and said that lunch was served in the cafeteria today, and only there. Dines thanked her as she bowed out.

'And if there was any such thug beating anybody up, then he needs to be left alone as he has important work for me, very important.'

'Just like taking a gun to someone?'

'You need to get on with that, James. And yes, a job like that. But my preference is for there to have been no thug, no beating up and no you telling them anything of any value. Shall we?'

He indicated the door and escorted James downstairs

to the cafeteria, their walking sticks just out of unison.

On the way, he said, 'you know, James old soldier, there are many here as you know who have flung wide the door to the twilight zone and rushed straight in, never to be seen again. You, I have to say, have opened the door but so far have only put a curled toe or strange foot in. Come back before it's too late.'

'You know, Ralph, I beg you to get some help before it's too late and you've dragged us all into madness with you.'

The men smiled at each other but said nothing more.

Lunch was a hurried affair, with several residents still quite anxious and confused. Some it transpired had asked the police to take somebody or other away or investigate the sighting of rats in the dining room. Those who seemed to be the most rational were the most suspicious.

Timmy Greenwood topped the list of nutters they were compiling, and as each interview took longer than planned, they talked to people while they ate – soup and sandwiches or jacket potatoes with baked beans. That was it. One officer had to help some poor old sod feed herself or it would have been all over both of them.

It was a regular visiting afternoon. Families began to arrive. The weather was fresh, chilly but dry and better than being imprisoned indoors. Many residents engaged with their precious ones outdoors.

As he walked outside to wait for his own darlings to arrive, he overheard snippets about the death of the doctor, each account different with a tendency to exaggerate the only common feature, her demise.

He realised that while visiting families sympathised and

made the right sounds, none offered to get their loved ones the hell out of the place. He waved to Samantha, Henry and William making their way towards him, his daughter eyeing up a free bench to commandeer.

One of the pretend police officers suddenly stepped into James' path, almost knocking him over. 'Mr Ellington? We're ready for you now, if you'd be so good as to step this way.'

'But my family have just arrived!'

'It won't take long. They can wait a minute. We've just a few questions.' Samantha nodded her understanding and made for the free bench.

Middle-aged with that world weary seen-it-all-before air that some people have, she stood about a foot shorter than James with more width but a strength that would deter most people from crossing her willingly. She led him into a small office off the main foyer, with the entrance cage in full view and invited him to sit.

She'd already piled a stack of files – the people she'd talked to. His was a fat one, directly in front of her. As she flipped through, he spotted photos, press cuttings and intelligence reports from his public life and his record at Sir Thomas More.

This he couldn't fathom upside down and in dense typing, but clearly there was a deal of information about him they'd logged and now shared with the 'police.'

'Confirm your name, please.'

'James Ellington.'

'When did you last see Dr Zoe Frayn?'

'Last night in the garden. That is, I was talking to her, but I know she wasn't there, so I only saw her in my mind. What you really need to focus on, if I may so, is Ralph Dines and his functionaries here who are systematically coercing people into leaving bequests in their wills before being bumped off.'

The officer watched him closely. 'I am alert to it and I shared it with Dr Zoe. She seemed to understand how I'm rather alone here. But I'm determined to do my level best to make sure Dines doesn't get away with it.'

She scribbled notes on a pad.

Encouraged, he went on, 'you need to dredge the pool and ponds, check the ash in the crematorium, dig up the internments, forensically examine all the accounts and you may know about the old toxic tip on the A12? Get a squad in there to dig down. God knows what white vans and bodies you'll find in there...'

James drew breath to continue to tell her all he knew. It came out a bit rushed and garbled. As she wrote she kept looking up at him, peering closely through her glasses. He pressed on, 'you need to look up when I went to visit that prison, the Tommy Cross case, murdered his wife, Lennie Sanders' daughter and I get the blame, and there was the father of the offshore worker who died tragically, I'm being blamed there as well. Oh, it's good to explain all this at last. They want you to think I'm mad. They want me to think I'm mad so I am putty in their hands.'

Saying nothing, she fished through a small, separate pile of paper at her side. He wasn't going to give up now. 'They lay on elaborate charades of things happening, beatings and murders and then deny it.'

She found what she was looking for, and added to

what was already a substantial list of names and comments:

'James Ellington, confused, possibly delusional, unreliable witness.'

He read it from across the table and realised that it was actually quite unhelpful to him. If she thought he was unreliable and confused, how would she take what he said seriously?

'What did Dr Zoe die from, Mr Ellington?' she asked.

'Old age. She's not dead, is she?'

'Thank you, Mr Ellington, you've been very helpful. Don't go far away; we may want to talk again.'

Act Two, Scene 18

James waited for Maisie in the foyer. He'd neither asked permission nor told anyone where he was headed. The gun in its gift box was tucked inside his coat, held in place by a gloved hand in his pocket.

He was in what was called Obit Corner, where a large area of spot-lit wall was covered in press clippings, tributes and funeral booklets. Here, news of the demise of any former colleague anywhere in the country was posted.

The material stayed up for a month after which he'd been told it was stored in the Archives. Where else?

It was a popular little facility. He had only so far read of the sending off of a couple of people he knew, though he recognised the names of a handful who'd been there well before his time.

The little shelf below the display carried seven pairs of spectacles and a single arm off a pair, left and forgotten by residents. They served as a free library, just like the teeth, so residents could help themselves whenever they realised they'd lost their own.

James stood reading, listening carefully to what was going on behind him, aware that he could be tackled from behind and squashed into a bin and wheeled out for disposal.

He heard Dines in affable form leading out the alleged

police officers, who seemed to have finished their enquiries into the murder/suicide/accident/high dramatic disappearance of poor Dr Zoe.

Imagining that Wyford would be in tow but that others might have tagged along, he was astonished to hear Dines quote, 'am I so short of madmen that you have to bring this fellow here to carry on like this?'

'You can never have too many madmen, hey Mr Dines?' asked the senior officer, fully in tune with the place, evidently.

'From the Bible. *1 Samuel 21*, if I'm not mistaken, and I rarely am.' Dines had only occasionally sounded more smugly satisfied with himself. James was absolutely gobsmacked to hear Timmy Greenwood chip in with a quote of his own.

'I am but mad north-north-west. When the wind is southerly, I know a hawk from a handsaw.' James swung round to look; he caught the officer nodding politely. 'The question is which is the more insane, Hamlet or Ophelia? She appears to be genuine while he feigns his lunacy.'

'My dear Timmy,' Catchpole shouted putting an arm round his shoulder as he joined the party. 'I think Dr Zoe should take a look at you. You seem to have had a moment of lucidity! Oh no, we can't. Poor Dr Zoe is no longer here.' And he roared an entirely inappropriate belly laugh.

James recalled yet another funeral they'd attended of an old man who'd been crushed by a cement mixer on the A47 and had been a stalwart in both their constituencies equally. Sebby had tried to chat up the young girl assisting the undertakers' smooth running of the occasion and had told her a joke.

He'd roared at it; she'd looked uncomfortable, while the congregation were openly appalled. James had curled up, embarrassed and annoyed. Sebby never even noticed, he was enjoying himself, sad occasion or not.

With that, Dines chivvied the visitors out before the entire stock of residents turned up to say something stupid. An Imelda opened the door without any expression on her bland face. The police trooped out, shaking Dines by the hand, rather deferentially, James thought.

'Ah James, old stick, loitering in the Obits are you? Hopefully you won't be pinned up there just yet.'

'Not till you've made a bequest in your will,' roared Wyford before he got a glance from his boss.

Dines raised an eyebrow. 'Going out are we, James?

'Well, I don't know about you, but I'm going for a drive with my granddaughter and he patted his coat with his hand still clutching his stick.

'Of course, of course, enjoy yourselves,' Dines smiled, noticing the gloves James was wearing.

He exited through the cage and front door and waited for Maisie outside, glad of the fresh air. The short wait gave him time to process what he'd just seen and heard.

Nobody was taking Zoe's death seriously enough for it to be real, Timmy speaking coherently if briefly and Wyford being upfront about the bequest they were anxious for him to leave.

He watched her drive his car in, scattering gravel, at a speed that was not approved of with just a twinge of regret that he was no longer allowed to get behind the wheel and take himself wherever and whenever he wanted to go.

'Hi Grandpa!'

He climbed in, placed the gift on his knee and belted up. 'Hello, Maisie. You just missed all the excitement.'

'What in Sir Thomas More House? Somebody healed? Somebody remembered something that happened yesterday? Somebody got younger?'

'Somebody got murdered.'

'What? Why wasn't it all over the news this morning?'

'Because it wasn't real. It was a pantomime they laid on for some reason to terrify everyone into submission. I bet tomorrow that Dr Zoe reappears as if nothing had happened. Most people here wouldn't remember she was supposed to be dead.'

'Dr Zoe? But you like her, you get on with her!'

'Yes, but she has to dance to Ralph Dines' tunes, so I must be careful.'

'Where are we going, by the way, Grandpa?' They were already out of the grounds and well on the way towards the town. 'Are you really cold enough for gloves? I'll put the heater up if so.'

'No, I'm fine. No need to fuss. You sound like your mother. He unfolded a typed slip of paper from his pocket and gave her the address. 'Do you want to put it in the satnav?'

'Nah, you're my satnav. You want to take that present to someone?'

'Yes, an old friend. One that you don't know. One that hasn't been forced to live at Sir Thomas More. One who is not expected to live long.'

'Oh dear, I'm sorry to hear that. What did you get him?' She nodded at the package.

'A gun, so he can shoot himself and save everybody a lot of trouble.'

She laughed. 'And how did you get a gun?'

'Dines gave it to me. It's clean. You and I were never here. I imagine this one will hit the news eventually, so when it does, remember that I was forced to play a part. The game is very serious now.'

She said nothing further while concentrating on going the long way round to a village three miles north of the town at his directions. Their destination was a semi-detached cottage, small but comfortable with ivy up the walls hiding the cracked plaster decorating the walls. An ideal retirement home, so much nicer than a bloody great care home full of lunatics, fantasists and murderers.

'Do you want me to come in with you, Grandpa?' she asked, turning off the engine and apparently being entirely unrepentant about a shocking piece of non-parallel parking.

'No, Maisie, better you don't. Keep the engine running for a quick getaway. Don't make eye contact with any neighbours.' She nodded with a smile, playing along.

Her grandfather limped up the short path, careful on the cracked and misaligned flagstones. He rapped on the door, glancing behind to check that Maisie was still in the car and nobody seemed to be about.

A very bent, small man with eyes that saw little detail peered at him. The man gripped the door jamb and drew breath with rasping difficulty. 'Hello, Tiger Smith, happy birthday, our old friend Ralph Dines suggested I bring you a little present.'

Maisie heard that much and watched him enter the house, but didn't realise that Tiger Smith had no clue as to who he was. He may have been a 'tiger' in his youth; now he was a poor shadow of humanity who'd lived way beyond his time.

An ancient golden retriever looked up at James from the hearth where no fire burned. James felt the chill of decay.

Little sunshine made it through the small grubby windows against which hung curtains so dusty their original colour was impossible to guess.

The dog put its head down again and ignored the two men. 'This is my dog, my best friend, he's getting on. Like me. You're not Ralph Dines!' The light had dawned.

'No, I'm a friend of his, from Sir Thomas More House.'

'What?'

'Mr Dines says you will know what to do with his gift and it'll be better for everybody. Well, for Ralph Dines. You have lived too long, I see.'

'Lived too long? Aye, he has that,' the tiny man nodded sadly. James pictured Ralph Dines who had lived too long. 'Will you take a glass with me?'

'Ah very kind, but I don't drink alcohol.' He could have added not in a dirty glass, not in what was probably a rat-infested junk shop masquerading as a home.

'What?'

'No matter, I must go now. Dines says you'll know what to do with his gift.'

'Oh I expect so.' He stood looking puzzled and as James moved to the door the old man bent to look at the package closely. James left, bid a loud farewell and safe journey to the next world into the room and closed the door carefully.

He'd got some way down the path, Maisie at the wheel but absorbed by her phone when he heard a gun shot from the house. It paused him a moment. Maisie hadn't noticed. Blimey, James hadn't expected that the old man would know what to do and carry it out so swiftly.

'Let's go,' cried James, climbing in, buckling up, breathing heavily.

'Did he like the present?'

'He loved it.'

'Grandpa, you're more than an errand boy,' Maisie said as she drove away and back towards the home. 'I'm thinking that we should get you out for a time, so you can settle your thoughts a bit and not be so dark all the time.'

He didn't respond as he took his gloves off and shoved them into his pocket. He imagined being squashed into a massive clear plastic sack by the A12 men and pushed the imaginary bag out of his face.

'You can stay with us or go to Essex for a few days. I'll argue the case with Mum and Aunty Rebecca. What do you say?'

'I'd have jumped at that a few weeks ago. But now I have a mission. I'm going to confront my demons, my enemies in that place. And when I have brought about a new regime, I'll decide what to do. Perhaps I might run the place myself!'

She nodded, surprised he'd turned down her offer to wangle a few days away. They said no more. He pictured the old man and his brains on the floor by the hearth.

Then he wondered what would happen to the poor old dog.

He needn't have troubled. Inside the cottage, the old man was sat in his armchair by the hearth holding the gun; the dog lay still, a bullet hole in its head.

Act Three, Scene 1

When the rearranged annual speech contest finally arrived, all the attention it usually received was diluted by news of Dame Winnie Carswood's illness which was the over-riding talk of the place.

Members crowded in, those coming via the entrance foyer noting that a large group of what were clearly relatives was being held back by the cage and offered cups of tea.

Anybody who knew what was actually wrong with her was saying nothing. Ralph Dines announced it from the Speaker's Chair and lamented the fact that they'd be without her always brilliant, lucid, perceptive and witty contribution. Members already in their places on the green benches set off a round of bleating, murmuring. 'ere-'ere' sounds to support Dines' statement.

He continued, basking in the moment to inform them that he'd arranged for a solicitor, a priest and a handful of her family to attend, in that order. Amidst a second round of approval noises, Catchpole whispered to James, 'that's it then, James; she'll be gone by morning. If the solicitor was brought in, it's to change her will to leave a bequest...'

Old Sebby Catchpole was not as crazy as he behaved. Of course, he was right. James wondered if they'd postpone the event yet again out of respect for Winnie, who'd not only been in Sir Thomas More since the start but was a well-respected former MP across all sides.

'I believe that out of respect for Dame Winnie, we should set to and make the most of our annual speech contest. She'd expect nothing less of us. So, I call upon our first speaker, the much-loved and widely respected Lord Ronnie Wyford.'

Amid supportive bleats from most of his audience, old Wyford used the table in front to haul himself upright, supported his bulk on his elbows on the Dispatch Box and launched into what would have been an excellent oration for her funeral.

She was a doer, a mover and shaker, only interested in solutions not problems. If someone dared to voice any doubts or have pettifogging questions, she didn't hear them. She just repeated what she'd last said and waited for them to jump to it. She'd have made a fine minister, but had never been offered a post.

Wyford then slipped seamlessly into the actual speech he'd drawn – 'Democracy as a model in a post-democratic world.' Of course, Wyford knew little about the topic and so delivered bits of his greatest speeches just to allow everyone to appreciate his deep voice, finely polished by nicotine over decades.

'I reckon she's gone already. That was definitely a funeral tribute.' James nodded agreement to Catchpole. He was getting nervous. He always used to in days in Parliament. Never an easy place to hold, that rectangular chamber, with the bright lights, the heckling and interruptions and the unpredictability of the Speaker's patience and temper.

As Wyford dropped back into his place amidst a further flurry of crowd bleating, James was called to speak as 'our newest Member to the Sir Thomas More community to speak from his heart, if he can find it.'

All the predictable ingredients were baked into his speech – some humour, some serious policy proposals, some changes in pitch and tempo, some courtesies as he gave way to others who wanted to ask him something. It was average.

As he sat down, having warmed and enjoyed himself as it progressed, Dines stood.' The Honourable Gentleman may be new to our community, but he will know that in the annual speech contest, there are rules. And one such rule is that the speech on the topic drawn from the bag shall be no more than six minutes and no less than five minutes. The Honourable Gentleman spoke for 59 seconds less than the minimum. He will oblige the House by supplying a further 59 seconds.'

In the real Parliamentary world if a Member had spoken less than expected or allowed, everyone would have rejoiced. But not Ralph Dines. He beckoned James to stand and sat himself so James could stand, as no one could stand if the Speaker was.

'Mr Speaker, I do apologise to you and the House if I fell short of the minimum.'

Dines stood. 'You did fall short. I timed you.' He sat.

James stood. 'My apologies, Mr Speaker. I shall pick up a point I made earlier, then.' He sat at Dine's gesture.

Dines stood. 'The Honourable Member will not try the patience of the House by repeating earlier points.' He sat.

By this time, with the unpleasantness in Dines' voice, the embarrassment in James and the bobbing up and down to reply to the Speaker, James felt weary. It was a little dizziness, in fact.

'Mr Speaker, we know that in some parts of the United Kingdom there are people who...'

And like all good politicos James invented stuff to fill the now missing 29 seconds before he was waved down again by Dines.

'The Honourable Gentleman has now spoken for the required length. It is for the House to judge the merits, if any, of what he had to say.'

'Point of Order, Mr Speaker.' James, stood, annoyed enough to risk making a further fool of himself.

'Order, order. There can be no point of order on what I have just said from the chair. The Honourable Member will not seek to raise any spurious points of order in order to prolong the time the House must listen to his voice.'

James made to stand, determined to do whatever it took to reduce Dines to size. But his jacket was pulled by Sebby Catchpole, 'let it go, James. He's in one of his moods. You don't want to be Named and excluded.'

James didn't need that ultimate humiliation. There must be another way of dealing with Ralph Dines. He'd spend the next few speeches thinking it over, yet again.

Then he thought he'd slip out and ask how Winnie Carswood was getting on. He was fond of her. She'd often dropped pearls of wisdom in his lap when he shared some constituency difficulties with her, particularly when he was first in the House.

After an hour of Members boring for Britain with the evening stretching pointlessly ahead, James recalled he'd been told the whole thing rarely finished before 2am, and occasionally had gone all night in fond memory of the days of all-night sittings of the House where unpaired minor MPs had to sit there or doze in the library or prop up one of many bars till daylight came and the actual next day's business was wiped out.

Hollow-eyed staff were expected to work on, serving in Members' Tea Room and the bars or patrol the grounds. If it finished in the small hours rather than mid-morning the House laid on taxis to take staff to their homes. Of course, James knew that if these staff were mainly robots, they'd be fine.

But *he* wouldn't be. He needed his sleep. If he slept in the Chamber, Dines would call him to order. The only other appealing place to doze was his actual bedroom. He whispered to Sebby Catchpole his intention of calling it a night, when suddenly there was a disturbance at the doors.

Everyone looked. Douglas Gardener's tongue froze and his mouth fell open. He'd lost his brilliant train of thought now. One of the security guards, a robot dressed as a House usher, tried to hold back some intruders.

It was the bunch of actors who'd been there after Dr Zoe's apparent death. The senior officer stood in the space between the facing rows of benches, bowed his head at the Speaker. 'I apologise, sir, but I'm afraid we have an arrest to make. It will not wait.'

Dines stood to his full height, pulled his formal gown around him better, and said through lips that were visibly quivering with simulated anger, 'this is an outrage. What, are you the King's minions sent in to arrest an Honourable Member in this sacred chamber?'

Sir Ronald Hasbery, in his place at the lawyer's table leaned back to hiss at Dines. 'This is a replica House; we cannot impede the lawful execution of law by officers of the law, Ralph.'

Dines slumped down, but his face was the full red and his look was dangerously like a murderer.

'Brilliant acting, he should get an Oscar for this,' James murmured to Catchpole.

''Yes, but let's see who's to be arrested. That might be even better!'

Clearing his throat, the officer stepped closer to Lord Wyford, 'Lord Ronald Percy Wyford, I am arresting you on suspicion of financial fraud, attempted bribery and falsifying accounts. You do not have to say anything, but it may harm your defence if you do not mention when questioned something that you later rely on in Court. Anything you do say may be given in evidence. Do you understand?'

In what was more like a supporting actor role to Dines' full Oscar performance, Wyford nodded, shell-shocked, allowing himself to be handcuffed and led outside.

The Chamber erupted in more than murmurings. Here was high entertainment. A messenger whispered in Hasbery's ear and he in turn bent round and told Dines something.

The mighty Speaker rose to his feet and called for order. Several times. When he'd got the attention of most, he announced. 'I am informed that the company solicitor has completed the meeting with Dame Winnie, and is now available to assist Lord Wyford in his hour of trial.'

Amidst yet more of the rent-a-mob approval chorus, Dines adjourned the annual speech contest until a time to be announced.

'Well, I reckon that confirms it, poor old Winnie is gone now or very soon will be.'

'I fear you're right, Sebby. Shall you ring the Oscar committee or shall I? We've certainly had a piece of high drama tonight. I wonder if it's been filmed?'

'Oh it will be, make no mistake, James, everything is. You're never alone in Sir Thomas More House.'

Act Three, Scene 2

By the morning of the day after the dramatic arrest of Lord Wyford most residents had either forgotten it or absorbed it as part of the rich pageant of life in their favourite care home.

There was also the announcement of the results of the unfinished annual speech contest to excite them. By the tradition they'd made for themselves, the results came after a good night's sleep to give the judges – who seemed to be Ralph Dines acting alone – a chance to give careful consideration.

What nobody but James seemed to be aware of was that the competition had been barely started. Members had waited to contribute. Clearly, though, a minor detail wasn't going to stop the show going on.

The Chamber was almost full and while they waited to start, a handful were reminded of the arrest of old Wyford so discussed it with all the enthusiasm of those relieved not to have been arrested themselves.

Dines called them to order. 'First, the House will wish to know the latest situation regarding our honourable friend, Lord Ronnie Wyford. I gather he had a comfortable night and will be undergoing further questioning today.

It sounded like a hospital bulletin on a sick patient. 'I further gather that the police are not looking for anyone else in connection with the alleged offences they are charging him with.'

A murmur of palpable relief went round. Old Ronnie could fend for himself, as long as they were all safe. Sir Ronald Hasbery, in his place at the feet of the Speaker, turned and reminded him of something.

'It will, of course, be obvious that Lord Wyford's distinguished and memorable contribution to last night's proceedings will be discounted.' He looked around as many white, grey and silver heads nodded, the brains inside them desperately trying to recall anything that Wyford had said that was either distinguished or memorable, much less both.

Dame Henrietta Bolsome, who had not contributed, was judged to have made the most effective speeches in both categories and received a bout of order paper waving and 'ere-'eres for her pains. Sebastian Catchpole was given a special merit for having produced the most amusing and original impromptu speech.

James knew it had been on the attraction of opposites with special mention of mixed races, only because Sebby had insisted on rehearsing it in front of him in the garden, arguing that no matter what the drawn topic was he'd make it fit. And he did; he'd drawn 'Kaleidoscopes.'

Dines remained standing, indicating that he had more to announce and waved away Hasbery's turn-round towards him. 'The House will also be anxious to know the health of Dame Winnie Carswood. I understand from the medical team that after she'd had a private session with the company solicitor she slept well under sedation, but she has a long road ahead of her to full recovery.'

So long, thought James, that it led straight to the other side. Heaven or hell, depending on what she believed.

He thought back to an occasion when he'd had a bit of

difficulty with a female journalist who seemed to have taken a shine to him when he first arrived as a squeaky-clean new Member.

The young woman, not unattractive and evidently available, hung around the lobby, haunted the corridors where she was permitted to go, hoping to find him, invite him for a drink, tell him with fluttering eyelashes that she needed some deep background information...

Happily married to Elspeth and fully intending to stay that way, he made excuses if they met or took to not being round the corridors unless with at least one other Member.

Dame Winnie witnessed one fabricated encounter and, having got the instant measure of the woman, suggested she and James had a snack in the Members' Tea Room and she'd advise him what to do.

It felt like an adult had suddenly discovered a child's problem and was going to sort it. She asked him about the woman and James poured out all his fears and inadequacies at handling her.

'This place is crawling with leeches, vampires, hangers on, wannabees and hopeless hopefuls. She is one. Now I've seen her at work – and really she is not very subtle – I'll have my odd job man deal with her.'

Shaking with gratitude, James asked about her handyman. 'Get yourself one or two, specialists to deal with certain things. Information on people, digging up the past or guessing the future. They may be constituents in your patch or elsewhere. They may be council officials or just someone eternally grateful to you for personal help.'

'I have five of them now, built up over time. A bottle of Commons scotch at Christmas plus fifty quid in an envelope, and they're mine. One is an alkie, so he gets £75 instead and no booze.'

'That sounds like good advice, Winnie, thanks so much,' James was genuinely in awe of this ordinary looking, quiet lady.

'And if you ever hint that I suggested such action, I'll deny it and we won't be friends.' That James didn't want.

It took a fortnight before Winnie told him in the Chamber one night while a debate was plodding to a black hole of pointlessness that the journalist wouldn't be troubling him any longer.

James thought he hadn't seen her around for a few days. 'She isn't dead?'

Winnie laughed. 'My dear boy, this isn't Sicily. No, she's gone back to her home town to be lead writer on her local rag.' He sensed it better to ask no more, just be grateful for the advice and find himself some handymen, too.

Later when he was on an Education Select Committee visit to secondary schools in the north east, he picked up the local paper in their hotel and read a sad piece by her about how some sexual diseases cannot be cured by drugs.

So, the handyman had really done a work on the woman. Did she deserve that? James wondered. Someone needed to get past him in the bench row so he never finished the thought or answered his own question.

He stood, gripped the back of the bench in front of him and grasped hold of his stick. Everyone else had dispersed for the toilets followed by coffee and cakes to bridge the gap till luncheon.

A badge messenger approached him and whispered, quite respectfully, 'Mr Ellington, the Speaker wonders if you'd be so good as to join him for a few minutes in his Room at the Back of the Chair?' It was phrased as a question, but James knew if he didn't nod agreement, assistants would be sent to club and drag him there, by what remained of his hair.

In Westminster the Speaker enjoyed a room behind an office where his staff worked to advise, help and prepare him for his sessions in the Chair. Following the messenger, he gave Sebby a thumbs-up as he passed.

The messenger seemed to be under the impression that James didn't know the way, but all members know how to get to that office to table questions, requests and draft bills.

Dines, waiting in the office, gestured him straight through to the inner sanctum. Perhaps he was going to ask James to step up as his minion with Wyford out of the way. Not a bad idea, in fact, because it would give James access to confidential material he could use to bring Dines down.

'Sit yourself, take the weight off your moccasins, my friend.' James complied. An offer of coffee from a functionary at the door was waved away by an impatient Dines. 'Now listen, carefully, James, first I want to know about your taking that little gift to our mutual friend?'

'He wasn't my friend. And I did as I was ordered. I delivered the package.'

'Did you stay to see him use it?'

'No, but I heard a shot as I was on the garden path.'

'You bloody moron. He shot his frigging dog!' Amazed,

James gave it some thought.

'You'll go again next week, when he has another birthday. This time you'll take poison to put in his tea, a knife to slit his throat, a cricket bat to reduce his head to pulp and an incendiary device to burn his place down with his remains inside.'

James stood. 'No, enough is enough. I'm not going anywhere near him. If you want him dead, use your A12 white van people.'

'We'll discuss it later. But, James, I urge you to reflect and do what I ask. Poor old Ronnie Wyford had the finger pointed at him by somebody inside the House who delved around in the files and concluded he was up to no good. That person reported it to the cops. They liked him for a range of crimes and added a few more so now I have no sidekick.'

'You want me to take his place?'

'You're further gone than I thought. No, I don't want that. Just do what I ask. The police took him in because they thought he was less demented than most of the others they interviewed about poor Dr Zoe. There was just one other who was slightly less demented. You!'

That didn't square with what James had noticed the officer writing down about him. He kept quiet, though.

'And I'm still very keen to know who fingered Ronnie and on the basis of what evidence. Hercule Poirot will have nothing on me in my relentless quest to find the traitor and bring him or her to justice.'

James sat again, his knee screaming. Some days were better than others in his walking limbs, and this wasn't a good one.

'Well, you don't need to look at me. I had nothing to do with Ronnie's alleged arrest. I know next to nothing about him, except in terms of being your henchman. What I'm more interested in is you and your illicit business and other activities. I'll make it my mission, as I have done ever since I came here.'

'Just a minute, old boy, let me get a recording of this ready for the Oscar nominations.'

'Oh, I thought last night's performance was unbeatable. You will have this one recording already. I decided to stay here against my better judgement to find something against you. I shall up that.'

'I doubt you'll find anything against me because there's nothing to find. I can't think why the police thought you were less demented and deluded than many of our guests. I am a patient man, James, but ... '

James cut him off. 'It was John Dryden the playwright who said, beware the fury of a patient man, but I'm not afraid.'

Dines replied, 'somebody else said impatient people always arrive too late, so that's why I'm patient. I am patient with you, though you drive me to distraction.'

'If I can't find out what will bring you down, then I shall have to kill you.' James stood to reinforce his threat, but it didn't work as Dines saw him trembling with anger and possibly fear. He was biting off far more than he could chew; James was punching above his weight now. And it wouldn't end well.

The two stood a short distance apart, both clutching their walking sticks and if one had shouted *'en garde'* it would have been appropriate. Instead, Dines chose to break the tense moment with one of his unfunny laughs, waving James aside as if he was a troublesome fly.

'Very droll. I like you enormously, James, I don't know why you can't appreciate that. I have always counted you my friend, and been proud to do so, even in public and even when you had your difficulties with certain constituents, those conflicts of interest and when you crossed the line and got too helpful without maintaining your professional distance.

'You are mixing me up with others.'

'No, James, I'm not. Think about the Firearms Friendly Society.'

Act Three, Scene 3

Maisie had asked to visit James at a time to suit him and he was happy to accept. Perhaps his granddaughter actually needed his help or advice. It was a rare moment of satisfaction that the old feel when a younger relative seeks out their help.

He smiled happily as she swept in the drive, his car spurting gravel. Even the dent and long scratch in the passenger door failed to spoil his morning as he greeted and hugged her warmly.

'Hi Grandpa! How you doing?'

'Oh, you know me.'

'That's why I'm asking!'

'Well, Maisie, I know I'm not dead, but I don't feel entirely alive.'

'That's depressing. And a bit sad.'

It was one of those days that hovered between being quite chilly and just warm, so he decided they could talk outside. It would be more private, anyway. 'I have a plan which will cheer you up and make me feel far more alive!' he said as he took her arm.

In fact, he was determined not to let anything spoil his plan. Then news flying round and out of the house person to person, ear to ear, did spoil it. Dame Winnie Carswood had passed away.

She'd been as popular in Sir Thomas More as she had been in Westminster. She inspired respect with her no-nonsense approach to people and events and her drive to get things done. She'd once told him she never wanted to be a minister, even if it had been offered, as she didn't want to be shoehorned into a straitjacket of ministerial expectations.

Maisie put her hand on his as he took in the news; she led him to a bench with a little ornamental table in front. Coffee and a diet cola appeared in the hands of a waitress; he must have ordered it in advance. She gave him a minute.

'I'm sorry about your friend, Grandpa. Why don't I come back one day next week…?'

'No, my love. Let's talk now. I'll be alright. It's just one more example of a very clever removal of a person from here with no questions asked.'

'You should make a timeline of the events you know about. A spreadsheet, in fact. I can set that up for you. Then you'll have some evidence and ammunition in one easy to access place.'

'Yes, I'll take them all from my diary. You knew I'd started keeping one again?'

'You can never have too many truths in a diary.'

'Don't you start. Now, what's the worry for you, Maisie?'

'It seems small stuff now. But I need to decide pretty soon whether I want to be a doctor and get on with what is a very long road. Or whether I should take a year out after 6th form, see something of the world that is not a family holiday. Or whether I should bother about uni at all.'

'What would you do if not a degree?'

'Write. Play music. Work in the media. I don't know...'

'The media is a viper's nest of bastards, liars and backstabbers.'

'Or I could go into politics, like you did.'

'Another viper's nest of bastards, liars and backstabbers.'

'Mum thinks I'll regret not going to uni while I'm young. Leroy agrees with her but says a year out seeing some non-white, non middle class majority areas of the world will make me more ready for uni. And my real Dad, well, he hasn't written back to tell me.

'But what do *you* want to do, Maisie?'

'That's it. I genuinely don't know at the moment.'

'I expect Paul, your real dad, will say do what raises your blood pressure a bit. What excites you? I agree with him, even before he says it. You wanted to be in medicine even when you were little.'

'I still want to make a difference. Perhaps I could train and work here, so I end up helping you, keeping an eye on you!'

'I'll be dead long before then.'

'Don't say that.'

'If I were you, I'd apply for med school before the deadline and then plan to take a year out. They'd let you defer for a year.' She nodded, draining the last of her cola.

'OK, I will. Now, what about you, really?'

'Well, what I imagine is a detective, making a speech in the library with all the suspects lined up as I go though all the evidence I've gathered.'

'Do you ever wish you'd gone into the theatre?'

'I did. Politics and theatre, two sides of the same coin. Now, what I don't have is enough concrete facts to challenge Dines with. I'm not going to get any just doddering about this place. I'll be on a gurney to the crematorium before I could find out a thing.'

'So what are you going to do?'

'When are all my family due to descend on me next, do you know?'

'I heard talk of coming for your 99th birthday.'

'Cheek! My birthday, and all the family will be here, I mean all your cousins?'

'A three-line whip, Grandpa.'

'Good. I'm going to use the computer skills of all of my grandchildren to hack into the systems here, which I can't do, obviously. It will all be in plain sight. The younger ones can be a distraction, causing whatever chaos we need. Your parents and Rebecca must be kept in the dark, that way they'll add to the confusion unwittingly. Can I trust you, Maisie?'

'Of course, Grandpa. You can never be among too many vipers, bastards, liars and backstabbers.'

'I feel ten years younger. I have a plan, a plot. You young people can help me carry it out and I will see Ralph Dines crushed by what I've found out. He thinks it's all safely buried in a toxic tip, but I will bring it to the light of day and call the police. The real police.'

'What, as opposed to the mind police, the thought police, the jazz police?'

'As opposed to the actor police they keep dredging up here to perform their illusions, sleights of hand and deceptions, Zoe.'

'Maisie, Grandpa,' she corrected him, a bit puzzled about what he was coming out with now.

'What?'

'You called me Zoe.'

'Did I? I was thinking of Dr Zoe Frayn, she understands, but they've taken her away. I hope she comes back before I do my great denouement performance.'

'But isn't she dead?'

'I don't believe so. Winnie Carswood is dead. Zoe Frayn is part of the show. Are you with me, Maisie?'

'Of course, if that's what you want. Shall I warn Henry and William and Joe and Emily? You do know that hacking is illegal?'

'Yes, so is killing people for money. And no, don't warn them. They might let something slip. We'll get them involved when they're here. You see the beauty of doing it on my birthday is that everyone will be outside or in the dining hall, weather depending, so nobody will miss you youngsters going to Dines' offices to hack into his precious systems.'

'I dare say Joe could do it remotely, if you asked him.'

'I'm sure. No, what I want is the big spectacle. I'll make a lengthy birthday speech, give you maximum time. Then when we have what we need printed off, we'll have the big Hercule Poirot finale.'

'Sounds like a plan, Grandpa,' Maisie smiled, humouring the old man who seemed to be flitting between moments of lucid clarity and the most peculiar thoughts.

Spotting a waitress approaching, James asked her, 'More cola, Maisie?' 'No, thanks, Grandpa, I'll need to pee if I drink any more.'

'There are toilets here, you know.'

'Of course, but how do you know they're safe?'

It was an innocent enough, gentle ribbing joke. But it filled James' mind with a picture of her stifled in a sack over her head, dragged from the toilet stall, her head then pushed into the bowl while the chain was flushed and her captors demanding to know what her dear old grandfather was up to.

'We don't know, Maisie. You're right. Your mother would never pee at school when she was at primary, afraid of monsters and bogeymen leaping out from the poo and wet toilet paper.'

'Blimey. I was going to say you can never have too

many toilets, but perhaps not, now I know that about Mum.'

'Best not mention that to her, along with what we have planned today.'

'Mum's the word, Grandpa!'

Act Three, Scene 4

When he first got the message that his former neighbour Judy Blowers was coming to see him again, James was suspicious. Surely she didn't need to visit any more? Was this some new angle of attack by Dines? How would she get to Sir Thomas More? They'd been friendly enough overall, but what was behind a visit?

Too windy and wet to meet her outside, he decided a bar would be unsuitable, but the Old Winter Garden coffee outlet would do. It was a mini-Kew Gardens, a glass house built in homage to Victorian grandeur that had fallen into decay. Dines had had it restored, stuffed with exotic plants and opened as the second coffee and tearoom available to the local village and visiting relatives.

James had never met any of his own family there as the tables were too close together for private conversation. He didn't want Judy to tell him anything private, so, yes it would do.

He met her as she was being admitted through the foyer cage. Unchanged to outward observation, walking with a slight roll, her hair all over the place from the wind, James watched, unable to recall a time when her wild, gray curly hair wasn't all over the place.

They embraced. James was unsure why, but it was what everyone seemed to do these days. 'James, James, how are they treating you?' She clearly thought he was in prison.

'I'm surviving, Judy, thanks. It's not where I want to be nor do I wish to stay here till the end, but I have a mission that I must accomplish.'

'That's nice.' She heard him but didn't absorb it as they walked down a corridor to the west garden door, her eyes darting about, taking it all in. Outside it was still blowing and raining, but he grabbed hold of her arm with his left hand and they got outside, across the path to the Old Winter Garden, which had double doors so they entered successfully.

Still quite early in the morning the place wasn't busy. James guessed it would fill up soon enough, so he led her to a table against a rear window. 'We can order from a waitress, or you can do it at the counter.'

'Have they got any toast?' she asked, smelling toast.

'Yes, of course. Bread, crumpets, muffins, cream cakes, scones, tea cakes, stollen, whatever.'

Hoping that nobody would take their spot he led through a maze of tables and chairs to the counter. Judy asked for toast and homemade strawberry jam, but eyed the cream cake stand till she came to the rack of cakes on offer from sponges to slabs.

Once ordered, he led back to the table which was still free, though one adjacent now housed a couple of old men laying out a chess board. Why people willingly sat so close to others, was beyond James.

He'd noticed in a cinema on more than one occasion, in an empty row, someone coming in would sit right next to him. And in a public carpark one Sunday morning he'd parked his car, the only vehicle in the entire site. When he returned from seeing a constituent, there was one other car – parked right next to his, close to his driving door.

'Tell me all about this home, James,' Judy demanded after several moments of awkward silence, while they waited for their snacks, looking up to the magnificent glass ceiling and heavy planting of indoor shrubs round the perimeter. Outside, trees swayed, some bashing against the roof of the building, like a surreal off-beat drum.

He looked closely to gauge how interested she really was or just needed to blurt out her reason for coming. 'It's a care home, Judy, full of old, mainly gaga MPs, Lords, civil servants, several of whom can still hear and feed themselves, and we play act like we're still important. The management lay on little theatrical events to amuse us.'

Finally a girl began unloading a tray to their table. 'Every couple of days or so some resident passes on and is taken to the crematorium or the cemetery they have considerately provided for us.'

Judy poured her own tea from a genteel silver pot; James grasped his cup of steaming coffee. Her mouth full of the buttered and jammed toast, she asked if the crematorium could be hired by anyone to dispose of undesirables.

James shunted back a fraction, in case she shared toast crumbs in the same way that Catchpole did.

Surely she didn't want him to sort out somebody else troubling her? It turned out that was exactly what she wanted. He watched her fingers break up a slice of cherry slab cake she'd sat on the toast crumbs. 'That old woman who bought your house.'

He often remarked, mainly to himself, that old people frequently called other oldies 'old', suggesting that they themselves were still in their prime. His late mother had done it at 93, grumbling about an old woman down the street who'd been taken away by social services, unable to look after herself at 85.

The woman now next door to Judy was 'old', had a handicapped husband she'd packed off to a care facility somewhere, council run, she wouldn't spend on a 'swanky place like this.' She'd installed a large pond in the lawn to attract wildlife. Judy detested wildlife and in that, James concurred.

One big crime was that she'd gutted the house, had every room redone, including the lounge nine times because she kept changing her mind on the shade of the walls. When it was finished, she'd had the electric sockets moved so part of the room was re-plastered.

The woman was a hoarder; most weeks her bins didn't go out, so all the rotting food must be stored indoors. That is, when she wasn't putting the wrong colour wheelie bin out the night before collection to confuse neighbours and the right one out as the lorry approached.

She was bossy, impatient, rude, pig-headed and when she demanded that Judy replace the fence between their houses and Judy declined – there was another decade of life in that old rickety fence – she'd had it painted deep crimson on *both* sides without permission.

Perhaps her biggest failing after all that was that Judy claimed she was little, with a Napoleon complex. She'd nicknamed her, 'the Poison Dwarf.'

'What, and you want me to have her vanished!'

'Yes, James, you know people. You know people who know people. Look how you dealt with my problem with those kids. Haven't seen or smelt them since you sorted it. I just want the Poison Dwarf gone.'

'If anything happened to her in my old house, there'd be suspicions leading straight here to me, Judy.' The noise in the Old Winter Garden suddenly eased, James realised, so at least six nearby tables had overheard him.

In the silence James gave a moment's thought to agreeing to do something to get shot of her. This wasn't a matter he could pass to his contact Kerry Sinclair in the council. He could ask Dines direct to sort it but then he'd owe Dines even more. Besides, why did Judy keep pestering him with her problems?

'James, think about it. I shall be eternally grateful. She's had skips outside your house for months. The rubbish blows across my garden. She never even notices. Then she brought me round a box of dark chocolates and a plant in a hideous pot saying, 'I'm sorry for the disturbance with all my builders. I do hope we can be friends.'

'Well, not all bad then?' he offered, hopefully.

'The plant was poison. It killed the cat across the street. And I hate plain chocolates.'

'I don't have the contacts anymore, Judy, I really don't.'

'Is there a toilet here? I need to go very quickly now' she said, agitation beginning. 'I need to go now.' And she set off through the tables, bumping people, rattling one table dangerously and heading for the toilets, mercifully not far away.

James stood, thinking that if he just left the table and hid in the grounds, she'd give up and get herself home. Except she'd probably raise a stink trying to find him. His mobile inside his jacket pocket made him jump.

He peered at the screen. It was Maisie. Pleased with

himself that he remembered how to open it and talk to his granddaughter, he sat down.

'Hi Grandpa! You remembered how to use the phone!'

'Hello, Maisie. Not too far gone yet, my love.'

'Right. Just to tell you that I've lined up all of your grandchildren to help at your birthday. Only Joe knows what he's got to do, but Henry and Emily are really pretty cool on computers. They all know you need something done. It's a surprise. We're good to go.'

'That's great, Maisie. And thanks so much. Bye.' A girl arrived to clear the table in that hopeful way that a customer is taking the hint to leave; the Garden was filling, people anxious to escape the rain, clothing dripping on the wooden floor and creating a cloud of damp fug in the air above.

'Oh Grandpa? Make sure that you have everything in order down on paper – all the issues from your Parliamentary days and since – that you want found on the computer. We'll find evidence of whatever you think if there's any to be had.'

'Got it, don't worry about me. This will be the first birthday since I was eight that I've looked forward to.'

'List every slight you ever had from Dines. It's important to prepare yourself. You don't know what he'll throw back at you.'

They signed off. James stood, letting the blood flow to his legs before starting to make his way out, skirting tables, apologising for jogging one elbow and grabbing the back of the chair of another. Looking back he noted their table was taken at once. He lost his footing and skidded on a patch of water trickling from an umbrella leaning against a customer's chair.

As he crashed down, his leg under his body, he grabbed the nearest thing, which was the arm and shoulder of Douglas Gardener entertaining younger family members in the hope of not seeing many residents.

Gardener was pulled out of his seat right onto James. The two apologised and Gardener struggled up with family assistance. James was propped against the wall while his leg recovered; he declined an ambulance or for help to be called from the House.

Gradually the ambient noise rose to its previous level. People got over seeing an old man fall over. A waitress helped him stand up, gingerly move to the doors, wrap his coat round him and out into the strengthening easterly wind.

It took ages, with slow, cautious steps, biting down on the leg throb, head bowed against the rain but thinking about what Maisie had told him to do before confronting Dines in public. She was a smart girl, his granddaughter. In his own mould, in fact.

Only when he'd reached the calm of the house and peeled off his wet jacket, wiped his glasses dry did he remember that he'd left Judy Blowers in the Old Winter Garden toilets.

She'd been a long time in there. Perhaps she'd passed away on the throne; or flushed herself away. Could he have imagined the conversation with her? Or maybe she was even now complaining about his lack of murderous co-operation to Dines himself.

Act Three, Scene 5

After refusing to yield a drop for days on end, it rained so that his late March birthday morning dawned chilly and damp, with grey to black skies.

Walking down to breakfast, not sure how many knew he was a year older this very day, he commented to Lady Helen Fulcher, grumbling about the weather being so bad she couldn't go out on her adapted mobility scooter, 'well, I suppose it's quite early to look for good weather.'

'Yes, it's only 8 in the morning' the woman replied, peering at her wristwatch.

No member of staff made any mention of his birthday. What was one more in a place where somebody seemed to have one every single day?

As he sat to pancakes coated with lemon juice and sugar granules – James preferred the traditional variant – Kenny Sloan breathed in his ear, 'I hear your birthday bash is moved indoors today through the inclement weather.'

'I'd assumed as much. But how did you know? Why are you informing me?' He looked at the weaselly Sloan, thinning hair making what had been an early Beatles' cut ever since he was 15 look like an old, tufted rug.

Kenny replied with a grin, sitting down opposite him and snapping his fingers for service. 'We parted on bad terms years ago, James, and we've not really had a chance to make the peace. You never wrote to me after I was elected MEP. I'd have thought that was a chance to bridge the gaps.'

'Did you? Well, I didn't. What on earth would I write to you about? You knew how I felt about the European Union so why would I be glad you'd been elected to its pointless Parliament? And after all that lying and twisting, I was hardly looking to chew the memory fat over with you on what you said about my wife.'

'I'll have the full Continental Breakfast,' he barked at a waitress, enunciating each word as if she was a simpleton. 'French cheese, Danish ham, Greek olives, Sicilian orange juice and fresh baked Portuguese cob loaves. Oh, and some Swedish butter, too.'

Even now, Sloan couldn't help baiting James, who'd been against membership of the European Union long before it was fashionable. If they went down the road of discussing Sloan's attraction to Elspeth, they'd come to fisticuffs and he wanted to save that for Dines.

On the other hand, his birthday was being spoilt. 'Your family coming in, are they?'

'I'm having my indoor tea with them, yes, and looking forward to it.' He wasn't being polite, he said it sarcastically.

'Well, that's nice. And do you know what I admire about you, James? It's that you raised both your girls, as if they were yours, yet you must have doubted the fatherhood of the younger one?'

James said nothing, merely sipped his coffee. He was determined that Sloan wouldn't spoil anything else, much less his feelings towards his late loving, faithful wife. He'd let Sloan see his anger years ago; but not today.

Not on his birthday.

It fell on a Sunday, so all his family had confirmed their attendance. It was customary for numbers of colleagues in the home to drift in for a few moments, perhaps to share a cup of tea and wolf a few cream cakes. Birthday celebrants could have whatever they wanted, but of course, they had to pay for it.

The morning had yet to pass. He ate as much of his breakfast as he could – the old trencherman habit returning as they waited for the girl bringing Sloan's breakfast. Sloan enjoyed watching James eat.

As soon as he spied a trolley being wheeled towards them James, wiping his mouth on the napkin, stood and said, 'Sorry, Kenny, must go. I have some letters to deal with this morning. Perhaps you'll be somewhere else this afternoon.'

'Absolutely, the Dining Room! See you then!' and he began to demolish his truly continental breakfast.

Too wet for a walk, but James had to simmer down from Kenny Sloan and pass the time till the early afternoon. For the first time, it hit him that people in these care homes so often spent every morning simply waiting for the afternoon, and every afternoon filling time till the evening and bed.

Having dressed in his rainwear, he set off for the Archives and Records, splashing through the puddles, his stick hitting them angrily as he moved, looking neither left nor right.

He was hailed from a distance by Sebastian Catchpole, still in possession of his stentorian voice, who boomed, 'see you at breakfast, Michael, and don't be long...'

Deciding not to tell Sebby he'd already had it and was in no mood to listen to the man's running on, he waved in the air and pressed on. Sebby would find someone else to talk at anyway, possibly even Kenny Sloan at the table James had left.

The storage facility was meant to be open and guarded from 6am to 10pm, seven days a week. Well, it was open, but James saw no sign of any guard.

The walk-in lockers were supplied with shelving, plastic boxes, a small functional desk and chair. As one became vacant, the next Member moving in took it, so they were all randomly placed.

The inner keys were hung in a bank of key safes in strict surname alphabetical order. James went to his, bottom left only to find Lenny Sanders in his place. There had been both a death and new arrival, so the safes had been hitched around. He found his, keyed in Elspeth's birth date and took hold of his keys.

His room looked a little different from his last visit. Still present were his meticulously labelled boxes - pre-Westminster, Being the Candidate, one for each of his ten years in and then subsequent years. One large box was for family and a big cardboard art folder held his election posters, his and Elspeth's certificates and early artwork Samantha and Rebecca had created as infants.

To see them reminded him of that cruel seed Sloan had planted years ago about the lineage of his girls. He shook off the thought. His things all seemed to be here, but not in the right order.

The Tommy Cross file was on the top – as if someone had looked at it. Lenny Sanders, presumably. His file on the toxic tip was still open, laid across the top of the contents in another box. Ralph Dines, he assumed.

Someone had been going through his records. His diaries. His letters. His memories. When he'd first entered Parliament, old Winnie Carswood had told him to remember that there were always three sides to every story – 'yours, somebody else's and the facts.'

His records were both fact and his own version of what happened. He tidied them up as best he could. In his 'home' box his last gas bills, council tax receipts and correspondence with his solicitor had been given a going over. He always prided himself on his logical systems. What he faced now was chaos.

Yes, some material had been thrown back in the wrong boxes. He saw a screwed up sheet of A4 tucked down the side of 1987. He unfurled it – it was a list of the times that Dines had wronged, slighted or crossed him. It spanned all the time they'd known each other and was almost up to date.

He'd begun it a few weeks ago as ammunition in his case against Dines, which he hoped to play out this afternoon. His birthday bash! He looked at his watch which had slipped round his wrist, he must be losing weight. He stuffed the note in his pocket.

Still time for an early lunch and change before the family arrived. He replaced lids, still annoyed that someone had ruined his method of storing. As he locked up, he wondered if someone really had or was it all an illusion. Had he in fact never had a tidy system all along?

Outside, the rain was unrelenting, so holding on to his locker key against all the rules, he plodded back to the house. Once inside he shook himself off and made his way upstairs. By then, some of the nursing and cleaning staff had been told to wish him a happy birthday, which he acknowledged with a gracious bow as he passed each smiling greeter.

He peeled off his wet day clothes, thinking that a bath would be nice. He could relax in there and think. His list of grievances was nothing alone; but with whatever his grandkids could hack out of Dines' computer base they would add up to dynamite.

He needed to rest his eyes for just a moment.

The sound of Timmy Greenwood declaiming in the corridor about giving his crown to his wayward daughters woke him with a start. James'd got under the duvet and dreamed of Parliamentary battles over abortion, Sunday trading, government sleaze and MPs' pay lost and skirmishes won in rivers of blood, with swords and armour, with witches spells and goblins.

Again, his watch had slipped round, but it was late. Too late for lunch; the bath would have to wait. He dressed in his blazer, crisply ironed white shirt with a tie he was still fond of that had been given to him on a cassette factory visit in 1988.

In that uniform he looked like an MP in the House on a Friday – a sort of dress-down, smart casual constituency weekend. Leaving everything on the floor and bed he dashed out, clumping at a fair rate of knots along the corridor, only slowing to descend the stairs carefully.

Lunch was long done. The Dining Room had been cleared and set out for his party. There was a top table, laden with high tea edibles, including rolls and sandwiches, dips, cakes, biscuits, crackers, flagons of soft drinks and Bucks Fizz. A space had been left clear in the centre to park the requisite large cake later on.

Joseph and Emily, Maisie, Henry and William had arranged themselves on the two large sofas, all focused on different games on their phones. That left a pair of straight-backed mock Victorian chairs for Samantha and

Rebecca to sit head-to-head in a good yarn. Leroy and Simon stood looking out the dripping window, holding a glass of the fizz and sharing what could have been a dirty joke.

Everyone wheeled to greet James, who clumped in apologising for his lateness. The kids merely chorused 'hi Grandpa,' with William adding, 'happy birthday, Grandpa.'

James shook his sons-in-laws by the hand, kissed his daughters on the cheeks and went along the grandchildren either touching heads, shoulders or phones as he passed.

He gravitated to the women, but kept himself facing the kids so he could watch Maisie. They asked several times how he was, how the food was, nighttimes, entertainment and how other residents were and if he was expecting many colleagues to look in.

He replied that he expected a handful, but that Dame Winnie Carswood had just passed away so was unlikely to join them.

The men gathered round to ask how he was, how the food was, nighttimes, entertainment and how other residents were and if he was expecting many colleagues to look in.

He replied that he expected one or two and that Dame Winnie Carswood who'd just passed away had sent her apologies.

William got up to inspect the food and had his hand slapped away by Samantha as he reached for a custard slice. 'Not yet, William.' Emily turned from the table and looked at a monstrous portrait over the fireplace of some old fart who'd done something famous a century ago.

James announced, still looking at Maisie, 'when people start arriving, you kids are free to go exploring, keep to the ground floor and foyer. Maisie, you remember where?'

'Chill, Grandpa, I got it.' She sounded laid back, but that was a good thing. The doors swung open, James turned to greet colleagues. But it was staff with heavy teapots, jugs of hot water and a coffee flagon for James.

After a good twenty minutes the women let the kids attack the food with no sign of any visitors, James was puzzled. What had gone wrong? Had a sudden wave of bubonic plague killed everyone but them?

The doors opened again to allow two staff to carry in the cake. Three tiers, heavy with icing, it was a masterful cross between a wedding cake and a piece of kids' art work. It looked spectacular; it would cost him a fortune.

The kids had gathered round Joseph's phone, looking at some game that had highs and lows and kept them sane. The adults were running out of conversation. Several times, James thought he heard approaching footsteps followed by muffled conversations. But nobody else entered the room to congratulate him and snatch a good gawp at his family.

James walked by the food table for the tenth time, straightened the plates and cutlery and fingered the white linen cloth. He needed the toilet, suddenly, as he often did. He'd been several times, but still felt a little nervous.

He flung open the door to discover Ralph Dines and another man stood in the middle blocking the way in and out, talking to Sir Gerry Manders, Dame Helen Fulcher in her chair and Sir Michael Michaelson facing him.

'So, no, we think as James is a bit unwell, if you get my meaning, that we don't embarrass him by doing the birthday thing, if you don't mind.... sorry, go and have some tea and forget old Ellington.'

Ralph Dines was sending all the guests away with a cock and bull story! James opened his mouth to protest when the trio shuffled away, quite put out at missing a freebie. A few moments of glad-handing would have been well rewarded with quality nosh. Lennie Sanders approached, puzzled himself as to why the others hadn't gone in. 'James Ellington's birthday, Lennie? Sorry, my man, but a bit of a mix up and it's not today after all.'

Lennie was not so easily put off; he'd planned to open up the Tommy Cross saga in front of all James' family. Dines adopted a look that he must have learned from the Jedi in the first *Star Wars* movie, 'you don't want to come in, Lennie, go back to your room now.'

At that moment, Dines' ankle went over and, his stick flying away, he seized hold of Sanders' jacket, shirt and chest skin in a desperate attempt to remain upright. It worked, but Sanders was rocked. 'Sorry old man, go and have a scotch on me.'

Dines sensed James behind him, slowly turned round, being very careful and beamed, 'how's it going James? Enjoying your birthday? Food all good?'

James decided to go along with it, not show Dines he was really pissed off. 'Lovely, thanks, Ralph. May we have some more fruit loaf and coffee? Are you coming in to say hello? Just a few moments?'

'Of course, I'll see to it, James. And be with you in a minute.'

James smiled and returned to the room. 'My loves, it seems that my old nemesis Ralph Dines is turning away all my visitors and colleagues so we are alone. Eat up, drink up and if you kids are bored with this room, then with my blessing go and explore and if anyone challenges you say Mr Dines said it was OK.'

Maisie took charge and nodded at William to join their exodus because she knew they needed effective distraction in the house to give her and Joe maximum time to go to work in Dines' office.

She was a little concerned to see Dines still outside the Dining Room. If he didn't go in to James and the family, then he could return to his office almost at once. Then what would she do?

Act Three, Scene 6

However, true to his word, Dines swanned into the Dining Room like royalty, gushing welcomes and hopes they'd had enough to eat. He apologised that James appeared to have made no friends in the House and shook hands with all the adults.

'And where are your grandchildren, James?'

'Playing. Exploring. They've been cooped up here long enough,' James replied.

Dines nodded and added, 'of course, I understand. As long as they don't get up to any mischief or get themselves hurt.' He beamed at the family and made to leave.

James, calculating how much he'd be billed for Dines' under three minute appearance, already red faced and sweating, anxious to keep him in the room, mumbled, 'but Ralph, why don't you tell my family more about your plans for the estate here.'

Dines frowned.' Really? Oh, I don't think they want to hear about dry and dull business plans! No, this is your day. Have you made a little speech?'

'Not just to my family, no, they've heard enough speeches from me. No, I would have said a few words if you'd let anyone else come and hadn't actively prevented them getting in here.'

'James, are you feeling quite well? Or is this that old adage that you should humour the lunatic, mmm? Isn't that what they say?'

'Is that what they said of you, Ralph, because everybody here seems to humour you?'

'I'm just concerned about you, James, that's all, old man.' It was an awkward moment, made worse by Dines pretending concern for James' well-being.

'The truth will out, soon enough, Ralph Dines, you'll see.'

'Out, out damned spot? I thought for a minute there you'd come over all Timmy Greenwood.' He expected a polite laugh from the family.

'I think we should check on the children,' Samantha suggested, looking at Leroy for support.

'You stay here enjoying the party. I'll send them back in if I find them on my way.' And he made for the door, clumping around James as if he was a traffic island.

He couldn't leave. He couldn't be allowed to return to his office. Maisie and Joseph hadn't had enough time yet.

'Ralph, I insist. Stay a moment longer.' He put his hand up, palm facing Dines in exactly the same way Dines silenced others. Ralph smiled, amused. He took hold of James' hand and bent it backwards, the action hidden from the family.

'Work calls. We haven't all got a birthday bash to share with our family! Enjoy your day,' he bowed to the room, skirted round James again and left, leaving the door wide open. Lennie Sanders was still in the corridor ensuring no residents entered.

'Lennie, with me,' Dines barked at the man and the pair strode off in the direction of the central lobby, the stick punctuating his footsteps aggressively.

They turned the corner and James panicked. A moment more and he'd discover the kids. He hobbled out after them, followed by the four adults, all equally unsure what was the matter with James. 'I thought he couldn't stand being in Dines' company?' Samantha said.

Simon suggested, 'maybe he's fully institutionalised now?'

As James clumped after Dines and Sanders, he came up with a line to use to stop them reaching the office. He shouted, 'a moment! You are really the unacceptable face of rudeness. You're supposed to be polite and courteous.'

Dines stopped and wheeled. 'I am *always* the very model of politeness and courteousness no matter what the provocation!' he thundered.

Raised voices were drawing the attention of those in the corridors. It wasn't what James had wanted, but at least Dines was no nearer his office.

'Only when it suits you, when you're putting on your oily salesman act.'

'Putting on an act? If anybody in this place should be teaching acting classes, it's you James Ellington, always declaiming from the high moral ground, superior to everyone else, don't think we haven't noticed!'

'Oh yeah?'

'Why do you think nobody looked in on your party?'

'Because you and Sanders stopped them in the

corridor outside!'

'Dear God, James, I despair. Your delusions have reached such a point someone will have to write you up as a case study in a psychology book.' Lennie disappeared at pace.

Now that they'd adopted a child-like yah-boo, my dad is bigger than yours tone with each other, James carried it down to the next level by prodding Dines' chest with a finger, short sharp stabs. Dines stepped back; James followed.

The problem was that they were getting to the last corner before the foyer and the office. James pretended to stagger on his ankle, swung his stick as he 'fell' and clashed it against Dines' walking aid. On the floor, gathering up his stick he realised it had been a poor pretend fall.

'Oscars all round!' Dines cried.

Rebecca, Simon, Samantha and Leroy paused a few feet from the pair, wondering what to do, appalled at how things were turning out. Both mothers were also concerned about where the kids were.

Ambient mood noises were switched to the greatest opera arias of all time as enjoyed by Morse in the television series. Lennie returned, having switched the tapes on. What, he was taking over as Dines' henchman now, was he?

James spoke the thought. Dines stood, against the wall, took hold of James' jacket lapels and sprayed into his face, 'Lord Wyford is presently unavailable as you know because you told the cops something, and I need help from my friends and well-wishers to run this care home.'

Not wiping his face and keeping a steady stare on Dines, James eased the lapel free, stood to full height and replied loudly, 'In a matter of moments I will have what I need to put you away for a good stretch and Lord Wyford will be released.'

'You idiot! You see nothing except the madness taking hold of your mind. Wyford was even more in my black books and I don't mean the Whips' Black Book, than you. Yes, you! Otherwise, it would have been you arrested not Ronnie.' Dines gave him the full top volume shout, close as he was.

The change of background sound effects and the shouting brought Emily and Henry to the scene. They started jumping up and down, crying 'go Grandpa, kill him!' and running round in circles, thinking that had been their signal.

William remained in the outer office engaging the hapless Imelda behind the desk with a series of banal questions about the house and grounds using the big pictogram map, interspersed with the running commentary of his own thoughts on wind turbines and world view that most 11-year-olds have in large doses inside their minds.

In the inner office, Joseph and Maisie worked as fast as they could on the computer terminal on Dines' desk and the one inside the cupboard which had been left unlocked.

Parental cries across the conflict of 'stop that', 'come here' and 'Henry! Emily!' had no effect on the cousins who were having a whale of a time, but contributed to the rising chaos in the corridor. Others appeared at either end, and while some patients started gibbering nobody made any move to intervene when they saw it was Dines squabbling.

James took in that several Karls, a couple of Imeldas, a Matron and one of the alleged police officers wearing the uniform jacket but with torn blue jeans and trainers had joined the throng.

The combatants took to pushing each other, to trying to slap each other's faces and to moving gingerly around, equally scared of genuinely falling.

When James, darting a look, realised that a pair of thugs he surely saw in the white van at least three times appeared, he needed space to evade them and deal with Dines. They closed towards him.

James left Dines, put his head down and charged at the pair. They'd not expected that and James, holding his stick like a machine gun, sprayed bullets as they jerked to blood erupting death against the immaculately painted walls.

Instead, he made it through to the foyer. The office door remained shut. They needed still more time. A circle of onlookers formed around James, broken by Dines pushing through, accompanied by a nurse with one hand behind her back. An injection.

'Stop them, Leroy,' Samantha screeched. Leroy bravely stepped forward only to be stopped by the Dines' upright hand gesture and told to 'fuck off, we've got this.' Dines was joined by more nurses, all with one hand behind their backs. Hell, how many injections were they going to give him?

In that second, he longed to have Dr Zoe administer to him. He wanted Maisie and Joseph to emerge from the office triumphantly holding aloft the incriminating evidence.

Still clutching his stick as if it was that machine gun, James stood rather unsteadily in the centre of the foyer, surrounded, but determined to take with him as many of Dines' minions as he could.

Nobody noticed Lennie Sanders grab Emily in a headlock, his free hand over her mouth and drag her down the corridor leading to the ground floor offices.

Or if they did, they did nothing about it. All part of the Sunday afternoon entertainment, of course.

And no charge levied.

Act Three, Scene 7

With a mass of what he fleetingly imagined were possibly marshmallows, for some reason, weighing his limbs down and partially covering glass shards that his bleeding hands were holding, James redoubled his effort to push Dines up the staircase, away from his office.

That was his only purpose as light came and went, a high-pitched whistle passed through his head from ear to ear and his breath came in sharp jags with all the energy he was pouring into defending himself. Get Dines away from his office.

And Ralph Dines' only purpose as light came and went inside his head, his breath rattling in gasps, was to get this shit down the stairs so he could be dealt with properly. And finally.

As an assistant came perilously close, brandishing a needle, James realised he needed more space between himself and the audience they'd now attracted.

Somebody changed the ambient music/noise, James was aware of an irritating journey through the opening seconds of a range of effects, from flying bats to Javanese dance and from motorway traffic to a dog left alone in distress.

Whoever was at the console finally settled on fairground-circus music, as if it was a clown show, this mock fight, and nobody would get really hurt. Sweeping away another nurse hell-bent on stabbing him, he shrieked, 'checkmate, old mate!'

He changed tack and pushed Dines into the assistant who almost stabbed her boss with whatever was in the needle. They paused. Dines' face appeared to be sliding off its skeleton, like dirty, melted ice. To him, the fight with James was everything he didn't want. If there was to be a staged fight, it should be his hirelings doing it; he should be directing.

Anger rose from within and flooded out his mouth like a spurt of vomit and down his arms like a bolt of lightning. He went for James' throat with renewed vigour.

A few steps up, one or two down, the fight moved. Now James was in the lead; then Dines took over. The family were swept up in the melee. Henry realised that Emily was no longer nearby, and stopped his riding warrior horses to look for her.

He dashed away, just escaping Leroy's grab for his arm, straight to the office where he knew help was. William was in mid-flow informing the bemused Imelda about how important it was to clean and floss your teeth and to be sure to treat the gums well.

He looked over at his brother. 'Emily in here?'

'No, haven't seen her. What is going on out there, can I come and look?'

'No, keep doing what you're doing. We need more time for Joe and Maisie to get what we need.'

Suddenly waking from the coma that William had talked her into, Imelda's brain clicked into life and she demanded as she stood, 'what's going on out there?'

'Nothing much, a piece of theatre, that's all, should be over in a minute or two and then normality will resume,' Henry shouted for the benefit of the hacking pair through the inner door. Leaving William to educate Imelda with everything he could remember about what the Romans did for Britain, Henry dashed back to the foyer.

By this point, the battle had reached the top of the stairs where a small balcony looked down into the hall below. James had the upper hand. A semi-circle of onlookers gathered, with the balcony forming a natural boundary. The needle-holding nurses waited their moment to pounce.

Both men stood, resting, still clinging to their sticks that they swung round, unpredictably, dangerously, their eyes daggers of hatred. A sudden burst of rapier fighting, cut and thrust, parry, lunge and Dines was speared. Dines lay at his feet, bleeding out, his eyes glazing, his lips struggling to form the words of an apology.

For a moment James thought he was in bed and had been dreaming. Dines rapidly weighed up his options. James could be injected and fall into a relaxing sleep enabling them to carry him to his room.

Or he himself could feign injury and get close to pin him long enough for the injection or to be bundled into a strait jacket and carried away. He had to consider the family, other visitors and the staff. What were they thinking? He had reputational damage to consider. He was conscious that somebody could sue him and the company. His lawyers charged by the minute.

Dines, at least, was in no doubt that all this was real. Neither dream nor fantasy. But James was waiting at the top end of the secondary school field as break-time ended, a whistle sounded and he and that other boy kept staring at each other, fists clenched, neither willing to be first to walk back to the school building.

It took the duty teacher's annoyed yell at them to get in

and wait outside the Headmaster's study to force them to walk in together, the fight forgotten amidst the consequences ahead. Fights rarely turned out well.

A scream from the lower floor cut through everybody's thoughts and noise. It was female; it was young. James looked down. Lenny Sanders had a knife to Emily's throat, holding her directly below the balcony. She was struggling to be free; Sanders wasn't letting go.

He shouted up to James, Dines and others who came to look down. This would have been a good moment to inject James, but below was a new emergency.

'Now you've stopped fighting like ferrets in a sack, you can watch the finale of this afternoon's entertainment. Happy birthday, by the way, Ellington, with no happy returns.'

Emily stamped hard down on his foot. It made him move to adjust his hold. He pricked her neck with the blade, producing an instant dash of red, trickling down and into her fluorescent-flavoured t-shirt.

'Let her go, Sanders, she's a child!' James yelled, starting to slide along the edging towards the stairs. 'Only a child.'

'A granddaughter for a daughter, James, hey? Seems a fair trade to me.'

'You're insane!' The Ellington adults started down the staircase.

Crowd voices concurred. Dines yelled, 'Let her go, Lennie, this isn't going to end well if you don't.'

'I'll die laughing, Ralph, old thing, I really will. Anybody filming this, it'll look good on the evening news.'

Sir Gerry Manders boomed down, 'The CCTV cameras have captured it all, Lennie. I imagine it will make compelling viewing for the jury at your trial!'

Dines slipped back to his quiet, calm self. 'Thanks, Gerry. Now, let's be calm about this. I'm coming down, you will hand me the knife, let the child go and ...'

'Just let her go, you bastard.' James was in his terrified, angry, impotent rage.

'What's the matter, Grandpa? Why is he doing this?'

Emily sounded as if her anger was rising too, just beginning to overcome her fear.

Either sensing a change of atmosphere outside in the foyer or being done with their task, Maisie and Joseph flung open the office door, William behind. They took in the situation at once and dropped the piles of white printing paper they'd been clutching.

The three youngsters with a savage cry like something out of *Lord of the Flies* dashed at Lennie and Emily, instinctively splitting like cavalry to approach from two sides. The parents reached the ground floor and poised, ready to strike at Sanders.

Again, Lennie adjusted his footing and his hold on Emily's neck allowing Joseph to reach him first and seize his arm holding the knife and give it a yank and a smack down on his bended knee. The knife hit the floor.

Maisie from behind picked up one of the foyer chairs and raising it high above her head, brought it down on Sanders' back, with a satisfying crack as it splintered and his back bruised.

William kicked the knife out of reach. Joseph took the

chair stump from Maisie and thumped him so he fell. The crowd had reached the foot of the stairs. Several cheered.

Rebecca darted in and out towards Sanders to reach her daughter. Leroy and Simon split up and waited ready to pounce. Samantha, last down the stairs, turned back to give Dines a piece of her mind about the whole afternoon. Two assistants hovered, still waiting to knock James out, while the others dashed down as well.

Dines yelled down, 'stop that you kids, I'll have you in an asylum till you're drawing your old age pensions...'

He stopped. James' stick had cracked him on the forehead so hard there was a line of blood and he staggered. The pair closed in a bear hug and wrestled madly, neither getting anywhere against the other.

If it had been possible to freeze frame the moment and put a thought caption over each person's head, the wide range of reactions would have been surprising. Douglas Gardener thought 'if I could stand next to Samantha...' Matron thought, 'why the hell don't they get on with the injection?'

One of the Karls thought, 'blimey, we need the real police now and an ambulance!' A second Matron's bubble would have said, 'where the hell is Dr Zoe when we need her?'

Dame Henrietta Bolsome thought, 'somebody, turn that bloody noise off...' and furiously wheeled herself to the stairs as if to go down and turn it off herself. A couple of visitors managed to stop her.

Dines himself might have thought, 'the cost of the chair, insurance claim, James is dead meat after this...' and Sebby Catchpole thought, 'old Dines has excelled himself with this circus...'

However, Dines, particularly, had no time for thought bubbles to inform an audience. He misjudged James' loss of balance as his ankle went over, but James fell the opposite way and true to his reflex of seizing something, anything to stop falling, he took hold of Dines in a new, stronger lock.

As the pair fell towards the balcony edge, Dines tumbled over, making a half turn as he fell through the space and hit the ground. Joseph felt an irresistible urge to applaud the man.

The sickening thud stopped almost everybody and everything.

At that precise moment, Dame Helen Fulcher who'd gone down in the lift, found the switches to turn off the ambient background noises. She stabbed every button in sight through the excitement of the chase that had seized her, and the arthritis that had long ago taken over her hands.

The stirring sounds of Chopin's *Funeral March* flooded the air.

Act Three, Scene 8

As it turned out, the fall was nowhere near as bad as the audience had feared, hoped or expected. Kenny Sloan was disappointed – he'd prayed that Dines and/or Ellington had broken their necks tumbling off the balcony.

Dines had landed on Sanders. If they'd rehearsed it, they wouldn't have achieved that precision. Sanders sobbed with pain and frustration; tears of rage.

Dines crawled off him, angry and embarrassed in his pain, reached the foot of the staircase to haul himself upright to draw breath and survey the scene. But his arms didn't have the strength he'd relied on earlier; his leg looked broken.

'Turn that bloody music off!' somebody shouted. Somebody else obeyed. The silence was filled by the noise of more people pouring from the upstairs corridors, the downstairs areas, the gardens and the nearest bars. Word spread fast. 'James Ellington threw Ralph Dines off the balcony!'

Leroy ushered William upstairs with a flea in his ear. Emily was escorted up out of harm's way by Rebecca with a comforting arm round her shoulder and a tissue at her neck to wipe away the thin line of blood.

To escape either a reprimand or a comforting arm, Maisie and Joseph turned back to the office door where the loose sheets were at the feet of a disconcerted Imelda who bent to scoop them up while looking over at her boss, still leaning against the balustrade. Still swearing and muttering.

'Get the fuck away from me, you mad lunatic,' Dines hissed, as if Sanders had been responsible for his fall rather than for breaking it. Happy to comply, Sanders got himself to his feet and scuttled to the side as fast as his bruised arms, left leg, back, shoulders, feet and forehead would allow.

He received a smattering of applause from some of the residents watching who had no idea what had actually happened. When he returned to his spot to pick up his knife several more joined in the clapping because it was a show. When Lennie looked to Dines as if he was about to take a bow, he was told again to 'bugger off' in louder tones.

Clearly the audience – a few wheelchairs were pushed through to the front – anticipated further highlights. The sight of Joseph and Emily snatching the reams of paper from Imelda and climbing upstairs was intriguing – these people seemed a bit young to be new residents.

Sanders stood stock still, fingering the blade lovingly, silently daring Dines to make him move. Dines stepped forward as if to grab Sanders, momentarily leaving the safe support of the handrail and fell forward on his face. Upstairs, William laughed.

Dines, very near boiling point, dragged himself up yet again, clung to the rail even more firmly and waved away an assistant who'd stepped forward to help him.

'Go on, do it again!' someone yelled from above. This invitation was accompanied by a chorus of supportive voices. James remembered he'd read of crowds gathering in streets to stare up at someone on a roof or at a window and shout 'jump! jump! jump!' at him or her.

For his part, safely upstairs, surveying the wreckage of Dines' pomp and ceremony, James looked over at Maisie and Joseph. That was a lot of paper to have printed off from Dines' computer but was clearly going to be the evidence of business malpractice, fraud, theft and murder James longed to find.

Back in his time in Parliament he'd visited one of his local 6th forms to take part in a debate in the school library on the topic, *'This House Believes Young People Should Run Schools'*. He'd agreed to speak against the motion supported by an intelligent, lucid sixth-former. His lefty-Labour opponent proposed the nonsense, supported by a gullible teenager.

James was impressed by his sensible seconder – she had done well – and had felt it was a big success. The students had all been polite, heard him out and party politics had played a minimal part on the speeches. When it was opened up to individuals on the floor to contribute, it got a little ragged.

The chair was the Head of 6th Form, an ineffectual bumbler, anxious not to offend anyone or contradict any viewpoint. The event followed the normal rules of debate – speak through the chair, one contribution per student from the floor and a right of uninterrupted reply from a selected student from each side at the end.

One cheeky youngster, who'd confessed Marxism was too right-wing for him, had three goes to argue back at people and generally make himself unpleasant. When James rose on a point of order, as he would in the House, to question the multi-interruptions from the young lad, there was loudly expressed disapproval from a large minority.

While the Chair vacillated in agonies of indecision, conscious of his two adult guests, the lad pulled a small, brown covered book from a nearby shelf, held it aloft and proclaimed, 'Chair, according to the rules of formal debating as laid down in Customs and Practices of Debate, 1932, which I have here, when a speaker makes points which are plainly against common decency or common sense, a vote may be taken...'

As uproar began, a vote on procedure was the last thing the Chair wanted. James didn't either; he needed to move to his next gig, visiting a care home. Noticing James glancing at his watch, the Chair said they must put the question and the motion was defeated by 34 to 97, a convincing margin.

The gathering broke up and after congratulating his seconder and shaking hands with everybody in sight, James made his way to the exit. The troublesome lad tossed the book he'd brandished at one of his mates, who opened it and laughed. *'How to Keep Rats.'*

James nodded and smiled at the youth and was rewarded with an upright middle finger. The lad clearly aimed to become a politician. He did become one. And was a friend of Ralph Dines, no doubt, despite being in a different party. He was a natural liar, twister and awkward sod.

It had made James think of the differences between his colleagues and himself. He'd never wanted his girls to grow up as devious as that. He always did his best to steer both gently away from the political path.

Maisie and Joseph came to James and passed him their piles of paper, now the worse for wear having been scooped from the floor and crushed in fists and arms.

James smiled in relief, grabbing a handful from Maisie. He shouted above the babble of people still hoping for something spectacular. Perhaps James was about to hurl himself down to keep old Ralph company? Of course, he wouldn't go without a speech.

'Ladies and gentlemen, friends and acquaintances, I'm sorry you were unable to join me in my birthday tea earlier.' There were a few murmurs about being prevented from doing so. 'I know, I know, Ralph stopped you.'

He took centre balcony, his back to the space, leaned back against the stonework and waved the papers about.

'The man who has fallen below is Ralph Dines, with a string of letters after his name, a host of bank accounts in his pocket and a stream of lies and falsehoods frothing from his mouth.'

Below, Dines attempted to move again, but the pain was too great and he toppled forward. Manders, leaning near James, noticed and cried out, 'he's also a very good comic turn!'

At once heads turned down as people surged to the balcony front, James feared for the strength of the structure and pictured falling down into a crocodile infested lake while being laughed at by the crowd.

But they were laughing at Dines, hopeless, helpless. His face was red. 'Stop that laughing. Would you laugh at a man who'd just been run over by a bulldozer?'

Some chorused yes! Others shook or nodded heads. But they all laughed at Dines, at the man who'd helped them, done things for them, covered up their crimes. Even those too far out of it to know what was going on, laughed at Dines.

James took back his audience, 'My granddaughter Maisie and grandson Joseph have hacked into the Dines' systems in his office. They have printed off all this evidence. The days of the Dines' empire are numbered. All this material is going straight to the police, the real police.'

Amidst cheers, one or two inmates looked uncomfortable. If James was right, their names could be among the evidence.

'That's not possible! Ellington is deluded, we'd better lock him up for his own safety. And others'. Bring us a straitjacket.' Dines looked up at what he could see over the balcony top.

The crowd began to disperse; suddenly it was no longer a laugh a minute. Some of the nurses bent to their more susceptible charges in fear that there'd been just too much excitement for them to process in an hour.

As he saw Sebby sidling up to him to make some fatuous comment, James glanced down at the still disorganised paper evidence he held and wondered at once how he could safely get it to the law.

Every sheet was blank. The kids had just grabbed paper and made out it was evidence.

'Sorry, Grandpa, we couldn't hack in, too many firewalls and false trails.' Joseph was disappointed for his grandfather and for himself at failing.

'Some of it seemed to destruct when we got close, Grandpa,' Maisie said, softly. 'But we thought you could make out we'd got the evidence against Dines. He seems to have fallen for it. And fallen for the balcony as well!'

She was a natural liar, twister and awkward sod. It gladdened James that he'd never let his girls grow up as devious as that. He couldn't be responsible for how his grandkids were growing up.

Act Three, Scene 9

Ralph Dines had not been drawn to the shady world of politics years ago merely to exercise power, enjoy authority, enforce changes and get things done. Nor had he done it to make money, build networks in business and government and use his skills to oversee things.

No, those were bonuses. He'd partly carved a career in the swamp because he was addicted to the sound of his own voice, as so many politicians are.

In how many areas of life was a person not only expected to voice an opinion on absolutely everything, but actually encouraged to speak out by the media and public expectation? Where else could a person stand on his or her feet and pontificate in a magnificent Chamber with every word immortalised in the *Hansard* verbatim records?

Sitting in the Speaker's chair of their mock Parliament, he felt a buzz. Here, everyone playing the game of Westminster theatre just like the good old days, afforded him due respect if not deference. But he rarely got to speak to an audience these days, except the occasional Rotary lunch or charity event where he was a guest invited to promote his old folks' home.

So, signalling to two minions to support him, he left the prop of the balustrade to adopt a position a little out from the overhanging balcony. He assumed his audience was still there, awaiting his guidance (orders).

Beginning his address with the lie of false modesty universally beloved by egotists everywhere, he boomed loudly and clearly, 'I did not go into public life and commit to a lifetime of service to others for reward, recognition or deference.'

Those were exactly the reasons, of course. When a few who had started to make their escape realised there was more amusement to be had, they reassembled in the foyer and on the balcony, leaning over. At least Dines had a small audience.

'Many years ago, one evening in the Commons waiting for a late-night division of the House, I sat with my best friend James Ellington and that wise old bird, Dame Winifred Carswood, sadly recently departed and soon to be laid to rest. It was a rare quiet moment, few other members around. James was grumbling in that whingeing, whiney way of his about all the casework we got from constituents that took up so much time and which people thought mattered.'

James recalled that it was Dines who'd moaned about it, but let it pass. Dines continued, leaning heavily on his helpers. 'James said something along the lines of what is all that stuff to us, grand and mighty as ever, people should see their councillors, the CAB, the churches or their Great Aunt Mary, why bother us MPs?'

'Do you know what that great lady replied to James? Of course not, you weren't there.' James said to himself, 'but I was there, Ralph.'

'She told us that to MPs, every single thing was of interest and mattered to us as well as the common people. And while I'd been doing that all my life, caring and listening about people's worries, however trivial, I watched as the lesson dawned on James.'

James could only shake his head, look at Rebecca who caught his eye; she nodded, she understood. Dines was warming up. 'And so, I have never expected gratitude from anyone I've helped. I've not looked for recognition. Hey, how many lords and ladies are living here while I'm still just a plain Mr?'

'That being said, how many of you here owe everything to me? A place in a warm, secure home-from-home at Sir Thomas More? A loan, turned into a gift, from time to time? A hamper of food sent to a relative? Advice, practical help? Why, I even had to sort out a bunch of young hooligans harassing an old lady for a friend of one of us here! Yet I asked for nothing in return. Nothing.'

With confirmation that Dines had been behind the sorting of Judy Blowers' problem and would undoubtedly deal with the Poison Dwarf if commissioned, James expected Saint Ralph to wipe away a crocodile tear while sad violins played in the background.

Dines made a herculean effort to pull himself together. 'If one of our residents sees fit to leave a small bequest for our work, that is reward enough for me. I don't go shouting it from the rooftops, look what someone has done to thank us, no I don't. But I tell you this..."

Dines took hold of his stick which had been returned to his fist. 'Note this, I think that to mock me, make fun of me, laugh at me rather than *with* me is a despicable act of cruelty which I shall take on the chin, like the man I am, but inside I'm bleeding.'

James led the smattering of applause. He clapped slowly, jokingly. One or two loyal residents and staff joined in, not realising Ellington was being sarcastic.

Dines looked up, expecting to see the heads of dozens leaning over the balcony enjoying his performance.

Accepting that enough was more than enough, he hissed, 'take me to my office, get Karl to come at once and some medic to come and see how badly hurt I am.'

Realising that Dines was leaving the stage, Rebecca and Samantha dashed back down the stairs, their men in tow and further back came the kids, with Maisie comforting a still shaking Emily.

Rebecca stood in his path. 'Before you skulk away to your office, Mr Dines, to lick your wounds…'

'Ah, yes, to lick the fatal wounds both literally and symbolically that your father has inflicted on me in my own house, dear lady, the house where I took him in, when you begged me to take him in.'

'That's not quite the case. I think this afternoon has revealed much of what my father has been trying to tell us ever since he got here.'

Samantha joined them. 'Before he came here, actually. I'm sure I speak for the whole family when I say that he really can't stay here any longer.' She looked at Rebecca for some support in that hasty statement.

Leroy gulped, wondering who the old man would be staying with, as if he didn't know. Simon stared wide-eyed, realising that though 100 miles away, they had the spare room which his father-in-law could take indefinitely. Maisie considered it, but couldn't see it working, but then the old boy could no longer stay in St Thomas More.

Joseph quickly thought of his GCSE exams coming up and Grandpa in the way; Emily wouldn't mind Grandpa with them for a few days. Henry felt indifferent either way while William liked the prospect of an adult who could teach him to play real chess and listen to his stories.

'You're ahead of me, ladies. I think we all agree that Mr Ellington has outstayed his welcome and must pack his bags tomorrow morning. Of course, he has sold his house, but he should have thought of that before embarrassing me today. And for your information, he has been a pain in the arse from day one and we've all tolerated it. But no longer. It's not fair on other residents who loathe and detest him and the staff who just can't please him.'

'I can hear what you're saying,' James shouted, still on the balcony. 'Don't let's rush things, not with all this evidence we have on Dines. Once the police get this, he'll be in a home courtesy of Her Majesty.'

James held up the bundle of paper, desperately trying to shuffle them together into some order while waving the whole clump over the space in front of him, to emphasise the trump cards he was holding. Several sheets escaped his clumsy clutch and floated slowly, gently to land at Dines' feet.

Looking down, he stirred them with his stick. 'Oh, very droll, James, most amusing. Blank paper! That will go down very well as evidence in a court of law. Blank sheets, the story of your wasted life!'

Dines was cheering up by the minute. 'We'll accept three months' fees in lieu of notice, payable in the morning.'

Both Rebecca and Samantha opened their mouths to protest. 'You both have copies of the Contract, I believe. If you read it carefully you see that we have a three-month notice period unless caused by death, in which case it's one month.'

Cursing his clumsiness, James began the descent, to check with Maisie and Joseph what they'd actually found in the office.

'Move!' Dines ordered his assistants and the party shuffled towards the office, the family of James Ellington shouting increasingly angry, incoherent phrases at the boss and following him.

At the outer office door, he paused, held his hand up, palm facing James' family and said, more in sorrow than anger, 'I'm sorry it's come to this, as James and I go back a long way. But when trust is dead, like in a relationship,' said the man who'd had more relationships than hot dinners, 'it's over.'

Imelda stood holding the door for him to hobble in, 'And you, Imelda, what the fuck were you so busy with that you let these two kids slip past you and get into my private office and try to hack my computer?' Imelda trembled, lip quivering.

'I'm sorry, Mr Dines, I didn't see them, they must have crawled past when I was talking to the little one.'

'Crawled past? You'll crawl past. From now on you take up cleaning duties. Get me another Imelda.'

One of the Karls appeared at the doorway. 'Karl, about time. Get in and check my computer systems, make sure nothing has been accessed without my authorisation.'

'Ah, Mr Dines, I'm the kitchen Karl, I misunderstood. When I heard you wanted Karl, I came running.'

'Who do I want then, you moron?'

'You want Computer Karl, Mr Dines, sir.'

'Well, fuck off and get Computer Karl. Are you still standing here?'

James had reached the foot of the stairs. Using the walls for support as he edged towards the office, he carefully circumnavigated an old man who was trying out different hearing aids from the Lost Property Box, where an ever-increasing pile of aids and dentures sat amongst the spectacles, odd gloves, a slipper and assorted detritus mislaid about the house.

James ached already but didn't feel the fight had done him lasting damage. He paused, close enough to Dines and his family to make an impact. 'Thank you for arranging my departure, I'm obliged. However, if I'm to leave, I will live out my notice in order to accomplish two things.'

James was enjoying his rebellion. 'One, it will give me time to find accommodation that does not involve me invading my daughters' homes. And two, it will give me time to finish bringing down the Ralph Dines' Empire.'

Clearly unimpressed, Dines barked to Imelda, still stood looking miserable, 'Get me Ronnie Wyford here. He has the legal advice at his fingertips,' evidently forgetting that Wyford was currently off site assisting the constabulary. Or was he?

'And if you can't find him, bring Ronald Hasbery, he's a legal adviser.'

'Ralph, before I say goodbye to my family, I'm going to give you some advice I received a few weeks back, from Dr Zoe Frayn.'

'God rest her,' Dines responded, crossing himself.

'I don't believe either you or she is religious. But

what she said was that I must learn to defeat my handicaps by facing them, not letting them define me, command respect by working through them accepting they are part of me.'

'And your point?'

'That you should do the same. Work through your handicaps, not stuff them under the carpet with the dead bodies. You've just never tried.'

'And what handicaps am I supposed to have, apart from a little arthritis in my knees requiring a stick?'

'The biggest handicap of all. Being Ralph Dines.'

Act Three, Scene 10

Finally, the right Karl was in Dines' office. He stood from looking at the systems in the normally locked cupboard room. 'I'm confident there was no successful hack made to any of your systems, boss.'

Dines nodded from his desk where he sat, uncomfortable, aching from his fall and fight. 'The firewalls and the *Repel* program held up. Not to say a more experienced hacker couldn't have got in, but these were kids and they didn't know enough.'

'Thank you, Karl. That's good to hear. Do whatever strengthening you need to do at once, or even sooner.'

Imelda hovered by the door, notebook and pen in hand awaiting Dines' orders. 'Imelda, be more vigilant in future. Normally if one of my people fuck up, like you did, they are buried alive in a very deep hole.'

As she looked shocked he gave her a blast of his non-funny laugh which did nothing to reassure her. But it cost him – his ribs were extremely sore.

Robert Fosdick, was a former MP, who rarely left his room, receiving all meals there and taking exercise in the middle of the night when he roamed the corridors, followed by a nurse. A doctor before going into Parliament back in the day, he'd been talked out of his afternoon nap to check Dines over in the absence of Dr Zoe.

'Doc, how am I, considering what happened?'

Fosdick was nudged awake. 'Mr Dines, you're in good shape as far as I can tell, but do please remember that it's fifty years since I practised medicine...'

'Don't give me that. You kept your hand in, prescribing select meds to MPs and Lords, sorting their sexual diseases and erectile dysfunctions,' Dines smiled, wagging a finger.

'Well, I don't know about that. But I do know you should let them have a look at you in the medical wing, 45, just for a proper check up.'

'Opinion duly noted. I have a busy day, today, a lot of rubbish to clear up. My day looks like what, Imelda?'

'Oh, Mr Dines,' she replied searching for his timetable in her pad. 'You have the Carswood funeral in the crematorium this morning followed by meetings with colleagues and others throughout the day.'

It was the standard reply a Prime Minister gave to the formal first question from a Member enquiring about his or her day ahead of asking a real question. Dines spread his hands to Fosdick.

'There we have it. I'll look in later this evening to wing 45, just to make you happy.'

'Oh, I'm ecstatic, Prime Minister,' Fosdick mumbled before nodding off again, his breathing laboured, similar to a weird last gasp.

The door opened to admit Lord Wyford, looking much as previously seen, overweight, jowly and reeking of his unique blend of nicotine, body odour and halitosis. If he could bottle it, he'd make a fortune.

'Ah Ronnie, they let you go!' Dines laughed and

slapped his desk.

'Yes, we had a laugh and a few refreshers and then I kept low, went to Brighton where I have a sister who was thrilled to accommodate me for a few days.'

Also scattered around the room on the spare chairs were Lennie Sanders, Gerry Manders, Kenny Sloan and Michael Michaelson. They dutifully stood and shuffled to Wyford to thump his back, releasing clouds of dandruff and making 'ere-'ere noises of approval.

'Thank you, gentlemen. Yes, I'm a free man again. Just a little misunderstanding,' and he attempted to wink, but it twisted up his face.

'You heard about James Ellington's pantomime yesterday afternoon?' Dines demanded. 'It can't go on. He's leaving. Very soon.'

A silence descended, while each man and Imelda thought for a moment of the various ways he could be leaving. Packing his bags and going off in a taxi was a possibility. Being wheeled out at night to the morgue and on to the crematorium was credible. Or leaving without trace and being reported absent in a week's time?

Anything was possible.

'Well, time to start the day. Thank you, Dr Fosdick. Good to have you back, Ronnie. And thanks for your sympathy, gentlemen. This old dog isn't ready to be put out to grass just yet.' The mixed metaphor passed unnoticed.

'Your speech, Mr Dines, for the funeral.' Imelda handed him a small pile of postcards on which had been typed his spontaneous thoughts, praise and kind words about Winnie Carswood.

The party broke up. Wyford remained standing, waiting for specific orders relating to him. Dines looked him up and down as he sighed. This was his right-hand sidekick, the best he had at the moment. It was a pity that James Ellington had gone crazy. He'd have made a surprisingly effective henchman.

'Ronnie, have a walk round, take the congratulations on being home, if any remember how you went. Say that you enjoyed your little break, but now you're back at work, helping me. Take complaints, but no details. Listen out to make sure Ellington is packing his bags.'

'Will do, roger and out,' and he made for the door.

'Ronnie, then go and change, black suit and tie and join me in the crematorium.'

'How is James leaving us, Ralph? And when?'

'I haven't decided yet, Ronnie.'

As soon as he was alone again, Dines carefully hauled himself up on the edge of his desk, winced as he wall-walked to the cupboard and returned with one of his secret phones. Relieved, he sat again and made a call.'

'Any fresh news on our Mr Ellington?' He listened. 'Well, he's leaving soon. I think one of the traditional ways might raise too many eyebrows after yesterday, so I'd like something to interest the real police.' He listened again.' His old house? Ah. I wonder why he didn't ask me to help? Yes, that sounds like a plan.'

He replaced the phone, pulled out a black tie from the desk drawer and clipped it on. He eased his way to the door. Passing Imelda he snarled, 'this is impossible. Get me a wheelchair, it'll look more convincing that Ellington did me some serious damage but I'm carrying on.'

As she called to have a chair sent down, Dines listened to a sudden noise in the foyer outside. It sounded like a squabble over a set of false teeth in the Lost Property corner. When he opened the door, it was exactly that.

He noticed James emerging from the stair area, the scene of yesterday's display and went back inside, closing the door. James was in his best suit, white shirt and black tie. All set to see Winnie off; so not getting on with his packing.

James averted his gaze from the squabble in case he was asked to intervene and take sides. It had happened to him before – residents always got very excited about ownership of teeth. He made his way to the garden door, like his antagonist much the worse for wear after yesterday, but he hadn't been thrown down a floor.

Outside it was chilly but fresh and dry. Ideal for a funeral, in many ways. He'd really miss Winnie, she'd been a friend. And James still couldn't shake off the feeling that Dines was behind her passing, though he had no proof. As usual.

Thinking back over his disastrous birthday, he hoped his grandkids were not in any prolonged trouble with their parents. A telling off, a period of grounding would surely be enough. And everyone would blame James, in any case, blame old Grandpa and his strange phobias.

On the other hand, his girls and their husbands had seemed very supportive after they'd seen Dines in something like his true colours. Stopping guests to the tea arriving. All that anger and schoolboy punching.

No, the adults saw it his way now.

And rather than accommodate him, he was confident he'd find somewhere else in three months. Of course, they'd keep on at him not to buy a small bungalow on his own but to go into somewhere where he could be cared for, that is, managed.

He was early inside the crematorium, but he always preferred to be early for timed events. He'd frequently been the butt of the old comment about being so early for his own funeral he'd be at the one ahead of him. But in public life, people liked their representative to be timely, not swan in late, apologising in a gush of half-hearted sorrow.

Somebody was trying to get the music playlist in order. *My Way, Can't Get No Satisfaction, How Much Is that Doggie in the Window?* and *O Sole Mio* seemed a strange selection for Dame Winnie Carswood A voice then barked angrily at some hapless operative, 'no, this is the list, you cretin.'

The building was suddenly filled with a range of classical extracts James didn't recognise and it seemed that the finale was to be *We'll Meet Again*, which was entirely fitting.

Growing cold and to stretch his leg he stood and clumped round the tasteful, mock art nouveau arena that Dines had built. Making small talk with some he knew, by the time he made his way back to the front row seat he'd wanted, it was gone. Indeed, the front five rows were filled with relatives, friends from outside and within Sir Thomas More House.

Dines was wheeled in and parked at the front, beside the coffin, facing the audience. He made a great play of being helped to stand, using the lectern for support.

The custom, designed by Dines himself, was that if the deceased had been religious, a priest conducted the ceremony, inviting the great man to speak first. If no religious element, Dines was the master of the ceremony and invited himself to go first.

For this one, a Lord Bishop was dredged out of the peers' wing of the house to bumble through his script with occasional bursts of memory giving it some sense of rationality. When he lost his way during the second section, Dines clicked his fingers and a nurse gently escorted the old buffer from centre stage, leaving it to Dines.

He paid tribute to her by reciting her political achievements, her good works outside politics, her natural humour and goodwill towards everyone. She was never too proud to help others cope with their misery. She dispensed the wisdom of age with a rare lightness of touch and sensitivity. It was more or less the same speech Dines used at every funeral, regardless of the deceased's real achievements, if any.

For his grand climax, Dines declared 'and as a measure of how much she cared, I can confirm that our beloved Dame Winifred Carswood left a modest bequest to help other residents in the home. God bless.'

This last came as news to her sobbing, distraught family, news of the most inconceivable and upsetting kind. Dines called three members of her family and ignored the gestures from the end of the row that another one had wanted to pay tribute to his mother, grandmother, great-grandmother, cousin, aunt or whatever she was to him.

With a glance at the clock, he started on his list of selected colleagues who spluttered a range of kind platitudes about her, with one or two genuinely upset that she was gone. After the whole thing had endured beyond long enough, James was called last by Dines who introduced him as Mr James Ellington, one of their newer residents who'd sadly decided to leave.

This was the cue for a round of tutting and 'shame' from Dines' henchmen strategically dotted around the area. James crossed the open space to the lectern, but Dines wasn't moving so he had to stand leaning against the coffin.

'Like many here, I met Winnie Carswood when I first entered Parliament. She immediately befriended me and gave me advice that has proved priceless to this day...' He intended avoiding repetition of the remarks of others, though that was not a skill usually exercised by politicians when they felt moved to speak.

'I want to share with you an incident that happened when I had been in two or three years. Mr Dines here had become a junior whip, the whip for my area indeed.' Dines bowed his head, as if acknowledging praise.

'I was urged to look around for a junior minister I could work with and grovel to the whips to see if I could be made a Parliamentary Private Secretary, a ministerial bag carrier and eavesdropper. This was often the first step up the greasy ladder in Westminster, so I did just that and made a couple of suggestions.'

This was different from expectations at a funeral and James noted that some of his crowd had nodded off; others clearly hoped there was still time for lunch. 'I was later informed that I'd missed the boat on the PPS jobs, I wasn't a match and that ship had sailed. It was a deliberate humiliation. Dame Carswood advised me to ignore it, rise above it; be a firebrand on the backbenches.'

He received a few claps of relief it was over, but James wasn't done. 'When I was offered a fee to act as Parliamentary spokesman for the Firearms Friendly Association, I wanted to accept it. Everyone else had side earners, why shouldn't I? We had expenses, same as others. The whips gave consent. Only Dame Carswood told me not to take it, it was a trap; it would blow up in my face. I'd shoot myself in the foot if I took it.'

This was new, so one or two rediscovered their public 'showing interest' faces. 'Shortly after that, there was a robbery of a bank in Edinburgh where three innocent members of the public and four staff had been shot dead. A number of documents were stolen from the vault. Nobody ever said what they were.'

James momentarily pictured the seven coffins of the victims on stands across the front, it had been so vile an experience. Pulling himself back to the single coffin in front of him, he continued, 'there was such a massive outcry about guns. Against firearms of any sort. People wanted them banned, no sports shooting, no Olympic shooting, no hunting, no farmers getting rid of pests. Nothing. And I was a week into my term as the new spokesman for the Firearms Friendly Association!'

'Ralph Dines told me to tough it out and earn the thousand a month they'd pay. Winnie didn't say I told you so, but just urged me to resign quietly. Say nothing. And I did and so averted a huge embarrassment. She was that wise voice in my ear, and I shall miss her so much.'

He paused to compose himself. 'That she left a bequest to this place I don't for one moment ...'

At that point Dines leaped to life, clapped loudly which others followed on and with a signal to the side, Wyford got *We'll Meet Again* on the speakers with the Dines' sycophants joining in heartily.

About half way through, the curtain opened, the coffin slid back and was gone from sight as the curtains closed.

Dame Winnie Carswood was on her way to a better place.

Act Three, Scene 11

After all the recent excitement, Dines wondered if the annual Easter egg hunt would not come as something of an anti-climax. But he'd underestimated the capacity of his residents for lapsing into childhood in their feverish greed to find and devour chocolate before others.

Frailties counted for little; a few motor scooters were enlisted, but most succeeded in struggling around the grass, under the trees, within the bushes, behind the flower pots and by the lake. Everywhere the Karls usually placed the mini eggs, there were plentiful supplies.

Matron Mercury circulated during the hunt topping up favoured spots with fresh supplies, pounced on eagerly with delighted cries from happy pensioners. At one point she had to give a handful to Gerry Manders who was inconsolable that he couldn't find a single egg.

Timmy Greenwood pronounced a large egg he ripped from its cardboard and plastic packaging which he strewed everywhere, the skull of 'alas poor Yorick' from *Hamlet*. He shouted he'd known the man and if this was all that was left of him he should be buried in the cemetery.

He set off to act on the idea before being restrained by staff, one holding a needle behind her back. As soon as he saw that, old Greenwood sobered up and stopped moving, sat on the grass and ate the egg, nodding and telling himself this was 'damned fine chocolate, Miss Suellen.'

While the hunt was on – 'all outdoors this year, outside' – staff assisted those who were missing out or had dropped or lost their reinforced cardboard buckets provided for the occasion. Misunderstanding the instruction, some folks stayed indoors, and became distraught they found no chocolate.

A squabble broke out by the main back door; an argument took place among three old dears, including Kenny Sloan, over a larger egg wedged between the lower branches of the weeping willow. A full-blown fight erupted between two women over a chocolate bunny.

Dines watched from his window. Normally he'd go out and encourage them. This year he was in too much pain and was momentarily disgusted at the behaviour of a majority of his paying customers. After decades of public service, often in high office, they couldn't provide a snack for themselves these days yet behaved like kids to get at morsels of chocolate.

He thanked his god that he wasn't like them. He was still running a host of busy enterprises employing many, making much and yet, here, he had to provide chocolate to greedy, grasping old fogies, at least one of whom would make him or herself very ill over scoffing and several would suffer headaches and demand painkillers.

And right on cue, Dame Henrietta Bolsome threw up, excusing herself with, 'I can't stand dark chocolate, who gave me that? Where's the milk chocolate?'

James took the opportunity of the distractions of the egg hunt and cleaning Henrietta up to ring round to discuss with his daughters, sons-in-law, Maisie and Joseph any and all avenues down which they could pursue Dines and his evil empire.

He sought out Sebby Catchpole, near the front gate, stuffing his mouth with a large egg, the flakes falling down his front and/or spraying the face of a new young assistant nurse who was hearing about his amazing Parliamentary career, all long before she was born.

Standing away from the chocolate fountain, he apologised to Seb and the nurse, and then to Douggie Gardener who was bearing down on them to introduce himself to the nurse, for interrupting, but did he know an honest solicitor, if that wasn't an oxymoron?

After a moment's thought Seb came up with two names. Kenny Sloan had studied law and some man in Bilgemouth he'd used himself, Rotary friend and lifelong chum of Ralph Dines.

He even thought of talking to the Chaplain. The House engaged a local clergyman to come in for Christmas and Easter events, some funerals, a wedding of two old dears who found they would be better as a pair and even on one occasion, the baptism of the great grandchild of a resident who could no longer travel.

James waited outside the broom cupboard allocated to the aptly named Reverend Peter Parsons, at the times stated on the faded, lopsided notice taped to the door. Nobody came. So, he tried different times of day and night. Finally, he found the door ajar, a light on within.

'Reverend Parsons? I'm sorry to disturb you, but do you have a minute?'

Sir Michael Michaelson stuck his grizzly head out, squinting. 'Ah hello, James, looking for old Parsons, hey? Something you want to get off your chest, I dare say. Parsons is off sick, he's not expected back if you ask me, a candidate for the crematorium, I believe. Can I help? I sometimes offer him backup.'

James pictured a machine gun toting Reverend Parsons in white robes holding back a crowd of demented, frothing inmates and Michaelson arriving like the cavalry with bigger and better guns blazing.

'No, thanks, Michael, good of you, but I really wanted some spiritual input just now. I can wait.'

'Very wise,' nodded his former Agent, biting back the natural loathing he felt for Ellington who'd been such a poor MP in his humble opinion. 'Anything here take your fancy?' indicating a rack of dusty leaflets, many bent over with age.

He stepped from the cupboard so James could enter and peer at the offering. Information about bunions, AIDS, Holy Communion, the local Foodbank, tax free gift aiding, how to mention Sir Thomas More House in your will, a local florists specialising in funeral wreaths and the Samaritans – that should have been left in every bedroom, James thought.

He took one on the Monastic Life and another on the Prayers of St Francis and palmed one about Serenity which rang a bell, so that Michaelson didn't notice and couldn't report on his choice.

But the old fool saw nothing, instead rattling an ancient biscuit tin with a coin slot cut into the lid, drawing James' eye to it and his conscience to reach into his pocket.

James ignored both gesture and tin. 'Thanks, Michael, and good to see you. I'll read these and come back another day.'

'Suit yourself, but if you want me to hear confession, just call on me in my room. Sebby Catchpole is also available, as, I believe is Kenny Sloan.' James would have to be on the gallows itself before he'd confess anything to those buffoons.

In his room, he tossed the Monastic Life and the St Francis pamphlets away and studied the one on Serenity. The Reinhold Niebuhr's Prayer of Serenity came back to him. He'd used it in speeches, though not for years.

The prayer contained the essence of all that MPs tried to do. Change things, but sometimes they had to admit defeat. They should often retreat to fight another day. They had to pick their battles. Parliamentary life had taught him that as he'd lost more endeavours than he'd succeeded with.

"Lord, grant me the strength to accept the things I cannot change, the courage to change the things I can, and the wisdom to know the difference."

He talked to Samantha on her next visit and had a similar discussion with Rebecca over the phone. Both understood that he couldn't win the fight against Dines. Accept and move on. Don't let the man of power crush him mentally. Oh, and by the way, had he thought any more about where he'd live after his notice was served?

Finally, he messaged Maisie and she rang him back when she had half an hour. Broadly agreeing with her mother and aunt she said that, depressing as it is, 'Goliath sometimes wins and David loses. He's no less a man, a genuine man for all that. It's just that he knows when to stop flogging a dead donkey.'

'Flogging a dead horse, Maisie, it's a dead horse!'

'Same difference. It's dead. It's hopeless. It's a deceased parrot. Move on and make new friends elsewhere. Let the Westminster past go, you've held on long enough.'

Priceless wisdom from a young head and he knew she was right. And all his family who believed the same. Even Elspeth wouldn't have wanted him to fight on, but would have hoped he'd find a new life and fight battles worth winning for the greater good.

With a final walk round the grounds, through the corridors and wings, the Chamber and the Archives where his records would be collected for storage in the town, James made his way to Dines' office. With a nod to Imelda at her place in the outer space, he entered straight into the control hub of the organisation and sat down in the big chair at the polished, empty desk.

Swinging back, he took in the surroundings, the trappings of power, the luxury. All this, it might as well be his as much as go to someone else.

Imelda poked her head round the door, 'Coffee?'

'Yes, please, Imelda. It's a coffee day, not a brandy one. How did you guess?'

'Are you,' she asked hesitatingly, 'are you well today, sir?'

'Never been better, Imelda. The trouble-makers are all either locked up or dead. Every madman has been caged, and I'll have extra of those caramel dunking biscuits with my coffee.'

As she served him from the side table on which sat an industrial sized coffee machine, with a range of drinks on the shelves below, she still looked a little wary. 'What's the matter, Imelda, you look worried.'

'Are you, sir, Mr Dines today or Mr Ellington?'

His reply took a moment. 'I'm Ralph Dines today, as I

usually am. James Ellington is a footnote in the history of this house, a scribble in the margins of life and a smudged full stop in the annals of Parliament.'

He snapped out of the reverie. James Ellington was sitting opposite Imelda in the outer office waiting for Dines to condescend to see him. Why had James thought he could double for Dines?

He was invited in to see Dines at his desk, Wyford on the sofa,

'Ralph, I'm off soon. I just wanted to say I'm sorry that things turned out as they did. I still think you're a piece of shit so big you'd block a sewer, but I can't prove it. I'm going to let it go. Let you go.' Turning to Wyford he added, 'let all of you go, the whole ludicrous charade, including joke actor police officers at one end of the scale and murderous scams at the other.

Dines gave him both a roar of unfunny laughter and the palm raised in his face. 'Stop there, James, old partner. It's been a journey, hasn't it? We've had some laughs on the way, and some fun. I wish you all the best in your new life of counselling and supporting the mentally ill.'

James opened his mouth to respond, but Dines was flowing on, 'and I'm glad you have accepted that sometimes the little man cannot be allowed to win. It upsets the balance of life.'

Again, James came to. What's with the fantasising weird scenarios? He just needed to tell Dines straight. And get the hell out of there, glad he could walk out and not be wheeled out to be slid into the furnace.

He pronounced to Imelda, 'I've been kept waiting long enough. Please be good enough to inform Mr Dines that I did the polite thing and waited to say goodbye, but I'm not a worm to be ignored. He can find me if he has the balls to face me.' And he stomped out, leaving the office door wide open.

During the evening as he packed his bags he found himself entertaining a welter of ways that Dines would die, sometimes alone, occasionally in the company of his minions and hangers on. Hails of bullets, endless gallows drops, gasping in a gas chamber, head rolling from a guillotine blade and being tarred and feathered before burning slowly like a piece of firewood.

The reality, such as it was, came the next morning when James made three trips to carry his suitcases to a taxi parked outside, 'helped' by Sebby Catchpole who managed one trip in the same time as he talked on, even to the empty room.

Several residents stood about to say goodbye. Only Sir Ronald Hasbery meant it when he wished James well. Sir Gerry Manders kept asking him to surrender his keys. Lenny Sanders came to stare, running his fingers across his own throat and pointing at James.

Kenny Sloan stood in the doorway and announced he was taking the room; it was better than his. Not for the first time had he been in James' bedroom, he said with a wink and a grin. James resisted the jibe.

He shook Douglas Gardener's hand by the front cage and then wiped it on his trousers. Dame Henrietta Bolsome wheeled up to say he owed her a game of bridge which she expected from him next Christmas.

He got through the exit and was outside the front door when Dines and Wyford appeared from the rear. 'James, time to say goodbye, toodle pip and all that.' Wyford proceeded to treat James to a burst of the First World War song, 'Goodbye-ee: goodbye-ee, goodbye-ee, wipe the tear, baby dear, from your eye, don't cry, don't sigh, there's a silver lining in the sky-ee.'

Unsure for a second if he was imagining this, Dines added to the surrealistic flavour of the occasion by slapping him on the back and saying, 'I'm really concerned, old man, that your rather hasty rush to leave us has left you without any clear purpose in mind, no destiny in life anymore?'

'On the contrary, Ralph old thing, I'm going to write a book. If I can't find the proof I need to bring you down and make the real police look into you, then maybe as a piece of fiction it'll work. Surely nobody could invent that, people will think.'

'Who on earth would publish that drivel, James, do you think? Besides if you name me, I'll sue your arse off.'

'Oh, I'll take the risk. If no publishing house will touch it, I'll self-publish or put it out on social media. I have young people who'll help me with that.'

'Where will you start on this fascinating saga of boredom? I was born in the back end of Nowhere in 1948 to a one-legged cowboy and a woman with three heads?'

James smiled, taking his diary from his pocket. 'No, this is how I will open the story, the birth details can come later. Listen. It will start with an old man, in his 70s, former MP, leaving his daughter's house in Essex and driving home along the A12. He stops to buy something to drink from a stall he's never seen before.'

Checking that Dines was following, he continued from the diary, *'He's handed a can, not as cold as he would like. 'That's a quid, mate.'*

Everyone watches him. They're criminals up to no good, pretending to be a roadside stopover. There is one staring at the back of his head.

Having found a coin among his pocket change, he turns towards his car, catching a flash of what one of the men is wearing under an outer-coat. Looks like a police uniform.

They're police pretending to be a roadside stopover to catch criminals. They continue to watch him get in, slam the door and belt up.

As he reaches the lay-by, he brakes, all clear and edges forward ready to rejoin the A12, needing a space in the fast-moving cars, vans and heavy lorries.

Stationary, his lights not yet on as he reaches for the switch, he is inches from being crushed by a white Ford Transit coming off the A12 at speed before screeching to a halt by the refreshments.

In his mirror he watches the passenger opening his door to exit but falling back, shot. A man flings back the drivers' door and fires into the cab five times, the noise lost against the A12 traffic.

What the hell? Shaking hand paused on the light switch, he clocks the pickup truck roaring into life and immediately swinging round to reverse to the van.

The hook is attached so the van's front wheels are hoisted up leaving the rear wheels on the road.

The truck will veer round towards him in a second so he pushes forward and finds a tiny gap in the traffic as he puts his lights on, being rewarded with a loud, angry horn blast for his trouble.

'The man drives towards home, followed and then overtaken by truck and van, till they reach the old toxic tip opposite the holiday camp. You know the one?'

And again he quotes from his notes, '*he slowly cruises past, grabbing a glimpse of the place he hasn't entered since just before closure and the official sealing off.*

The gates stand open; E403 CDP, towing the Ford Transit is being driven in. Flashing torches point the way into the site.

Dear God! The two dead men and their van are being dumped into the toxic pit, never to be seen again.

And the killers saw him at the crime scene.

Some relief, as he arrives home. But they have his car number, they can trace him. He replays the scene in every dark corner of his street, fighting the rising panic.

He has seen enough films and read sufficient crime literature to fully imagine five miles away Ralph Dines, not unlike him, a fraction taller and putting on weight too, sometimes limping, Member of Parliament from 1987 to 2019, one-time minor whip and very junior minister in the business department answering his phone.

'Job done; all good,' he is informed. 'Fee received.'

'Thank you.' He listens to a question from the other end before stating, 'Oh, the secret of successful lying is to include as much truth as possible, don't you know.'

The caller is satisfied. Dines wishes him or her, 'Good night.'

Returning the diary to his pocket so Dines can't snatch it, he smiles, 'I think that's quite an opening, don't you?

Should grip readers so they want to press on and see who's responsible!'

'Yes, I'm sure. Do it. And then watch out for a copy of the medical file on the insanity treatment you received here to accidentally find its way into the public domain.'

James clambered into the taxi without further word; Dines and Wyford watched it go, also with no comment. Each was sure the other was too big a liar to do anything, published or not.

Epilogue

Six months later on a glorious late summer day, Ralph Dines feels good, secure in the empire he's built. The finances of Sir Thomas More House are in fair shape and improving all the time. His private companies are all doing quite well.

The crematorium is at full stretch some days while the graveyard with its annually incremented storage fees is filling up, but not too quickly.

And now they are developing a new system of adding soil, woodchips, alfalfa and straw grass to cremated bodies and keeping them in containers for a few weeks to produce 'naturally, organically reduced' fertiliser.

It had already generated interest – 'Granny is now environmentally friendly soil enricher.' Dines was delighted.

The people around him now are mainly trustworthy and reliable – it's always amazing what a bit of threat, blackmail or splashed cash will do. The occasional bad apple, such as James Ellington, can be seen off.

He sits at a large garden table, under a colourful gazebo, freshly supplied with glasses of Pimm's when he raises a finger. Beside him, Wyford works through a list of items for discussion.

'Did the mental and physical check go well, Ralph?'

'Clean bill of health on all counts. I'm fighting fit, but if we start screening residents for blood groups, DNA and other essentials, our proposed body part transplant service should replace any of my organs that might fail.'

'That's a great reassurance, Ralph, it really is, but don't we need younger donors than most of our residents?' Wyford wonders, sucking his vape.

'Yes, we do, younger and cleaner. None addicted to nicotine like you, but I'm advised that a healthy old kidney is better than a raddled younger one. Besides,' he adds for good measure, 'we have branches of the company who from time have to dispose of younger, fitter bodies, though they tend to be mental defectives or drug addicts if not physical disasters.'

Timmy Greenwood gabbles incoherent gibberish across near the roses while two assistants are attempting to talk him away from Sir Gerry Manders entertaining an elderly couple who are considering double places in the house.

Wyford picks up a folder. 'On that, we have planning approval to extend Wing 45 into a proper state of the art medical facility with operating theatres. The third operating theatre will be doing transplants. Our legal team are looking closely at the consent agreements.'

'Encourage them to get on with it. We need them yesterday. How far are we with the Out of The Box Club?'

'Well, it's gathering some interest from the internet, I'm told. Our social media team are plugging away at this. The slogan is: *'keep out of your box as long as possible with a stay at Sir Thomas More House.'*

'Good, a simple idea,' smiles Dines, thinking about the scheme. 'People like to keep out of their boxes till well beyond their time – look at how many residents cling on, long after making a bequest, if they can't be shuffled off.

And others like to think they're out-of-the-box thinkers. Almost nobody is.' He laughs. 'And that artificial intelligence, illusions thing?'

He waves at a couple of residents enjoying the gardens and sunshine.

Wyford nods, grabbing another folder. 'Lennie Sanders has been testing out the one made of his daughter, Rachel. He says it's almost like the real thing. He can sit with her image in a dark room and talk to her, share jokes and stories from her childhood. It's got real possibilities.'

'Have they finished the illusion of beating someone up from the past to get revenge?'

'Almost ready for trials. The old barn behind the Archives is ideal for the base. Good wi-fi, I'm told. We thought an image of James Ellington which Sanders can set about, with a daily replenishing, would go well.'

'Ha ha, it will. I'll try that one out,' Dines smiles again. 'You know, Ronnie, this illusion thing, reality more real than reality itself can really take off and make us a decent pile of ready cash.'

The sound of people welcoming someone comes across the grass. Dr Zoe Frayn strides towards them, her summer dress billowing like a moving flower. Her hair is now shoulder length. She looks the picture of health.

'Hello Ralph. Ronnie,' she beams, giving both men a kiss on the cheek. 'How are things now, Doctor?'

'Thank you, Ralph, for giving me the time off. I looked after my old mother till the end. She was riddled with cancer so no body part could be transplanted.' Dines nods, understandingly. 'Then I had a couple of weeks in

Portugal, soaking the sun and reading lots of medical books and murder mysteries.'

'I'm glad to see you back, looking so well,' Dines smiles, sips his drink and nods at her. A flunky brings a glass over and Wyford struggles up to fill it with Pimm's for her.

Raising her glass to the men in turn she asks, 'how did the murder scene go?'

Both men laugh. 'You should have seen James, it was most entertaining!'

'I'm sorry to have missed it. But, you know, I was rather fond of him, he was genuine and realised what was going on ...'

'Some of it, my dear!'

'Some of what was going on. I'd like to have said goodbye. Despite what you say, he was a good man.'

'And still is, I believe. Where is he now, Ronne?'

'Still helping the real constabulary, I understand. He's not yet explained away the discovery of the body of the little woman who bought his house.'

'What did they decide to do with her?'

'Well, some of the lads thought it would be amusing to bury her up to her head – not a deep hole – and then nick a beehive from somewhere and place it over her head!'

'That's not a nice way to go,' Zoe says.

'You're the doctor.'

'Right, Zoe, back to work. If any residents think you're reborn from the dead, it'll feed their neuroses quite nicely. We need to clear out some of the dead wood around here, so make me a list. Work with Matron on that.'

Both Ronnie and Zoe nod agreement. 'I was thinking about retirees from other strata of society, not just MPs and Lords. What about teachers and Headteachers? What about wealthy medics? Solicitors and judges? Senior law enforcement? We've plenty of room here to expand, and we need a steady, reliable supply of bequests, transplants and work in the crematorium.'

Wyford chips into this exciting set of prospects, 'yes and that cemetery isn't going to fill itself!' The three laugh and sip more drink, enjoying the day in every way.

Zoe grins, 'don't forget the cemetery is large enough to host concerts and performances, summer fayres, barbecues and winter wonderlands...'

'Nice little earners, unusual surroundings!' roars Dines.

Back in the town, James Ellington is on a statutory break for coffee and toilet between bouts of questioning by the real police about the death of the Poison Dwarf. Or has Dines had a set built in town?

After a week with Samantha and family, a week with Rebecca and hers, he'd enjoyed an extensive world cruise with a difference. Themed cruises had become very popular – perhaps Dines was running them? James had chosen one which visited famous murder spots around the globe.

These were both fictional and actual murders, but few passengers grasped the differences. Farms, city apartments, creepy houses, disused factories, mines, open fields, forests, jungles – wherever a murder, assassination or massacre had occurred, the tourists trooped around the sites, guided, to appreciate every horror in full gory detail.

To make more of it, the organisers included atrocities from actual wars and civil unrest. Guests traipsed round more museums, memorials and abandoned prisons and asylums than they thought possible. Days at sea were filled with worthy lectures and slide shows to whet their appetites for more.

While on that, James had pictured Dines as the power behind every one of them. The cruise had blown most of his savings, but he really didn't care. Maybe he'd turn up at Sir Thomas More House and beg to be taken back in return for helping Dines come up with madcap ideas.

On his return he'd been arrested on suspicion of causing the death of the old dear who'd bought his house. He hears his interrogators returning to continue grilling him. Will they carry a straitjacket? Is this actually the Dines Asylum?

No, of course not. That is Sir Thomas More House.

Yet again his mind slips back. It wasn't all bad. Several inmates were reasonable. Dame Winnie, Sebby Catchpole and Dr Zoe had been his friends.

Now, two of those three were dead. Perhaps even Sebby had gone by now.

Back in the grounds on a sunny afternoon, he imagines Dines and Wyford plotting. And there is Dr Zoe with them, not dead, of course. Around the grounds, his lovely family are talking and laughing with other residents, Sir Gerry, Sir Michael, Timmy, Henrietta, Helen, Kenny and Sir Ronald Hasbery.

Lenny Sanders is in a padded cell; the last vestiges of sanity slipped through his fingers ages ago.

Staff are not robotic, but caring, sharing people. Karl opens doors politely, Imelda answers all questions and the Lost Property box is almost empty, just a lower molar on a plastic plate lying unclaimed.

As the interrogators pull back their chairs to sit, shuffle paper and ask him yet again about his old house and the lady who bought it from him, James feels nostalgic for his past, all of it.

If he asked, would they let him ring Dines? James has this great idea for a film company shooting a murder mystery about bodies being disposed in the old toxic tip.

James has lots of other ideas, too, if only someone would listen.

www.ingramcontent.com/pod-product-compliance
Lightning Source LLC
Chambersburg PA
CBHW070526010526
44118CB000128/1065